ROUTLEDGE LIBRARY EDITIONS:
FAMILY

Volume 10

AGEING AND FAMILIES

AGEING AND FAMILIES

A Support Networks
Perspective

Edited by
HAL L. KENDIG

Routledge
Taylor & Francis Group

LONDON AND NEW YORK

First published in 1986 by Allen & Unwin

This edition first published in 2023
by Routledge
4 Park Square, Milton Park, Abingdon, Oxon OX14 4RN

and by Routledge
605 Third Avenue, New York, NY 10158

Routledge is an imprint of the Taylor & Francis Group, an informa business

British Library Cataloguing in Publication Data
A catalogue record for this book is available from the British Library

ISBN: 978-1-032-51072-9 (Set)
ISBN: 978-1-032-53051-2 (Volume 10) (hbk)
ISBN: 978-1-032-53173-1 (Volume 10) (pbk)
ISBN: 978-1-003-41071-3 (Volume 10) (ebk)

DOI: 10.4324/9781003410713

Publisher's Note
The publisher has gone to great lengths to ensure the quality of this reprint but points out that some imperfections in the original copies may be apparent.

Disclaimer
The publisher has made every effort to trace copyright holders and would welcome correspondence from those they have been unable to trace.

AGEING AND FAMILIES

To our parents

AGEING AND FAMILIES

A Support Networks Perspective

Editor
Hal L. Kendig

ALLEN & UNWIN
Sydney London Boston

© Hal L. Kendig 1986

This book is copyright under the Berne Convention.
No reproduction without permission. All rights reserved.

First published in 1986
Allen & Unwin Australia Pty Ltd
8 Napier Street, North Sydney, NSW 2060 Australia
Allen & Unwin New Zealand Limited
60 Cambridge Terrace, Wellington, New Zealand
George Allen & Unwin (Publishers) Ltd
18 Park Lane, Hemel Hempstead, Herts HP2 4TE England
Allen & Unwin Inc.
8 Winchester Place, Winchester, Mass 01890 USA

National Library of Australia
Cataloguing-in-Publication

Ageing and families.

Bibliography.
ISBN 0 86861 962 0.
ISBN 0 86861 946 9 (pbk.).

1. Aged – Australia – Family relationships –
Addresses, essays, lectures. 2. Aged – Australia
– Care and hygiene – Addresses, essays, lectures.
I. Kendig, Hal, 1948–

305.2′6′0994

Library of Congress Catalog Card Number: 85–73514

Set in 10/11 pt Times by Graphicraft Typesetters Limited, Hong Kong
Printed by Bright Sun (Shenzhen) Printing, China

Contents

v

Contributors

Alice T. Day is a sociologist who was a Visiting Fellow from 1982 through 1983 on the Ageing and the Family Project conducted by the Research School of Social Sciences at the Australian National University (ANU). She is now an Andrew Mellon fellow at the Population Reference Bureau in Washington DC.

Diane Gibson was a Research Fellow on the Project from 1980 to 1984, and now lectures in Sociology in the School of Humanities at Griffith University.

Hal Kendig established and co-ordinated the Project, and will be returning to a fellowship in the Urban Research Unit in the Research School of Social Sciences at ANU.

John McCallum is a sociologist who was seconded to the Project as a Visiting Fellow from Griffith University during 1984 and 1985.

M. Victor Minichiello is a research scholar completing a PhD thesis in ANU's Department of Sociology in the Research School of Social Sciences, and a lecturer at Lincoln Institute of Health Sciences.

Stephen Mugford is a Visiting Fellow seconded to the Project during 1984 and 1985 from ANU's Department of Sociology in the faculties.

Gina Roach has been a Research Assistant with the Project since 1982.

Don T. Rowland was a Research Fellow on the Project from 1980 to 1984, and now lectures in the ANU Population Studies Program.

Tables

Figures

Foreword

This is a landmark study of ageing in Australia as well as a major contribution to the study of gerontology in general. The authors have systematically placed their Australian data into the larger mosaic of research findings. As a consequence, this book highlights major themes on ageing in 'western' industrialised societies, as well as pinpointing new, emerging themes. For instance, the initial speculations in the 1960s that informal groups such as the family, neighbours, and friends play crucial helping roles for older people has reached full fruition in this book. The systematic international documentation is impressive. The book also presents data and summarises past studies that show the common characteristics of those delivering and receiving services, such as the special role of women; and within that, gender related services, the special importance of children and spouses, the importance of close proximity when people are chronically disabled, the fact that most retired people manage their own lives without help and in fact provide services to their children, and much more, is dealt with.

However, the authors do not make the mistake of many of those who assume that the informal group can operate without the help of the formal agencies. They also pay attention to the role of formal agencies, such as nursing homes. The partnership between formal agencies and informal groups has often been overlooked in the excitement of the 'rediscovery' of the informal support systems. Many policy makers, confronted with the evidence that relatives, neighbours, and friends provide the bulk of household care to retired older people, and faced with the costs of maintaining agencies for the aged, have eagerly encouraged those who saw the informal supports as a substitute for nursing home care. Some have even gone as far as to argue for the reinstitution of the laws on filial responsibility. What such policy makers have missed is that the full use of informal supports, such as relatives, neighbours, and friends, was made fully possible only with the development of social security programmes that gave older people a financial basis and avoided bankrupting the helping group. Furthermore, it meant the development of agencies, such as nursing homes, that took in those needing 24-hour continuous care, which was beyond the resources of the ordinary informal support system. This book brings to the fore the limits of informal support systems by its discussion of 'care givers burden'. If the 1960s and 1970s were devoted to establishing the importance of the informal support systems, the 1970s and 1980s are being characterized by studies of the costs to the helpers who provide support. This book is in the forefront of presenting this emerging theme. It suggests that the informal supports and formal systems are not alternatives but partners in the care of the elderly.

The systematic study of how informal and formal systems link together is one of the great lacunae of current gerontological research. Its centrality becomes important only as the researchers understand the partnership role of informal and formal support systems. Perhaps this will be the major theme of the 1980s and 1990s. At this point it is still at a very embryonic stage with several important exceptions.

Yet another issue which has newly emerged with the 'rediscovery' of family, friends, and neighbours is the respective role each plays in the delivery of services. Early students in the field often started with the assumption that these groups were more or less interchangeable. What most discovered was that this was far from the case. *Each* seemed to supply some *special* services. This was generally noted without an attempt to present an alternative explanation. As a result, the reader often saw it as a puzzling piece of information with only secondary interest. However, with the mounting evidence of the viability of informal supports, researchers have become increasingly interested in the specialised roles of family, neighbours, and friends. This emerging theme is pursued in this volume through two lines of inquiry. Using the language of network theory, it searches for the underlying dimensions of informal supports which permits them to provide different types of services. At the same time, it pursues the view that primary groups have become structurally differentiated, and, because of this, can manage different tasks. These two lines of inquiry are not inconsistent with each other. Hopefully, future investigators will integrate them. Though the authors of this book make no attempt to do so, they do provide a very important service to students of the field in highlighting the need to systematically account for the specialised roles of different informal supports and uncovered two major modes for explaining these differences.

The rapid growth of the older segments of western societies has made gerontologists especially sensitive to change. This book goes further than most in its sophisticated presentation of future demographic changes affecting the aged. As such it provides a model for future researchers. Yet there is one major gap in the literature of change that is not discussed, despite its obvious importance, and that is the role of science and technology. If one considers three basic services—providing emotional support by talking, providing ad hoc household help to those temporarily bedridden for a week or more, and providing continuous household help to those chronically disabled—then the role of science and technology is apparent. Two hundred years ago the only way that family could provide such services was by living very close to the older person. It took the invention of the telephone to liberate the delivery of emotional support from the demands of geographic proximity. It took the invention of the car, train, and plane to liberate the second service from geography, and the third service has not as yet been freed. However, it is quite possible it will be. It is precisely these technological inventions that many argue have permitted the evolvement of new kinship structures in modern societies. Yet very little has been done to really study how much technology has liberated informal supports from geographic boundaries.

Little, moreover, is understood about the dynamics which return to the informal supports duties previously managed by formal systems and thereby reintroducing the importance of proximity again, for example, the evolution of technology that permits home dialysis for those with poorly functioning kidneys; the development of home medical tests; the teaching to lay people of how to deliver injections. These are a few of the technical developments which put a great stress on helpers who live very close to the older person. Despite the obvious importance of technology in shaping the form of informal supports as well as the services they deliver, gerontologists have provided little systematic research or theoretical evidence on this subject. It is a difficult and elusive subject but one which must be tackled if we are to know how enduring the present trends are.

To summarise, the field of gerontology has now evolved systematic international data on the role of informal support systems and the characteristics of the helpers and those being helped. The initial speculations have resulted in a large array of findings that increase at a rapid pace. It is easy to see that in the immediate future we will all be buried under the blizzard of facts and figures being produced. Books on gerontology are rapidly taking on the characteristics of dictionaries. They are handy for reference to specific topics but almost impossible to absorb in totality. It is a field that could benefit from an overall theoretical scheme which can put into order this bewildering array of facts. One almost longs for frameworks, such as disengagement theory, around which order can be introduced.

More specifically, one of the major lacunae is the absence of theoretical schemes to organise the rapidly growing empirical data around us. It is not an easy job. It may mean several theories rather than one overall embracing one. But I would hope that some of those interested in gerontology would spend time in providing order to the data already gathered and that those gathering data would see the virtue of trying to produce order.

Finally, let me comment on one very important attribute of this book. It has drawn on a wide array of data, ranging from a major survey, to demographic data, to the qualitative observational data of the field observer. It falls into a tradition of science which I most wholeheartedly endorse. Some people see science as a game which can only proceed if the scientist follows certain rules. Each discipline sees its own methods and vocabulary as providing the form and substance of the rules. I see science and the field of gerontology as more akin to a fight in which one does anything necessary to defeat an adversary. There are no simple rules or single method.

In conclusion, the readers of this volume will have an intellectual feast in which they can see the documentation in Australian data of basic themes developed elsewhere, the emergence of new themes, and the suggestion of themes not as yet researched.

Professor Eugene Litwak
Department of Sociology and School of Public Health
Columbia University
New York
November 1985

Preface

This book presents some of the principal research findings produced by the Ageing and the Family Project, conducted by the Research School of Social Sciences at the Australian National University (ANU) over the past five years. While our research has addressed many topics and audiences outlined below, this particular publication focuses on the interpersonal ties developed by older Australians. Emphasis is placed on the variety of social support networks evolving out of earlier life experiences and broader social circumstances. In the pages that follow, we are speaking primarily to advanced undergraduate students in the social sciences in Australia, and an international audience of specialist researchers in social gerontology and networks analysis. We have tried, however, to limit the complex statistical analysis and academic jargon in order to also reach professionals and social scientists in related fields.

When the Research School of Social Sciences established the project, it placed its reputation and budget behind the pursuit of two important objectives. First, a new area of research in Australia was to be explored purposefully by a multidisciplinary team brought together for a limited period of time. Second, high quality academic research was to be conducted on an applied topic of national interest and importance. The school has funded two and one-half academic posts, a research assistant, a secretary, and most fieldwork expenses. My efforts as project coordinator have been supported by two school directors, A.J. Youngson and G. Max Neutze, a School Advisory Committee and a number of colleagues at ANU and elsewhere in Australia.

The research program was carried out in three overlapping stages.

Don Rowland and Diane Gibson, the first of the academic staff to join me on the project, were co-investigators in developing and conducting the 1981 survey on which many of our findings are based. While the survey was a collaborative effort, Don took primary responsibility for sampling and fieldwork, and Diane worked primarily on the questionnaire, particularly the sections on health, expressive support, social interaction and social networks. Among the many other contributors were Pamela Manley, fieldwork supervisor; Roger Jones, who developed the sampling frame; Terry Beed, who provided a fieldwork base in Sydney; Gabrielle Braun, Naomi Kronenberg and Gillian Unger; the thirty interviewers; and, most of all, the 1050 respondents who graciously opened their doors and their lives to our study. Averil Fink, and her staff at the NSW Council on the Ageing, provided strong support throughout the effort. The Commonwealth Department of Health provided a grant which enabled us to increase substantially the number of interviews with people aged 75 or over.

As the analysis began on the survey findings in 1982, the second stage of our research program was launched, with qualitative studies by M. Vic Minichiello on older people entering nursing homes and their families; Alice Day on very old people in the community; and Jan Carter on younger members of older people's families. The Institute of Family Studies covered some of the fieldwork costs of the latter two studies. While the gulf between quantitative and qualitative research can be difficult to bridge, the research has benefited considerably from the complementarity of the different research approaches as well as the different disciplines.

A third stage of research was marked by the arrival in 1984 of John McCallum and Stephen Mugford, who have been analysing survey findings on retirement and social networks respectively.

Many people have assisted ably in bringing the research findings together into this book. Jane Halton, Sue Freeman, Bruce Shadbolt, and especially Gina Roach, took responsibility for converting the complex network data into orderly computer printouts. Susan Wells had the equally trying task of translating illegible handwriting into text and tables. The job she began has been completed capably by Ros Gresshoff, Coralie Cullen and Gillian Scott. Nigel Duff drew the figures, and Rita Coles proofread the text and prepared the index. Two visitors, Philip Taietz and Eugene Litwak, brought a welcome balance of enthusiasm and expertise to our efforts. Of the other colleagues who helped in various ways, Lyn Richards and Sidney Sax played an especially important part by commenting on a draft of the entire typescript.

It should be emphasised that only a small proportion of the project's research is presented in this book. In order to meet out multiple objectives, a variety of publications have been tailored for particular topics and audiences. A companion volume, *Ageing and Public Policy in Australia* (Kendig and McCallum, forthcoming, 1986a), covers a wider range of policy-related topics, includes contributors from outside the project, and is directed to a broad audience of professionals and social scientists. *Greying Australia* (Kendig and McCallum, 1986b forthcoming) aims to inform a lay audience about the future of ageing in Australia. An earlier report (Kendig, Gibson, Rowland, and Hemer, 1983) presented survey findings that have a more direct bearing on health and welfare services in the community.

The bulk of the project's findings, however, are presented in individual articles and reports. Studies with a more direct bearing on policies have been conducted on older women by Alice Day, for the National Womens Advisory Council; Commonwealth policies for aged care by Anne Brennan and John Hemer, on second must from the Commonwealth government; and income adequacy by Larry Cromwell, for the Australian Council on the Ageing. Work is now under way on further networks analyses by Stephen Mugford and myself; retirement and income support by John McCallum; policy development by Sidney Sax; and political action by Marian Simms. Particular emphasis will be given to the ethnic aged in my own work.

The principal aim of the Ageing and the Family Project, over its five year span, has been to make a specific research contribution to the development of social gerontology in Australia. It is a vast field and I am keenly aware of my own responsibilities for our having covered but a few of the most pressing topics. At the same time, it is encouraging to note the substantial progress being made throughout Australia: funding, recognition, and publications of research on ageing have increased substantially over recent years. While the Research School is redirecting its resources to conduct limited term projects on other topics, the individuals who have formed the project will be continuing their participation in Australian research on ageing.

Hal L. Kendig
Research School of Social Sciences
The Australian National University
Canberra
July 1985

Part 1

FAMILY AND NETWORK STRUCTURE

1

Perspectives on ageing and families

HAL KENDIG

Ageing, and family relationships, have been central forces shaping individual lives throughout history. At each stage of life, virtually everybody has close interpersonal ties which are major sources of emotional joys and pains, and of practical supports and demands. However, our personal immersion in these concerns stands strangely divorced from any broader understanding of the close bonds of older Australians. The new-found interest in the family, within government and academia, has so far yielded studies which focus almost entirely on marital and parenting experience in early and middle adulthood. The fledgeling field of social gerontology has the substantial challenge of uncovering the scope and nature of family relationships in the latter stages of life.

This book aims to make three basic contributions in developing a comprehensive knowledge of ageing and family relations. First, we provide Australian findings on the remarkable diversity among older people in negotiating support through family and other close personal relationships. Second, we move away from idiosyncratic and per-sonalised accounts by drawing on the rich insights forthcoming from social networks and life span perspectives. The life span approach provides a way of discovering how experiences in old age are influenced by enduring bonds formed in mid-life as well as transitions out of them with child-launching, retirement, and widowhood. The social networks approach provides powerful methods for identifying the many and subtle interconnections between people, and the importance of these ties for quality of life. Finally, we demonstrate the value of combining quantitative research, showing the basic dimensions of social ageing, with qualitative research revealing the individual meanings and actions which lie behind the summary statistics.

Our study is set in the academic and popular debate over the historical transition from traditional to nuclear families in advanced societies (Harris, 1983). One view is that older parents have become relatively isolated as bonds between spouses, and those to their dependent children, become the basic unit of family obligations (Parsons, 1955). Others have countered that older people are embedded in 'modified extended families': the generations may be living in separate households but they are still found to maintain close contact and reciprocal support (Litwak, 1960; Sussman and Burchinall, 1962). In addition to these concerns for the broader structure of families, we focus more specifically on the processes of primary relations, defined by Cooley (1909) as expressive, diffuse, and consensual bonds based on an intrinsic regard between the actors. The more direct parentage of our study can be traced from pioneering British and United States studies documenting the continuing importance of family in the lives of older people (Townsend, 1963; Sussman and Burchinall, 1962; Shanas, et al., 1968).

The scope of the book also can be introduced by providing some basic definitions. While 'social ageing' does not always fit neatly with any chronological age cut-off, we set 60 years of age as our entry point into later life, because it is increasingly becoming the age at which people are expected to retire from work and have a right to income support. We thus include people having a wide range of circumstances across the span of 30 or more years. The often vague notion of social support is conceptualised in two specific ways: expressive ties which reaffirm identity and provide companionship; and instrumental assistance with household tasks and other practical aspects of daily living. Rather than limit ourselves to particular kinds of family or other relationships, we consider any individual or organisation involved with providing or receiving support in these terms. This enables us to carry out comparative analyses of informal bonds with family, friends and neighbours, as well as ties with formal organisations.

The remainder of this first chapter introduces our key concepts and research approaches. In the next section, we apply the concepts of age stratification, status, and exchange to an understanding of older people's personal relationships. These ideas are developed further by considering the nature of different informal and formal bonds, and the ways in which relationships are influenced by the positions of older people within broader social structures. Our research approaches, including a large community survey and three qualitative studies, are briefly reviewed. Finally, an overview is presented on how the concepts introduced in this first chapter are applied to in the findings reported later in the book.

INDIVIDUAL ACTION AND SOCIAL STRUCTURE

The ways in which older people are able to form personal networks, and interact within them, depends on both the underlying bases of the bonds and broader social structures. As a preamble, it is worth emphasising that ageing is as much a social construction as a biological fact. Many changes in old age take place irrespective of any physical decline, and those that do occur are interpreted and given meaning by their social context. Moreover, the gerontological literature shows that the experience of ageing is strongly conditioned by the period of history in which one becomes old, as well as a lifetime's accumulation of orientations, resources, and vulnerabilities (Riley, 1979; Hagestad and Neugarten, 1985). Even among people in the same birth cohort, the experience and timing of major life events, both in old age as well as in earlier years, can vary markedly. Over the passing of many decades, life 'trajectories' can diverge markedly, and the aged may well be more diverse than other age groups (Neugarten and Moore, 1968; Kalish, 1975).

The concept of age stratification provides a useful starting point in understanding the social world of older people (Riley, 1972; Bengtson, Cuellar and Ragan, 1977). Age acts as a social marker structuring expectations for appropriate behaviour and various rights and privileges. Diversity in terms of class background, family circumstances and gender can be conceived as interlocking statuses which combine with age in 'locating' people within wider social structures. Much of the gerontological literature, drawing on role theory (Rosow, 1976) and functionalist sociology (Bengtson and Dowd, 1980), takes these status positions and the transitions out of them as explanation in themselves of older people's behaviour and quality of life.[1] Our use of the concept of status, however, is limited to predisposing (rather than determining) influences on the actions of individuals.

For our purposes, social status has two principal impacts on older people's options and abilities to form and maintain supportive bonds. The first of these is that particular statuses are associated with expectations and resources which influence power and options in interpersonal relationships. The second is that status group membership sets the pool of people who have similarities which facilitate affiliative bonds. Social ageing can thus be understood in terms of reduced social opportunities as people lose positions of power and respect, and become increasingly dissimilar from those in the mainstream of adult life. As an example of both effects, retirement releases people from some obligations but can be accompanied by losses of the income, esteem, and power forthcoming from employment, as well as social ties with co-workers.

The concept of exchange provides a valuable way to understand the interactions which take place within (and indeed form) informal as well as formal relationships. Exchange and the exercise of power are by no means limited to financial and instrumental transactions; they extend in equal measure to 'currency' in purely social and emotional terms (Dowd, 1980). Those who have the least resources can offer only approbation and compliance as their part in the relationship. The retracting social world of older people, far from being a necessary disengagement, can be understood as the withdrawal both of dominant younger people (who no longer receive returns commensurate with investments), and of subordinate older people (whose independence and self-esteem is compromised in each encounter). An exchange approach can incorporate social norms as establishing the agreed understandings which serve as the starting point for negotiations. In this sense, the exchange perspective has close parallels with the symbolic interactionist literature, which conceives of roles as being negotiated, rather than simply 'played' (Marshall, 1979).

Relationships

In understanding interpersonal exchanges, it is important to take into account the comparative statuses of the actors and the expectations they have for each other. In this way Cooley's (1909) conception of the nature of primary bonds can be specified for different kinds of informal relationships (Litwak, 1985). While individual relationships vary considerably, various family and friendship ties tend to involve distinctive patterns in the characteristics of the actors and the terms on which they interact (ibid.; Dono, et al., 1979). We will see that the kind of relationship has a major bearing on the fundamental bases, limits and potentials for the support exchanged through them.

Close family relationships commonly (but by no means always) involve high levels of attachment based on complex patterns of obligation, exchange, and affection built up over the entire life course. Spouses characteristically have especially strong bonds due to long-established interdependencies and shared orientations. But the small marital unit in old age can be rendered vulnerable by low levels of resources, skills, and knowledge. Adult children—although usually evincing less commitment, commonality, and accessibility when compared to spouses—have lifelong attachments to parents, and they are likely to command the greater resources available to the middle generation. While bonds with other relatives typically are weaker and even more variable, it is notable that siblings are age peers exhibiting some of the features of friends, as discussed below, and other relatives can be summarily described by their generation, kin distance, and whether the tie is by blood or by marriage.

In *The Family Life of Old People*, Sussman (1976: 218) goes so far as to say that 'Exchange . . . provides the most viable explanation of primary group relationships'. The norms of filial duty and obligation (Adams, 1968; Hill, 1970) may predispose, but by no means determine, relationships between older parents and their adult children. Their lifelong bonds provide them with a uniquely powerful emotional hold over each other, and the knowledge of how to wield it, for better or worse, with pinpoint accuracy (for some graphic examples, see the case studies reported by Bengtson and Treas, 1980). The difficulty and rarity of completely withdrawing from the bond enhances the power of guilt and approval as levers in these transactions. It also opens the possibilities for complex patterns of intergenerational exchanges over long periods of time in many different 'currencies'; individual families, for example, can develop 'lineage themes' (ibid.) which order the exchanges. It follows that conflict and negotiation potentially are as common and powerful as consensus and selflessness in the dynamics of families. The comparative invisibility of these contests in the eyes of the actors (as well as the hapless researcher who tries to explore them) can be explained by the strong norms against their expression. Indeed, the unstated possibility of making conflict explicit is an influential bargaining tool.

Among non-kin, the category of friend is even less specific, yet usually involves freely-chosen age peers, with whom relationships are often relatively short-term and limited to specific spheres of life; friendship tends to be organised around principles of more immediate and direct reciprocity (Dono et al., 1979). While neighbours are highly accessible, they seldom have the obligatory and long-term commitments of family bonds, and usually have less of the freely-chosen and peer bases characteristic of friendships.

In comparison to close family, friendship evolves within a more voluntary and less normative context. A friendship is always open to the possibility of dwindling away, with little disapproval accruing to either party, and its continuance reflects high levels of reciprocity. The homogeneity which characterises friendship reflects a substantial degree of status equality, and the similarities between friends facilitates interaction which is mutually rewarding and reaffirms the identity and esteem of both parties. Self-esteem is enhanced by having been designated as worthy of being chosen as a friend (Lee, 1984). This contrasts sharply with the demoralising realisation that obligation, rather than mutuality or affection, may underlie relations with family.

Two counterposed perspectives consider the interrelationship between different informal bonds. Litwak and his colleagues (Dono, et al., 1979; Litwak, 1985) argue that the particular structures of groups lend themselves to performing only certain kinds of tasks; hence the absence of particular bonds is seen to risk a 'lost function'. Cantor (1979, 1980) has developed an alternative 'hierarchical compensation model', in which more distant bonds are thought to become important only when the closest relations are unavailable. From this second point of view, 'functions' are more likely to be transferred than lost, and there is an explicit ordering of responsibility from spouses and children through to other relatives and friends and neighbours (Townsend, 1963). The important question, then, is whether different kinds of social support are specific to certain relationships, or substitutable between them (Simmons, 1983-1984). The answer to the question is central to the quality of life of people whose exchange power and pool of informal bonds can be eroded substantially as they grow older.

The various questions pertaining to primary relationships also apply to the distinctive support potentially provided by formal organisations. Cantor's substitution approach conceives of services as a 'last resort' if no informal bonds are available: other researchers have conceptualised the complementarity of 'shared functions' between formal organisations and informal relationships, especially in meeting instrumental needs (Shanas and Sussman, 1977; Litwak, 1985). While formal organisations potentially have far greater resources and skills, primary groups are more flexible, accessible, and personalised. Another view is that the two sectors are competitive: services have been considered as displacing family support (Green, 1983) thus undermining family bonds (Glazer, 1971) and adding to the financial burdens of government (Morris and Sherwood, 1984). The interpretations are closely related to ideological assumptions regarding the respective responsibilities of individuals, families, and the State.

Questions regarding the interrelationship between informal and formal support lie at the heart of the burgeoning literature on older people's support networks (Cantor and Little, 1985; Johnson and Cooper, 1983). While most of these studies merely apply a now fashionable label to the old concept of informal support, a new element is introduced, and the message is as much ideological as it is substantive. Having noted the importance of informal networks, many of these studies then proceed to propose ways of strengthening and extending them. It is no accident that this kind of social engineering was initially proposed in the United States, during a time of sustained and substantial cutbacks of welfare expenditure. There is the explicit assumption (implicit in most studies of substitutability) that family and others in the informal sector should have, as well as do have, first responsibility for the care of the frail aged. When government argues for increased care in the community rather than in institutions (House of Representatives Standing on Expenditure, 1982), there is the risk that the burdens of family care will be heightened rather than lessened (Finch and Groves, 1980; D'Abbs, 1984; Kinnear and Graycar, 1984).

DIVERSITY AMONG OLDER PEOPLE

Having reviewed the concepts of exchange and relationships, we can now turn to some of the major influences on the negotiating power of older people. As we will see throughout the book, the various statuses of older people organise the press of social forces and opportunities over the entire life course (Taylor and Ford, 1983). They structure the arena within which informal bonds evolve, and the skills and resources which influence their negotiation. To paraphrase Marx, people may well lead lives of their own choosing, but they do so within firm constraints over which they have virtually no control.

Before reviewing diversity amongst the aged, it is important to recognise that the power of virtually all older people is eroded by two widespread influences. One of the most damaging is 'ageism', in which age-based expectations include a negative stereotype of the aged as incompetent and dependent (Butler, 1980; Bassili and Reil, 1981). However inaccurate the negative label may be, it can become a self-fulfilling prophecy if older people accept the distorted reflection of themselves (Rodin and Langer, 1980). Older people also may be forced into the difficult position of dealing with others who view them with a 'presumption of incompetence' (Dowd, 1980). While family may in some senses be a 'safe haven' from these harsh realities (Shanas, et al., 1968), two Australian studies have found that close personal bonds can also serve to express and apply ageism: Job (1984) emphasises the active efforts made to resist the stereotypes, while Russell (1981) concentrates on the 'spoiled identities' resulting from the 'stigma' of being aged.

The other widespread influence is forthcoming from the newly-emergent welfare state. While government clearly does ameliorate many problems in an immediate sense, Townsend (1981: 5) presents a convincing argument that '. . . the dependency of the elderly in the twentieth century is being manufactured socially and that its severity is unnecessary'. He shows that government pensions legitimate and allow forced retirement and poverty. The dependencies imposed by disabilities are exacerbated when services deny self-determination and encourage passivity. Policies thus express and perpetuate broader ideologies regarding the devalued status of those who are outside the workforce, and the responsibility of family rather than the public sector in caring for the frail aged in the community. Townsend (1981: 13) strikes an optimistic tone in noting that: 'The defensive and restorative mechanisms of the family temper the dependency created by the State'. It is equally noteworthy, however, that inadequate pensions and services can enforce a family dependency which undermines the affective and affirmative qualities of personal bonds.

Marriage clearly is one of the major factors shaping older people's informal relationships. As numerous studies have shown, marriage brings an accumulation of shared experiences and interdependencies which is virtually unparalleled in any other relationship (Troll, et al., 1979; Russell, 1981). Moreover, it adds a potential set of ties with in-laws, and is usually combined with childbearing; the number and characteristics of descendants set obvious limits to family relations. While 58 per cent of Australians aged 60 or over are married, becoming widowed (29 per cent of the aged) or separated or divorced (6 per cent) involves major adjustments and renegotiations of personal bonds; both can cut off or attenuate social ties (Lopata, 1979; Furstenberg, 1981). Those who have never married (7 per cent) appear to have developed very different orientations, personal skills, and support networks in mid-life (Penman and Stolk, 1984), and these carry over into old age (Johnson and Catalano, 1981).

Gender is equally influential, and interacts closely with marriage patterns. While women comprise 56 per cent of all people aged 60 or over, they are especially common among those in more vulnerable circumstances. Widows outnumber widowers by a four to one margin, and women are similarly over-represented among those who are disabled, impoverished, or living in institutions or their childrens' homes (Kendig, Gibson, Rowland and Hemer, 1983). The two sexes are also conditioned to have different orientations towards family and friends, as well as towards dealing with major life events (Bengtson, Cuellar and Ragan, 1977; West and Simmons, 1983). In her Australian study of life histories, Job (1984) typifies men as being oriented toward 'event confrontation', while women evolve lives around 'network maintenance'. These emotional and social differences, together with disparities of instrumental skills, have emerged primarily out of the social structuring of life investments in paid work among men, and families and homes among women (Weitz, 1977).

Social class is another of the 'social locations' which can facilitate or impede the formation of bonds. While most older Australians depend primarily on a government pension, the material inequalities associated with class background continue in the form of home-ownership (Kendig, 1984a, b), ownership of cars and other useful capital assets, and superannuation benefits. All of these resources directly enhance abilities to maintain independence and contribute in exchange relationships. A more advantaged class background also is related to the continuation of more effective personal skills and coping strategies (West and Simmons, 1983). There is a wide body of literature which shows that class is strongly associated with better health, higher morale, and a delay in the perception (and in many respects the social fact) of being old (Bengtson, Cuellar and Ragan, 1977).

Disability is discussed last, not because it is of any less importance, but because frailty is a contingent risk which typically emerges only late in life. Contrary to the popular conception of old age as a time of pronounced dependency, only 15 per cent of older Australians have a long-term handicap which renders them incapable of managing personal care, communication, or mobility, outside the home (Australian Bureau of Statistics, 1982). However, difficulties which are less severe, or acute and episodic, are much more common (ibid.; Kendig, Gibson, Rowland and Hemer, 1983). It is obvious that health limits can pose severe constraints on social interaction, and dramatically tip the balance of exchange through informal relationships.

There are, of course, many other features of older people which influence their interpersonal negotiations. We will be briefly examining the attrition of collateral kin and same-aged friendships as people grow older. Other topics of considerable importance will not be addressed because they extend beyond the scope of our study. Aspects of personality, such as likeability and orientations toward dependency, have a major bearing on relationships (Goldfarb, 1969; Russell, 1981; Job, 1984) but rate as a secondary priority given our primary concern for distinctly social processes. Ethnicity and migration are clearly major and growing concerns in Australia: our work on the topic has been conducted in collaboration with the Australian Institute of Multicultural Affairs (Rowland, 1983; Kendig, forthcoming 1986a). The primary reason is that a specialised study is necessary to identify rare groups and interview in foreign languages.[2] Finally, we were unable to carry out specialised research on the increasing numbers of older people suffering from dementia, although it is clear that the illness involves social constructions and has major consequences on social networks (Gubrium, 1978).

A RESEARCH APPROACH

Our project began at a time when Australian research on social gerontology was in its very early days. Even now, current information on older Australians is basically encapsulated in three books (Howe, 1981; Russell, 1981; Job, 1984); a report on the needs of older people at home (Australian Council on the Ageing/Department of Community Services, 1985); and small studies reported in the Proceedings of the Australian Association of Gerontology and the newly established *Australian Journal on Ageing*. There are only a few review articles available on ageing and family relationships (Lefroy, 1977; Howe, 1979). As a result, we have collected a wide range of primary information on a number of other topics besides family relationships. Our higher order abstractions have emerged out of a 'double fitting' between a variety of information sources and concepts (Wild, 1981).

The complexity of ageing and family relationships requires a range of methodological as well as disciplinary approaches. The literature attests fully to the importance of employing multiple units of analysis—individuals, dyads, and networks—and examining the views and circumstances of significant others as well as older people themselves (Mangen and Peterson, 1982). There also is the crucial question of the 'level' of analysis, particularly the distinction between quantitative and qualitative research. Too often, social research breaks into 'two methodological subcultures ... one professing the superiority of "deep, rich" observational data, and the other the virtues of "hard, generalizable" survey data' (Sieber, 1973: 1335). The debate is drawn between researchers who consider qualitative work to be unrepresentative and biased, and others who view quantitative analysis as being reductionist, deterministic, and limited to 'positivist' theoretical perspectives. Examples of the conflicting views, as applied to Australian gerontology, can be found in Russell's (1981) rationale for conducting a qualitative study, and reviews by Sweetser (1983) and Howe (1982).

There is an increasing appreciation, however, of the validity of both methodological approaches and the complementarity between them (Jick, 1979; Reichhardt and Cook, 1979). It is more accurate to dissolve the false dichotomies and conceive of a continuum along the poles of purely quantitative and qualitative information. The comparative strength of more quantitative surveys is in objectively identifying social patterns, as they diverge between groups, and in explaining social processes in terms of correlations between many variables. More qualitative studies are better suited to exploring complex meanings and interpretations as particular individuals view the active construction of their social relationships.

An integrated research design can yield findings which draw on the strengths of several research approaches. In recognition of this potential, our research included three levels of analysis and data collection: census data, a large quantitative survey, and three smaller qualitative studies. The topics and methods of the particular substudies were designed in ways which increased comparability between them. Each yielded findings which, in addition to being useful in their own right, are closely interrelated and illuminate different aspects of ageing and family relationships.

As the first stage of our research, we established some of the basic dimensions of the older population in Australia—in terms of demographic characteristics, family structure, living arrangements, and handicaps—based on the Census and national surveys conducted by the Australian Bureau of Statistics (ABS, 1982a).[3] A specially prepared matrix tape from the 1976 Census proved to be particularly useful. These sources cover only a limited range of topics but are available on a national basis, and for earlier periods of history.

In the second stage of our research a community survey of 1050 persons aged 60 or over was conducted in Sydney late in 1981. In order to increase our ability to explore diversity in the experience of ageing, the sample was stratified to over-represent persons aged 75 years or over and under-represent those aged 60 to 64 years. The data were collected in a way which makes it possible to study individuals, couples, households, significant others, and personal support networks as a whole. Appendix 1 provides more information on the data items, fieldwork procedures and response rates, and sample weights; as well as specific measures of disability, occupational status, and various network characteristics.

Following the basic approach developed by McAllister and Fischer (1978), the questionnaire concentrated on identifying the personal networks of individuals with whom respondents exchanged various kinds of instrumental and expressive support. The information on older people's contributions, which is seldom found in the problem-focused literature, proved to be essential in analysing patterns of exchange and reciprocity. The relationship, age, gender, and other key statuses of these significant others were recorded in order to explore the influence of broader social structures on primary bonds. Additional questions measured the respondents' personal characteristics, quality of life, social interaction, and attitudes toward care and family relationships.

Several strategies were adapted to overcome some of the limitations of a cross-sectional study. Respondents were asked about their own parents' experiences in old age, thus providing data linking the previous and present generations of older people. The life span approach was developed in questions on respondents' family and employment experiences earlier in adulthood. The questionnaire also addressed recent changes of social relationships and capabilities; these included adjustments and support associated with widowhood, retirement, and illness.

While many methodological treatises view qualitative studies as exploratory exercises, mere preliminaries to quantitative research, our experience is that the two approaches are fruitfully viewed as parallel and equal partners in a research inquiry. The third stage of our research thus consisted of three qualitative studies; these are described more fully in Appendixes 2 and 3. The first study explored the life histories and orientations toward care of 23 individuals aged 75 or over; the interviews were held with selected respondents in the quantitative survey to illustrate a range of life circumstances (Day, 1985). Seventeen of the close family members of these older people were interviewed in the second qualitative study (Carter, 1985)[4]. Finally, as part of a larger study of 'social pathways' into institutions, qualitative interviews were carried out with 90 recent entrants to nursing homes, and 79 of their close relatives who were involved with the decision (Minichiello, in progress). The qualitative studies widened the range of respondents in our study, in addition to developing a more complete picture of individual perceptions and actions.

In interpreting our various findings, it is essential to keep three major limitations of the data in mind. The first is that the people who are least successful in ageing are not included in our study. For the cohort of Australians born in 1920, only half at that time were expected to survive to age 60 (Australian Bureau of Statistics, 1984b); the chances of surviving to old age are least among men, the never married, and the lower classes (ibid.; Cox, 1970). While the Census data covers all surviving old people, our quantitative survey excludes the 7 per cent who are in institutions; and 30 per cent of the selected sample could not be interviewed (See Appendix 1). The study of people in nursing homes included only the relatively more capable residents (See Appendix 3). While many studies (such as Morris and Sherwood, 1984) fail to acknowledge the point, these inevitable limitations must be fully appreciated if one is to avoid developing a misleadingly favourable view of older people's circumstances.

A second caution is that cross-sectional data is of limited value in examining changes associated with ageing. Our analysis concentrates on the social impact of diversity in terms of marital status, gender, and disability—not ageing itself among the aged. The association between these variables and age is partly attributable to different cohort experiences (such as the higher proportion of never-married women in the cohort coming of age during the Depression); it is also affected by differential rates of survival and institutionalisation. Similarly, retrospective questions on the timing of certain events, such as retirement, will be influenced by the period of history when the event took place. While we believe that most of the age-related differences in our findings are due to ageing effects, this could be established definitely only by conducting a longitudinal study, and carrying out cross sequential analyses (Schaie, 1973) that separate out cohort, ageing, and period effects.

This brings us to the third qualification: our research on the Australian aged in the early 1980s is very much delimited by the prior experiences of the current cohort of older people, and contemporary historical circumstances. Elder (1974; 1978a), for example, has shown that the generation which came of age during the depression has been extensively and perhaps uniquely affected by this experience during a formative stage of life. Similarly, Australians born in the 19th Century have orientations towards gender relations, family life, and work which are very different from those found over more recent decades (Job, 1984). In concluding the book, we will consider the point that the aged are our 'future selves' (Blythe, 1979), and make a speculative assessment of ageing and family relationships in the future.

We are confident that our findings based on Sydney alone (which has a fifth of Australia's older people) reflect quite accurately the circumstances of the 60 per cent of older Australians who live in capital cities. A 1981 survey on the circumstances and needs of older people in Melbourne and Adelaide (Australian Council on the Ageing, and the Commonwealth Department of Community Services, 1985) has yielded findings very similar to those from our study. The age, living arrangements, and other characteristics of the aged in Sydney are very close to those found for the nation as a whole (See Appendix 1). In rural areas and small towns, however, there could well be different patterns, particularly in terms of available family and services (Dempsey, 1981; ABS, 1984a; Wenger, 1984). Finally, we are struck by the close parallels between our findings and those from a wide variety of American studies (Kendig and Rowland, 1983), which suggests that the place of the aged has many similarities between advanced English-speaking countries.

CHAPTER OVERVIEW

This first chapter has introduced the primary concepts and research approaches in our study of the support provided and received by older people. Figure 1.1, which summarises our topics of investigation, shows the central attention given to the membership of personal networks and the kinds of support which flow through them ('B'). These ties are understood in terms of diverse experiences of individuals over the entire life course, and the status characteristics which situate them within the broader social structure ('A'). The importance of networks is assessed by the adequacy of support, and its impact on satisfaction with relationships and quality of life ('C'). The following chapters draw on our range of quantitative and qualitative research to identify and explain the interrelationships between these topics.

Figure 1.1 Primary topics of investigation.

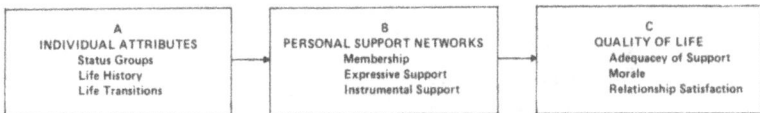

A INDIVIDUAL ATTRIBUTES Status Groups Life History Life Transitions	B PERSONAL SUPPORT NETWORKS Membership Expressive Support Instrumental Support	C QUALITY OF LIFE Adequacey of Support Morale Relationship Satisfaction

Note: This schema is adapted from a more complex one reported in Gibson and Kendig (1982)

The remaining two chapters in this first part of the book outline some of the basic dimensions of family structure and social networks. Chapter 2 uses census and survey data to show the family building and dissolution of present and past generations of older Australians, and their membership of traditional joint-households and modified extended-families. Chapter 3 presents survey findings on how life circumstances and backgrounds influence the formation of personal support networks as a whole.

Part 2 of the book examines more specifically the kinds of support provided and received through personal support networks. Chapter 4 draws on the survey findings to examine expressive bonds and their influence on quality of life. The next chapter, on instrumental support, provides parallel findings on the two-way flow of informal aid over the life course. Chapter 6 presents complementary case studies which identify the meanings and diversity which underlie the survey findings.

While earlier chapters consider stages along an ageing career, the final section of the book considers key transitions between them. Chapter 7 focuses on retirement and widowhood, the ways in which personal networks respond to these events, and their consequences on social relationships and quality of life. Chapter 8 explores negotiations with family while older people move from the community into nursing homes, a final transition prior to death. The concluding chapter considers the broader 'transitions' associated with social change, and sketches policy options which would improve the social circumstances of older Australians.

2

Family structure

DON T. ROWLAND

Older people look back on lifetimes spanning much of the 20th century. They remember events and innovations which have transformed society, including some that were thought to threaten the very survival of the family. Declining birth rates, rising divorce rates, the dispersal of sons and daughters and the institutionalisation of aged parents: all might seem to be signs of a break with the past and the loss of the family's role in bringing security and meaning to people's lives. Yet the pace and extent of change in the family circumstances of older people are easily exaggerated. There has been much continuity over time, and there have been improvements as well as losses. This chapter reviews the antecedents of contemporary family circumstances and discusses causes and consequences of ongoing changes in later life. Two categories of changes are identified: those occurring over an individual lifetime or lifecycle, and those differentiating the experience of each birth cohort (that is persons born in the same period of time, such as a decade).

Family structure is crucial to understanding relationships between family members during the ageing process (Townsend, 1968). Family structure also affects the availability of support and the participation of the elderly in society. This chapter discusses the nature of family structure and its implications for instrumental support for the elderly. Family support is a two-way process, however, and the chapter is intended also as background to later chapters which examine the exchange of instrumental and expressive support between family members.

For decades the family and the aged have each been subjects of misinformation in Australia and, inevitably, family life in old age has been unusually misrepresented. So misleading are popular stereotypes that it is not only research findings that offer surprises, for even research questions deserving priority are not necessarily obvious ones. A number of questions are addressed here including: Why has declining family size had little effect on potential family support? Why do older generations prefer to live apart from their younger relatives? Why are the poor, under-represented in institutions? Why do the great majority of the disabled elderly live in private households? Why do cultural factors only partly explain the formation of joint households by the ethnic minority elderly and their sons and daughters? Answers to these questions mainly emphasise the enduring and pervasive importance of the family, as well as the limits beyond which its resources should not be stretched.

In studies of the aged in industrial societies the family is commonly defined as the network of relatives, related by descent or marriage, with whom the elderly have frequent contact (Shanas, et al., 1968; Troll, 1971; Townsend, 1977). Thus family structure includes relatives in the same household, together with others who live elsewhere. These two divisions provide a basis for organising research into the family situation of the aged. On the one hand there are questions about choices of living arrangements and relationships between members of the same household. On the other hand are questions about social interaction with relatives who live separately. This dual approach, supplemented by comparisons between co-residents and others, enables the frequency and practicality of different forms of family support to be made clear.

Generally, the household is the 'front line' of support in times of need, since co-residents are best able to give high levels of assistance. Less effective in situations of continuing need, but very important where regular contact is necessary, is the second line of defence represented by relatives, and others, who live in dwellings close by. Finally, the 'reserve defences' consist of family members who live in more distant places. They can help in emergencies, take a needy relative into their own home, or provide some support through telephone conversations and occasional visits. Hence the adequacy of family resources can be assessed according to whether people have relatives in the same household, in the same district or in more distant locations. The availability of family resources further depends on the characteristics of family members and the nature of their relationships. Nevertheless, family structure is a useful starting point in establishing the numbers of the aged who potentially have sufficient family resources to enable them to remain in their own homes, or at least in the community, in the face of frailty.

CHANGES THROUGH TIME

Diversity is the overriding characteristic of the elderly. They span an age-range of more than thirty years and they cover the full spectrum of categories of income, health and ethnicity. Similarly, family structure varies considerably; in the survey of the aged in Sydney, 44 per cent of respondents had no spouse, 37 per cent had no daughters, 17 per cent had no surviving children, and 20 per cent had no living siblings. The lack of a spouse or a daughter is especially significant since, as shown in later chapters, they figure most prominently in the networks of the disabled aged.

The pool of relatives with whom the elderly can interact inevitably diminishes with age, particularly through deaths of members of the same generation: spouses, siblings, friends and long-time neighbours. The numbers in the younger generation of sons and daughters remain fairly intact during a parent's old age, and the great majority of the elderly have close relatives surviving. An indication of the size of the family is given by the proportions of the elderly having a spouse and one or more children and siblings (Figure 2.1). In the survey, fewer than 3 per cent of respondents had no such relatives, and men, in particular, commonly had several family members who might render assistance. It is clear that changes in patterns of family formation over time have by no means left the aged bereft of relatives who might give occasional help with shopping and other household needs, if not with personal care.

Figure 2.1   Respondents with a surviving spouse, child and/or sibling (percentages)

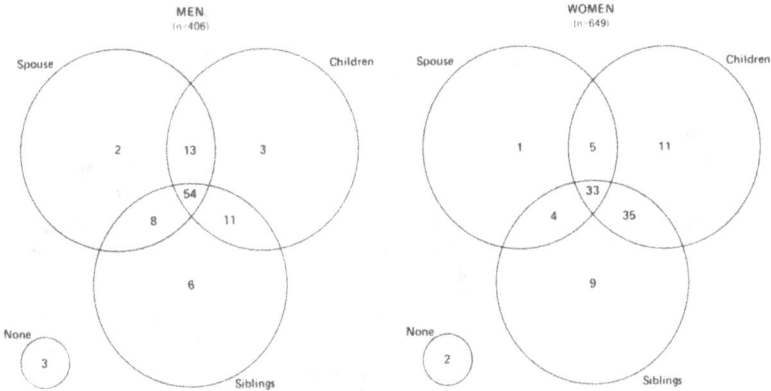

Note: Spouses of separated persons excluded
Source: Ageing and The Family Project Survey, Sydney 1981

The continuing trend over past decades is towards a decline in the diversity of family structures, since most people marry, have two or three children and survive to become grandparents. Thus in Australia, where birth and death rates are low, families consisting of three surviving generations of equal size are becoming typical. This pattern of similar size generations—below the ages of high mortality—will not be fully achieved until the 21st century because of the ongoing effects of past changes. The present transitional situation offers several advantages and disadvantages in relation to family support.

One advantage is that the numbers in the older generations are still relatively low; consequently the level of aged dependency is also low. In 1981 there were 23 people aged 60 years and over for every hundred of working age, and the former group comprised 14 per cent of the total population. Neither of these indices will rise appreciably until the second decade of the next century, but thereafter, the pace of demographic ageing will accelerate. Present conditions represent an opportunity to prepare socially and economically for this major change. Nevertheless, significant changes are already in progress: while the numbers aged 60 and over may increase by nearly 50 per cent between 1981 and 2001, the numbers aged 75 and over—who are most vulnerable to disabling illnesses—could increase by 100 per cent or more.

Another advantage of the present situation is that the number of potential family supporters for the aged will increase during the 1990s. This may seem surprising in that it appears to contradict the evidence of falling family size over time. Figure 2.2 shows that average completed family size for married women declined from more than six children in the 1880s to just over two in the 1930s. Such a decline would have reduced dramatically the number of sons and daughters present in their parents' old age were it not for the opposite impact of falling mortality. The diagram shows that, of children born in the 19th century, only about half survived to 60 years—the age by which a child would have outlived parents or would have seen them reach an advanced age. Thus a family size of six produced, on average, only three potential supporters for parents in old age: the large family system did not create an equally numerous stock of potential carers. Conversely, the small family system now prevalent has not reduced substantially the numbers of prospective carers. Low mortality rates virtually guarantee that the majority of people born since the Second World War will celebrate their sixtieth birthdays. Average family sizes of two or three children, therefore, ensure the survival of two children during their parent's old age.

Despite the predominance of small families since the 1930s, average family size has continued to vary, albeit within a narrow range. Women whose main reproductive years spanned the Great Depression and the Second World War had the smallest average family size and the highest levels of childlessness ever recorded in Australia. Since, by the late 1980s, all of them will have reached, the 'old-old' ages (75 years and over) where ill-health is more prevalent, this decade is distinctive as a period of restricted access to family support

Figure 2.2(a) Family size and survival of children for cohorts of married women at the age of 60

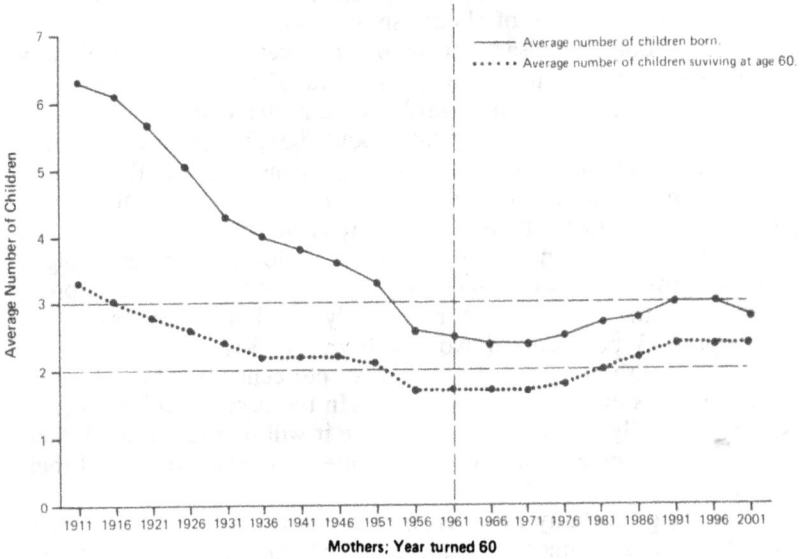

Figure 2.2(b) Percentage of childless for cohorts of married women at the age of 60

Sources: Rowland (1984);
1981 Census

for old people who are most at risk. During the 1990s the situation will gradually improve as the oldest age groups become dominated by cohorts which had higher marriage rates, larger average family size and a lower incidence of childlessness (Figure 2.2).

Apart from one disadvantage of the present situation already mentioned—the limited family resources of the frail aged in the 1980s—there is the further problem that the demand for family support will continue to grow until about 2031, by which year a more even representation of older and younger generations in the population will have emerged (Rowland, 1983a). Although the numbers of middle-aged persons in an average family network has not changed dramatically over time, the opposite is true for the numbers of aged kin. Improvements in survival are still increasing the proportion of families with aged, and more notably, frail aged relatives. For example, 53 per cent of women born in 1851 reached age 60, compared with a projected figure of 93 per cent for women born in 1950 (Lancaster, 1959; Young, 1969). In the past the elderly were a rarity in family networks; in the future it will be the norm for their generation to be as numerous, for a time, as the generations of their children and grandchildren.

Declining mortality at older ages is contributing to this process. Controversy surrounds the question of whether lower mortality is a sign of more years of life in good health; yet whatever the trend in health, there will remain heavy demands for family support in the declining years or in the final illness. This is more pertinent to the present than to the past because very high proportions of people are living to ages at which non-fatal disabling diseases are prevalent. There is thus no question whether many more families will be faced with decisions about providing for frail aged parents. The question is how or whether they will meet such demands.

One expectation, based on stereotypes of family life in the past, is that family support for the elderly is now less likely because fewer live with their sons and daughters. This belief is as misleading as that about declining family size and the supposed drastic fall in the number of potential carers. There is little evidence that extended family living, producing households of three generations, was ever frequent in Australia or in Great Britain and the United States (Laslett, 1977; Uhlenberg, 1977). In the survey of the aged in Sydney only a small proportion of respondents said that during their childhood a grandparent lived in the same household (Table 2.1). Overall, only 11 per cent of the Australian-born and 12 per cent of the overseas-born reported co-residence with any grandparents before turning fifteen. Contributing to this pattern were lower rates of survival to old age and the separation of generations through overseas migration to Australia. But also important then, as now, were preferences for separate households and the formation of joint-living arrangements only near the end of older people's lives, after their grandchildren had left home. Households of two rather than three generations generally resulted when an elderly parent moved to live with a son or daughter.

Table 2.1 Household membership of survey respondents when ten years of age (1901–1931) by birthplace (n = 465)

Household member	Birthplace of respondent		
	Australia (342) (%)	Overseas (123) (%)	Total (465) (%)
Mother/stepmother	94	90	93
Father/stepfather	90	84	88
Siblings (one or more)	86	79	84
Grandmother	8	9	8
Grandfather	5	3	5
Aunts	4	—	3
Uncles	3	—	2
Cousins	2	2	2
Other relatives	—	—	—
Boarders/lodgers	2	—	1
Servants	2	5	3
Other non-relatives	—	2	1

Reinforcing the frequency of separate living arrangements over time has been the trend towards more universal marriage. It is often forgotten that wives and husbands are the main supporters of the aged, as discussed in later chapters. In 1981, for example, 94 per cent of currently married handicapped persons aged 65 and over were living in private households, compared with 63 per cent of the never-married handicapped aged (Gibson and Rowland, 1984). The wider availability of the assistance of spouses is denoted in rises in the proportions of older people married: for instance, at ages 60–64 the proportion of men married has increased from 64 per cent to over 80 per cent this century. Higher proportions marrying also means that relatively more have the potential support of their own children. At the same time, declining mortality rates have postponed widowhood to later ages, extending the period over which married couples can maintain their independence through mutual support.

Changes in the composition of the older population and its needs result from the ageing of cohorts with differing life experiences. The cohort born from 1900 to 1910 is the most deprived in terms of family; about a quarter of them have no surviving children and they are necessarily more reliant on others. In contrast, the family resources of the cohorts born in the 1930s are the most abundant in living memory (Figure 2.2). For them, government policies which complement family support will be especially relevant. Variations in the size and longevity of cohorts are responsible for further changes in the amount and duration of assistance needed. Longer life, for instance, extends the time over which income maintenance is needed and increases the proportions experiencing disabling diseases. If death rates decline at 1.5 per cent annually for the last twenty years of this century, and are constant after that, the 1950s baby boom cohort will be at the current pensionable age (women from 60, men from 65) for 14 per cent longer than if its mortality is constant at 1981 levels. Also, because of its greater numbers, the baby boom generation could have a total of almost 45 million person-years at these ages, compared with 29 million for the 1930s cohort. Variations in cohort size and composition necessitate continual reviews of government and business activities which are age-specific in application. Preparedness to meet future changes resulting from cohort succession is largely dependent on the better use of census and survey information.

THE LATER LIFE CYCLE

Norman Ryder (1965) likened the study of cohorts to writing macro-biographies of generations. One approach to organising such biographies, and facilitating comparisons between them, is to use the life cycle concept. This describes the succession of stages through which the typical family passes (Spanier and Glick, 1980). Cohort differences in the timing and duration of life cycle stages highlight the extent of changes in the family through time (Young, 1977). The life cycle, however, is intended to be more than a representation of a sequence of events. It has important applications in identifying shifts in family needs and resources, as well as in demonstrating that the family is never static (Young, 1977). Criticisms of life cycle work have drawn attention especially to preoccupations with average behaviour, and an over-emphasis on the nuclear family household to the neglect of the wider family network. Nevertheless, averages are essential points of reference in comparative studies provided that variations are also documented, and life cycle related changes in household composition are central considerations in understanding the functioning of the wider family network.

Some writers have seen widowhood or 'the ageing family' as the last stage in the life cycle (Elder, 1978b: 45). Others, however, have identified a number of stages in later life, thereby giving better recognition to old age as a time of major adjustments (Townsend, 1968; Treas, 1975). Such stages, which Treas (1975) referred to as the 'later life cycle', are essential to an understanding of adjustments in living arrangements in old age, since they identify the major events precipitating change. Drawing on previous work, a new and more comprehensive later life cycle scheme has been proposed (Rowland,

Table 2.2 Later life cycle stages

Stages	
1st	Child-launching
2nd	Childless pre-retirement
3rd	Birth of first grandchild
4th	Death of last parent
5th	Retirement
6th	Birth of first great-grandchild
7th	Death of spouse
8th	Disability
	(a) locality-bound
	(b) house-bound
	(c) bed-bound

Source: Rowland (1982a)

1982a). The stages are a combination of life events, potentially experienced by all, and family events confined to people who have married and had children (Table 2.2). The later life cycle is especially relevant to the study of living arrangements or household composition (Rowland, 1982b). It is noteworthy that the stages of later life are mostly beyond the older person's initiative—nearly all are inevitable consequences of ageing. This feature eliminates some of the variability typical of earlier stages of life, which are more dependent on voluntary decisions.

There have been significant changes this century in the timing of later life cycle stages in the United States (Hareven, 1978; Uhlenberg, 1978) as well as in Australia (Young, 1977). Child-launching has been completed at younger ages over time, because of a decrease in the age of women at the birth of their last child, and the desire of sons and daughters for earlier independence. The childless pre-retirement stage, or 'empty nest', has been lengthening in duration because of the earlier completion of child-bearing and the later average age of widowhood. Retirement from the workforce has become almost universal, and is now more frequent at ages 60 or younger (Bureau of Labour Market Research, 1983). At retirement, living arrangements do not change, but release from work ties may enable a residential move to another community. Retirement migration has implications for future living arrangements according to whether other family members live in the new community, and whether the community provides services assisting the disabled elderly to continue to live at home. In retirement communities, responses to problems of old age are often institutionalisation or outward migration, because of a lack of family or home-based means of support.

The life cycles of the aged are intertwined with those of their younger relatives. The stages of 'birth of first grandchild' and 'birth of

Table 2.3 Living arrangements by ability to go out of doors (n = 1048)

Living arrangement	Without difficulty (923) (%)	With difficulty (52) (%)	Only with help (46) (%)	Not at all (27) (%)
Alone	24.7	34.6	21.7	14.8
With spouse only	46.8	32.6	30.4	37.0
With spouse & others	12.7	5.8	6.5	3.7
With siblings	3.8	5.8	6.5	3.7
With son(s) and daughter(s)	4.3	1.9	10.9	25.9
With family of son/daughter	3.1	15.4	15.2	7.4
With others	4.5	3.8	8.7	7.4
Total (percentage)	100.0	100.0	100.0	100.0

first great-grandchild' have implications for family relationships since young children provide social opportunities for older people but limit the likelihood of co-residence of the aged and their families. Also sons and daughters who are grandparents themselves may be too involved in other family roles to provide substantial assistance to parents. Thus while some stages of the later life cycle entail no change in living arrangements, they remain significant in that they can influence other aspects of family life and subsequent events. When the spouse dies, living arrangements inevitably change and diverge according to the situation of the surviving partner. Alternatives include living alone independently, remaining at home with support from the modified extended family and services, moving in with relatives, or moving to a retirement village or a home for the aged. Choices at this time depend especially on whether an elderly person is disabled. Following Gordon, et al. (1976), the later life cycle sequence identifies three stages of disability, each of which may lead to differing living arrangements (Table 2.2). The nature of the local community, in terms of the accessibility of essential services and the availability of domiciliary support, further affects decisions about living arrangements and housing as a person's mobility becomes more restricted (Table 2.3).

DECISIONS AFFECTING HOUSEHOLD STRUCTURE

The later life cycle represents events affecting family structure within the household, together with other events which influence the future course of changes. To this framework must be added an explanation for the divergence in living arrangements at particular life cycle stages. Decisions about living arrangements are generally made with reference to three considerations: autonomy, integration and security.

Autonomy, or freedom from the control of others, is a prized possession. Individuals' ability to achieve and sustain autonomy has increased over time on account of higher incomes, rising rates of home ownership, and the provision of subsidised housing and domiciliary services. Nevertheless, disabilities associated with ageing reduce capacities to live independently at advanced ages.

Integration, or participation in family life (Gibson, 1983), is another key consideration in decisions about living arrangements. In studies of the elderly in Western societies, a repeated finding is the prevalence of preferences for 'intimacy at a distance' with relatives (Rosenmayr and Kockeis, 1963; Shanas and Hauser, 1974). This form of family involvement is sustained by visits and other regular contacts between family members who live separately. 'Intimacy at a distance' is most accessible to the aged who are healthy and mobile; the frail aged often must accept a degree of contact with relatives that is well above or well below the norm.

Whereas changes associated with ageing lessen personal autonomy and cause divergence in relation to participation in family life, they increase the importance of security in decisions about living arrangements. Security considerations refer to the accessibility of personal help in the event of an accident or illness. Such needs loom larger at each stage of disability, and in decisions about living arrangements other major considerations may be sacrificed to obtain security. Consequences can include premature surrender of autonomy and excessive levels of institutionalisation.

Attainment of the goals of autonomy, integration and security depend on individual resources, especially those of family, health and wealth. Groups with the most resources cluster in the types of living arrangements preferred in Western societies—conjugal and single-person households, which afford high levels of personal autonomy. By contrast, groups with limited resources cluster in less commonly favoured situations, where autonomy is more restricted, especially households of younger relatives. Ensuing sections examine how abilities to achieve autonomy, integration and security in relation to living arrangements vary according to personal resources.

Family resources

Family resources may be considered in terms of the dual categories mentioned at the beginning of the chapter, that is, relatives within and beyond the household. The latter are especially important in

providing instrumental support after the crises in the later life
cycle—widowhood and the commencement of each stage of disability. Family resources for instrumental support are most favourable
for the married elderly, because mutual assistance enables them to
preserve autonomy, security and 'intimacy at a distance' with other
relatives. Men are more likely than women to be in this advantageous
situation: on average, they have younger wives, shorter lifespans and
a wife who is more oriented to providing care during illness. In 1981,
75 per cent of men aged 60 years and over were currently married,
compared with 45 per cent of older women.

When the spouse is incapacitated the married elderly, like the
widowed, necessarily turn to other relatives for assistance in times of
need. If their own health is good they may continue to live independently. Indeed, wishes to preserve personal autonomy and 'intimacy

**Figure 2.3   Proportions of older men and women in different types of living
arrangements, Australia, 1976**

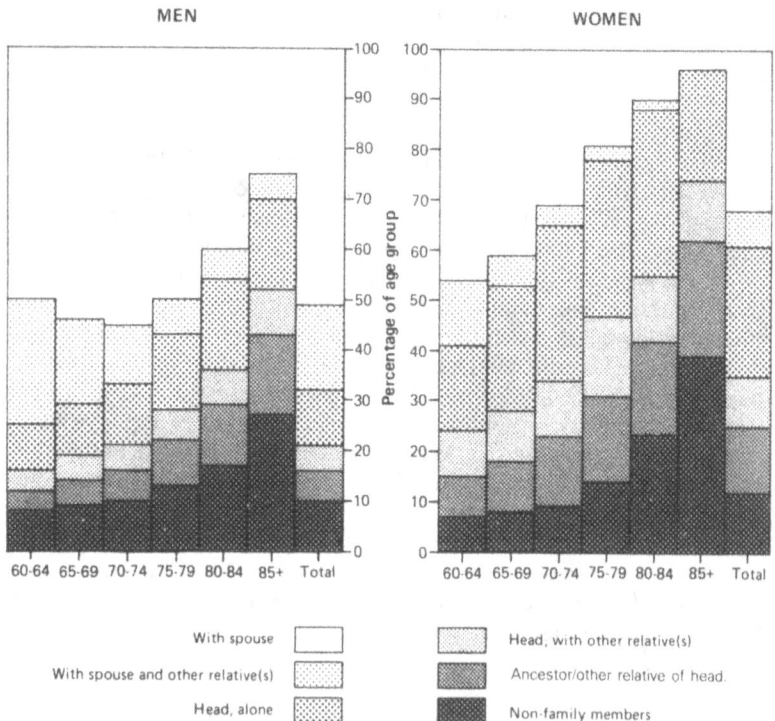

MEN

WOMEN

Percentage of age group

60-64 65-69 70-74 75-79 80-84 85+ Total

60-64 65-69 70-74 75-79 80-84 85+ Total

With spouse

Head, with other relative(s)

With spouse and other relative(s)

Ancestor/other relative of head.

Head, alone

Non-family members

Note: ('non-family' members include older people who are boarders, employees, guests,
          inmates and patients. The majority are in non-private dwellings, especially institutions)
Source: 1976 Census, Matrix Tape No. 25

at a distance' go far towards explaining the prevalence of living alone after widowhood. In Australia, 19 per cent of persons sixty-and-over live alone, compared with 46 per cent of widows (Figure 2.3). However, if the remaining partner's health is impaired, or if security is an issue, he or she may go to live with a younger relative. Since disabling illnesses become more prevalent with greater age, the proportion living in a relative's household also increases with age (Figure 2.3). Furthermore, security considerations prompt sons and daughters to persuade aged parents to live with them, even if security is not a major concern to the parents themselves. Thus, at the death or institutionalisation of the spouse, divergence in choices of living arrangements occurs according to the remaining partner's health and family situation.

After the spouse, daughters and sons generally have the closest relationships with the aged. One option for relatives of the frail aged is to provide assistance through joint-living arrangements, at the cost of 'intimacy at a distance'. As mentioned earlier, joint households more commonly consist of two rather than three generations. In the Sydney survey, only 4 per cent of respondents lived in three generation households, and three-quarters of these were living with a daughter's family. The likelihood of forming joint-households depends partly on family size. National census statistics (1976) show that 22 per cent of widows aged 75 and over with one or two children were in joint living arrangements, compared with 29 per cent of those with three or more children. The existence of households of the aged and their sons and daughters, however, is not necessarily indicative of need on the part of the older generation. Sometimes the children have not left home, and sometimes the aged are assisting other family members by providing housing: in the Sydney survey, half the respondents who were living with persons other than their spouse either owned or rented the dwelling. Moreover, even in the three-generation house-holds about a quarter of the aged said they were the owners or renters.

Provision of many kinds of instrumental support by sons and daughters is by no means dependent on joint-living arrangements. Whereas it is often thought that the high level of residential mobility in industrial societies causes a wide dispersal of different generations, survey materials confirm that dispersal is normally limited to an extent which permits the functioning of the family type described as the 'modified extended family' (Litwak, 1960). Despite high mobility during early adulthood, a predominance of short-distance moves within capital cities results in the majority of the elderly there having relatives living nearby. The Sydney survey revealed that 55 per cent of elderly parents had one or more children living in the same household or within about 8 kilometres, and 87 per cent had at least one child in Sydney (Table 2.4). A large family is not a prerequisite to having children nearby, nor is there a tendency for more daughters than sons to live close (Rowland, 1983c). Residential propinquity is particularly significant to the support needs of the elderly who live alone. Membership of a modified extended family helps to explain why so many of the aged can continue to live alone, even if disabled to the extent of being housebound (Table 2.3). Of respondents in the Sydney survey who had children but lived alone, about 40 per cent had at least one son or daughter within 8 kilometres, and over 80 per cent had at least one in Sydney. The kind of assistance that most of the frail aged require does not include personal care, and membership of a modified extended family is a sign of potential access to the kinds of support most widely required, such as with shopping, housework and transport. About a third of survey respondents who lived alone were housebound yet were able to maintain autonomy through outside help. Living with or near a sibling also offers potential access to social contact and some kinds of support. Four per cent of the survey respondents in Sydney lived with a sibling; these were mainly households of two sisters. Overall, family resources are a crucial determinant of living arrangements as different stages of the later life cycle are reached. Family resources are especially important in providing the alternatives of living alone with outside help or moving to live with relatives. These options are denied to most of those who never married or never had children.

Table 2.4   Location of nearest child, by number of living children (cumulative percentage) (n = 775)

Location of nearest child	Number of living children				Total 1–4
	1 (196) (%)	2 (346) (%)	3 (165) (%)	4 (68) (%)	(775) (%)
Same household	18.9	23.1	25.4	39.7	24.0
Neighbouring house	19.9	24.8	29.1	42.6	26.1
Same suburb	28.1	32.4	37.0	60.3	33.9
Within 8 km	47.9	51.2	60.0	77.9	54.6
Within Sydney	82.1	85.8	94.5	91.2	87.2

Life chances

Although the modified extended family is the most prevalent family type, it is not universally attainable or preferred. The elderly in disadvantaged socio-economic groups have fewer opportunities to live in their own independent households. Census statistics on individual incomes provide one measure of the way in which economic deprivation restricts choices of living arrangements. Analyses of such data show that the elderly on relatively high incomes—more than $12 000 in 1976—cluster in preferred living arrangements with high autonomy (that is, they live with a spouse or alone). Home ownership and the ability to afford paid-help with housework and home maintenance assist them in living independently after widowhood.

By contrast, the elderly on low incomes, of $3000 or less in 1976, cluster in less-preferred situations. This group, who are mainly people dependent on an age or widows' pension for their income, are disproportionately represented in joint-living arrangements with younger relatives. For example, among women aged 75 years and over in 1976, 19 per cent of those on low incomes lived in a son's or daughter's household compared with 8 per cent of those on higher incomes. The restrictions on the choices of living arrangements by the low income group is particularly significant considering that it includes about 63 per cent of total persons aged 75 years and over.

While the situation described for the richest and poorest groups is reasonably predictable, that for the middle income group is less so. A problem in interpreting their situation is that census figures do not distinguish adequately between persons in self-contained units in a sheltered environment, and the more dependent aged occupying hostel rooms and nursing home beds. Nevertheless, census statistics for 'old-old' women on middle range incomes suggest that they are more likely than others to obtain all forms of sheltered accommodation—in retirement villages, hostels, hospitals and nursing homes. In 1976, 18 per cent of old-old women were in institutional accommodation, but the figure for those with incomes of $3001 to $6000 was 44 per cent. The latter group comprised only 24 per cent of the total women aged 75 and over but they accounted for 60 per cent of the institutional placements for this age-sex group. Instead of merely reflecting a lack of choice, institutional accommodation is actively sought by some who are able to afford it. For the elderly with the lowest incomes, living with a son or daughter is a frequent alternative not only to living in a retirement village but also to staying in a hospital or nursing home. If wealth remains essential to obtaining retirement village housing, the majority of the frail elderly will continue to have limited access to the forms of sheltered accommodation which offer security in old age, without undue sacrifice of autonomy.

Health

Because of popular expectations that institutionalisation is the main response to failing health in old age, it is seldom appreciated that families bear the greater part of the responsibility for the care of the frail aged. Clear evidence of this is that more than two-thirds of severely handicapped older people live in private households (Gibson and Rowland, 1984). Such people require personal help or supervision with self-care, mobility and/or communication. If all severely handicapped older people were accommodated in hospitals, nursing homes or homes for the aged, 15 per cent of the total population aged 60 years or more would be in institutions, instead of the present figure of 5 per cent. The presence of family support, as discussed in Chapters 5 and 6, is thus a major preventative of institutionalisation.

Figure 2.4 **Age structure of the older population and numbers of handicapped persons in households and institutions, 1981**

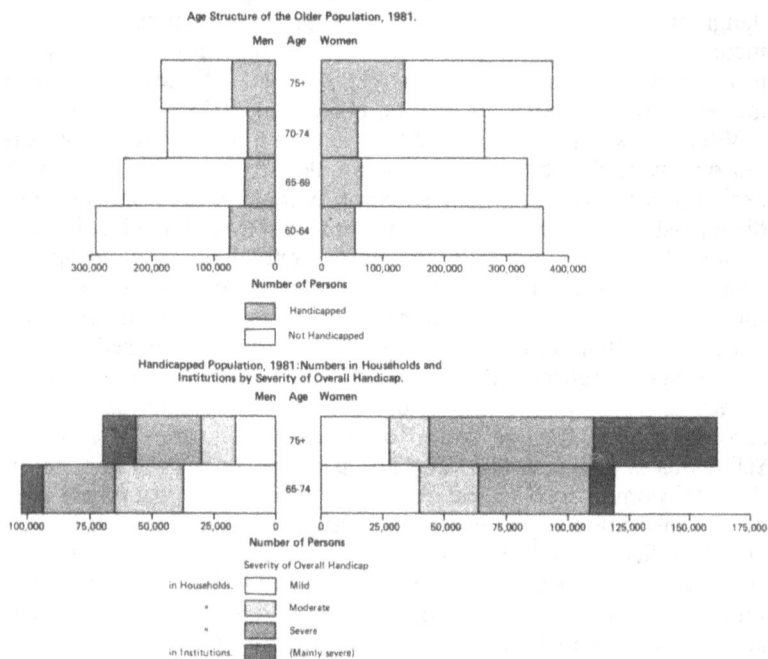

Age Structure of the Older Population, 1981.

Men   Age   Women

Number of Persons

☐ Handicapped

☐ Not Handicapped

Handicapped Population, 1981:Numbers in Households and Institutions by Severity of Overall Handicap.

Men   Age   Women

Number of Persons

Severity of Overall Handicap

in Households: ☐ Mild
"   ☐ Moderate
"   ☐ Severe
in Institutions: ☐ (Mainly severe)

Notes: Handicapped persons here are people who have a disability or impairment which limits, to some degree, their ability to perform activities in relation to self-care, mobility or communication. Self-care handicaps are difficulties in showering, bathing, dressing or eating a meal. Mobility handicaps include difficulties in using public transport, moving around one's own home, moving around unfamilar places, walking 200m and walking up and down stairs. Communication handicaps refer to difficulties understanding or being understood in one's native language. See Australian Bureau of Statistics (1982c) The levels of severity are defined as follows:
1   Severe handicap: personal help or supervision required or the person is unable to perform one or more of the activities
2   Moderate handicap: no personal help or supervision required, but difficulty in performing one or more of the activities
3   Mild handicap: no personal help or supervision required and no difficulty in performing any of the activities, but uses an aid. The highest level of severity in any one of the areas of self-care, mobility and communication determined the severity of overall handicap for handicapped persons. See also footnote to Table 1. Survey of handicapped persons. Cat. No. 43420.
Source: Australian Bureau of Statistics, Survey of Handicapped Persons, unpublished tables

Variations in family structure and economic resources lead to different living arrangements among the elderly whose ability to live independently is restricted. The likelihood of institutionalisation, however, rises markedly as health problems become more difficult to manage in a domestic situation.

The incidence of institutionalisation increases steeply with age, mainly because of the mounting prevalence of severe handicaps. While 14 per cent of persons aged 60 and over are severely handicapped, the proportion rises to 53 per cent for persons aged 85 and over, and 34 per cent of this age group are in institutions or non-private dwellings. Difficulties most likely to lead to institutionalisation in later life are limitations on the use of feet and legs, mental disabilities, blindness and incontinence (Australian Bureau of Statistics, 1982c). Institutionalisation cannot be postponed indefinitely through private support, and is necessary where community services cannot give sufficient assistance to families, or where the nature of the illness imposes excessive demands on relatives. This helps to explain why, before admission to a hostel or nursing home, 53 per cent lived with a spouse or other relative and 63 per cent of the former were still married.

Despite the higher probability of institutionalisation associated with advanced age and greater disabilities, the majority of the severely handicapped old-old live in private households (Figure 2.4), whether because of preferences, or because they cannot gain access to good quality sheltered accommodation. As noted earlier, the family resources of the present generation of the frail elderly are unusually scarce; in the future higher proportions of widows will have families which potentially could provide support.

Overall, decisions which affect household structure in later life are guided by several considerations, rather than security only. The living arrangements of married people are least likely to change in the face of impaired health, although having middle range incomes is associated with a greater likelihood of moving to sheltered accommodation. Among the never-married, widowed and divorced on low incomes ($3000 or less in 1976), the distribution of living arrangements does not change greatly as disabilities increase, but there is a very marked tendency for the non-married with medium incomes to congregate in sheltered accommodation. People receiving low incomes are more likely to live with younger relatives, not so much through choice as through a lack of alternatives, a feature observed in other Western societies (Shanas, et al., 1968; Soldo, 1978).

THE ETHNIC MINORITY AGED

Deprivation, rather than preference, is also applicable to overseas-born groups in explaining joint living arrangements. This runs counter to popular belief, which attributes co-residence between the ethnic minority aged and their children to traditions of extended family living. Maintenance of the language and lifestyles of the country of origin can be important to quality of life in old age, but it should be noted that large extended family households are uncommon in most societies (Bongaarts, 1983). Also, while cultural differences give rise to varying prerequisites for successful ageing in the family context, cultural practices may become modified in the country of settlement. Hence ethnic stereotypes of the role and status of the elderly in family life are misleading (Holzberg, 1982). Diversity has become the overriding feature of the family circumstances of the ethnic-minority aged in Australia (Rowland, 1983b). For instance the Sydney survey showed that many of the overseas-born from non-English speaking countries prefer the 'modified extended' family form, which is not surprising considering that most immigrants to Australia have come from urbanised, industrial countries.

Nevertheless, disproportionate numbers of older immigrants live with relatives. Whereas 13 per cent of Australian-born women aged 75 and over live in the household of a married son or daughter, the corresponding figures for Northern and Eastern Europeans are around three times higher, and four times higher for southern Europeans (Rowland, 1983b). The explanation for this situation goes far beyond lifestyle preferences and traditional obligations. Life chances, rather than lifestyles, underlie the formation of joint-living arrangements among the overseas-born as much as the Australian-born.

People who move house in old age have a high probability of going to live with relatives, partly because relatives are initiators or sponsors in such moves, whether from overseas or within Australia. Indeed, the entry of the ethnic aged into joint-living arrangements is due at least as much to movement within Australia as to immigration from overseas, since the majority of them have been in Australia many years. The main question here is: Why is living alone not a viable alternative for many of the ethnic-minority elderly? Proficiency in the English language is one of the deciding factors. Widows, formerly reliant on husbands' abilities in English, may be obliged to move because they cannot manage on their own. In Australia at the 1981 Census, 15 000 women aged 60 and over could not speak English; they represented 15 per cent of the total women in this age group born in non-English speaking countries. Co-residence may also be desirable, or even necessary, if moving to an unfamiliar community where the elderly know few apart from their relatives.

The majority of the ethnic-minority aged are further constrained in their choices of living arrangements on account of economic deprivation. Since immigrants must have lived in Australia for ten years to be eligible for the age pension, family reunion migration from overseas can involve an extended period of economic dependence on relatives. In the United States the concept of double jeopardy has been used to refer to the expectation that being old and a member of a disadvantaged ethnic group has more adverse effects than being younger, or being an older member of the majority population (Dowd and Bengtson, 1978). Double jeopardy is descriptive of the situation of the poorest of the ethnic aged in Australia, because immigrant origins initially deny access to the Australian age pension and can be further indicative of life-long economic deprivation.

Just as joint-living arrangements among the ethnic aged and their younger relatives are popularly considered to be cultural legacies, so too they are commonly interpreted as alternatives to institutionalisation. At first sight, the evidence seems to support this contention. Exceptionally low numbers of the aged from Southern Europe are inmates of institutions in Australia. The proportion of old-old women from Italy, Greece and Yugoslavia in institutions is in the range of 5 to 7 per cent, compared with 19 per cent for the Australian-born. Health statistics, however, negate the view that family care is more common among ethnic minorities and is chosen in preference to institutionalisation. Measures of health from the census and official surveys all show that the unusually high percentages of the ethnic elderly living with relatives are not matched by above average proportions of the handicapped ethnic elderly living in the community. For them, living with relatives is mainly an alternative to living alone, rather than in an institution. One reason for this situation is a lower incidence of disabling illnesses among the ethnic aged. The health selectivity of immigration, together with emigration to the homeland in old age, have so far restrained growth in the numbers of disabled ethnic aged in Australia.

Although immigrant families do not bear a greater burden of support for the frail aged than the Australian-born, there is reason to expect that the situation will change as the composition of the older population becomes dominated by people who migrated to Australia at a young age and have not recently been subject to selection on the basis of health. Given that high proportions live with relatives and are in situations where substantial personal care is practicable, measures designed to assist families caring for older relatives will be essential among ethnic minority groups.

CONCLUSION

A realistic view of contemporary family structure is a prerequisite for understanding family relationships and developing policies and programs to assist older people and their supporting relatives. This chapter has shown that family structure is not synonymous with household composition; rather, the concept of the modified extended family is the appropriate description of the family unit within which contact and support are maintained.

A supposed decline in the potential for family support is not borne out in historical evidence for Australia, or for Great Britain and the United States. The number of sons and daughters surviving in their parents' old age is similar now under the small family system to the number present under the large family system of the 19th century. The actuality of family support, in terms of help being offered and accepted, is a question addressed in other chapters, but the evidence presented here on the living arrangements of the disabled elderly demonstrates the pervasiveness of assistance to the disabled aged from family members in the same or separate households.

Over time, improvements have occurred in the family situation of the elderly, for instance through more universal marriage, longer joint-survival of spouses and a great decline in deaths of infants and children. There have also been losses, in terms of the access of older people to the assistance of relatives, through a decline in the stock of unmarried daughters and the greater commitment of daughters to employment and other roles which compete with that of a carer for the elderly. Divorce, which is currently the fate of 40 per cent of marriages and remarriages (McDonald, 1983), might also be thought to disrupt the support networks of older people. However, because remarriages are common, sons' or daughters' divorces potentially increase rather than decrease the number of relatives in an older person's network (Sussman, 1976).

In policies pertaining to the living arrangements of the aged, security is a dominant concern. Outcomes include unnecessary institutionalisation, an emphasis on custodianship rather than rehabilitation, and the neglect of considerations of personal autonomy and social integration. The goals of autonomy and integration could be made more widely attainable through the development of domiciliary services, assistance to carers—including some who are not co-residents—provision of low rental, self-contained or hostel accommodation in retirement villages, and help with home modifications to construct 'granny flats'.

Even practices which emphasise security do not necessarily provide equally for all. In the United States social policies for the aged have generally considered them to be white, English-speaking and relatively well-educated; this denies access to minorities or confronts them with culturally insensitive programs (Bengtson, 1979). Such inequalities, resulting from the policies and practices of institutions, have been referred to as 'institutional discrimination' (Palmore and Manton, 1973). One instance of institutional discrimination affecting the elderly in Australia is the inappropriateness of nursing home accommodation to the sizeable numbers of the ethnic minority aged who do not speak English. An alternative to housing people in unsuitable social environments entails extending assistance to ethnic communities which are seeking to meet the support needs of compatriots through family or institutional arrangements.

To counter institutional discrimination and increase individual choice, there must be better recognition of the diversity of needs and resources within the older population. Diversity is not simply a function of differences between individuals or social groups. It depends also on the succession of one cohort by another as well as on the progression of people through the stages of later life. Accordingly, the cohort and life cycle concepts help to clarify why policies with age-specific applications must be responsive to continual changes, why individual needs vary during later life, and why the ability of families to meet support such needs also varies.

3

Social relations: networks and ties

STEPHEN MUGFORD and HAL KENDIG

With rare exceptions, people in our society are linked to numerous others by a variety of social ties. These bonds—to family, friends, neighbours or workmates, within and without the household—may provide help and support but also, at times, exert pressure or make demands. Complete sets of such linkages form potential support networks, and are often very large. In practice, however, the set of ties employed to give, receive, or exchange support are much smaller. It may, for example, be appropriate to ask one's brother for help, or be asked by him, but in reality each might prefer to ask others or rely upon their own resources.

This chapter explores the support networks of our community sample of aged people. We concentrate on the size and membership of networks, restricting ourselves to bonds where specific kinds of support are provided, and excluding social interactions which are more diffuse and less important. Our examination shows that older people's interpersonal worlds are influenced by crucial turning points in mid-life, such as marriage and childbearing; by gender identities built up since birth; and by exigencies such as widowhood or disability which may arise in old age. The results portray the typically small group of people with whom the respondents negotiate the exchange of social support.

The chapter begins by describing our network approach. Then, after providing a detailed example of the network of one respondent, we describe the basic dimensions of networks—whether they are large or small, comprised more of family or of friends, include people similar or dissimilar to the respondents—and an analysis of the complexity of their constituent relationships. Finally we discuss network differences between marital status and gender groups which have made different investments in family life and have different situations in old age. In later chapters we present findings on the types of support exchanged within networks, including qualitative data on the processes that underlie such exchanges.

A NETWORKS APPROACH

Some studies of older people have been using network concepts for many years (Sussman and Burchinall, 1962), but using the social network as a basis for survey research has emerged only recently (Kahn and Antonucci, 1981; Antonucci, 1985). In this respect social gerontology has lagged behind other fields, where studying a set of relationships has increased the understanding of social support (Bott, 1971; Mueller, 1980; Mitchell and Trickett, 1980; Ell, 1984). For example, large and diverse networks of weak ties seem very effective for information seeking (Granovetter, 1973), while small and dense networks seem to maintain identity during times of stress (Stokes, 1983).

Our approach identified people with whom the respondent exchanged specific kinds of support. Generally, we elicited names by asking about particular activity areas rather than relying upon variable recall or highly subjective definitions. Thus, we did not ask: 'Who are your friends?' or 'Who do you feel close to?'. Rather we asked questions like: 'Who would (or does) help with X?', 'Who accepts you as a person ...?' and so on. Our network-generating questions covered the provision or receipt of a wide range of expressive and instrumental support, both actual and potential.

In the terminology of network analysis (Barnes, 1972; D'Abbs, 1982), we are working with 'egocentric networks'—the set of direct ties which respondents have with significant others, and do not venture into the complex relationships between these others (Mitchell, 1969). In total, 910 respondents answered all the questions required for the networks analysis, and we analysed unweighted data in order to better explore diversity among the respondents (See Appendix 1).

As we shall show, the social and demographic characteristics of significant others have a bearing on the nature of their ties with older people. Our exchange perspective (See Chapter 1) suggests that expressive support can be facilitated by similarity and reciprocity—features typical of age peers such as friends and siblings. Permanent bonds are not essential. Indeed, in friendships where one partner appears to be growing dependent, the relationship may be terminated by one of the parties. Instrumental support, however, often involves dissimilarity and asymmetrical flows of activity. Permanency of bond is often a necessity, and kin ties—especially intergenerational and cross gender ties—fit these requirements more than any other in our society. Furthermore, for both expressive and instrumental support, aged persons exchange support more readily through well-established ties, involving several aspects of social life, than through single-stranded relationships. There is, of course, no guarantee that bonds of particular types will be available. For people who occupy highly unusual statuses there is, by definition, a dearth of 'similar' others, and this may severely restrict opportunities for expressive support. Or, for childless old people, a lack of strong kin ties to people dissimilar in age and health, may restrict opportunities for instrumental support.

This brings us to a central theme in our discussion—the ways in which socio-demographic statuses influence support networks. For example, never to have married reduces potential kin ties, to have been divorced or separated may break them, and to become widowed late in life makes remarriage very difficult. As people grow older, ties with age peers are lost and they grow away from the mainstream adult status—the married person in middle age. Consequences can include restricted opportunities for friendships, and the increased importance of kinship in integrating people with dissimilar statuses.

Some of these themes can be brought out by a concrete example. For this illustrative 'case study', we chose a statistically representative case, used the detailed questionnaire data and added, here and there, items garnered from a number of similar cases to create a more rounded and typical picture.

Case study of a network

Born in Australia in 1920, Hilda Smith (as she then was) was the youngest of three children. Her brother Charlie, to whom she was always close—'I looked up to him all my life'—died three years ago. Her sister Irene (67), and husband Bob (68) live some miles away elsewhere in Sydney. Raised in a strict Methodist home, Hilda left school at 16, and worked as a clerk through the war years. In 1946 at the age of 26 she married Edward Brown, a successful small businessman—'We'd known each other for a while, but we waited until the war was out of the way and Edward's business was sorted out, to get married'. He was 15 years her senior. Now some 36 years later they are a happy and devoted couple aged 62 and 77 respectively, both in good health, living in material comfort. They own their own three-bedroom home in a 'nice' suburb and have an income substantially above the basic pension.

Our interviewer saw Mrs Brown as a friendly woman, close to her family and very fond of them all. Of their two daughters, the younger, Linda (24) still lives at home. She is a secretary and unmarried—'A bit of a career girl, our Linda, she likes the young men but there's no one in particular . . .'—and is good company in the evenings and weekends for her Mum and Dad. The elder daughter, Janet (30), is married to Kevin (33), and they have one son—Geoff (4). Janet works full-time—a clerical worker in a shop—as does Kevin, who is in technical advice and sales for a large photographic concern.

The Browns see their daughter, son-in-law and grandson two or three times a week:

> They don't live all that far away, only 10 minutes in the car, and usually I have them here for tea once or twice a week. It makes it easier for them, what with her working and Geoff in the creche. And we often go over there on the weekend, for Sunday lunch or for afternoon tea on a Saturday. Quite often Edward and Kevin will sit and watch the League together . . .

Mrs Brown also has an aged spinster aunt—Lucy (79)—who she sometimes sees and helps:

> She's a funny old dear, really, I really feel she should be in a home but, she soldiers on with a hand from me, and occasionally Irene [Mrs Brown's sister]. Sometimes, I think she'll outlast us all . . .

Mrs Brown is conservative. She is very involved in her Church work, and a staunch Liberal party voter. She feels the government (at the time, the Fraser Government) should do more to 'stamp out strikes' and was critical of:

> permissive legislation—I just can't understand how they can allow all this abortion and divorce. It undermines the family and leads on to all sorts of problems. Thank God our family isn't like that . . .

Although she and her husband are very close, they have a very traditional division of labour—he does outdoors work and manages the money while she tends to the cooking and household chores. She does not drive, but he has a licence and drives her regularly. Indeed, she mentioned that greater access to transport was one of several advantages of his retirement. 'In fact, I don't know whether she'd be able to manage money affairs now I think on it', said her husband Edward, part jokingly, 'perhaps she should think about it more'. But Mrs Brown did not make much response to this, 'Well, Kevin could advise me . . .'.

Who does Mrs Brown have in the way of important contacts, people who we count in her personal network? There are eight people. Of these, six are kin—her husband, two daughters, son-in-law, grandson and aunt—and the other two are her friends, Evelyn and Ken, with whom she shares some social activities and outings. Evelyn and Ken are a retired couple in their 70s (nearer in age to her husband than herself) and she feels quite warm towards them, but they are not 'close':

> Really, they are more Edward's friends than mine. We often do things together—barbecues or meals—and I like them, but I wouldn't have a heart-to-heart with Evelyn. We are friends because, originally, Ken was a sales rep. who came to Edward's business for years . . .

One person who was not listed, was her sister (Irene). Although they see her and her husband (Bob) about every six to eight weeks: 'Really, we aren't that close. Both Irene and I could rely on each other if we were desperate, but there's others we'd each see first . . .'.

Mrs Brown's network provides ample social support. Her material needs are well catered for and she does not lack people who could or would provide such things as nursing or financial aid, although this is hypothetical since both she and her husband are in good health and the need has not really arisen.

At the more emotional level she has several ties—she can confide in her husband and her daughters, all of whom accept her as she is. She says that her husband, aunt and grandson all make her feel needed and appreciated, and she has plenty of social activity available, especially through her husband and daughter, Linda. Perhaps not surprisingly in this context she is happy with her life, very satisfied with her marriage and family and friends, does not feel lonely or depressed and does not find time hanging on her hands.

BASIC NETWORK DIMENSIONS

As Mrs Brown's case illustrates, the essential questions to ask in assessing networks are:

1 How many people are in the network?
2 What sorts of people (kin, friends, etc.) are they?
3 To what extent are these people like the respondent—in terms of gender, age, etc.?
4 How complex are the ties that exist between the respondent and others?

The first two questions are relatively easy to ask and answer. Questions (3) and (4) require the development of certain measures—introduced and discussed below—to answer them.

Network composition

Consistent with previous studies based on social interaction (Shanas, et al., 1968), the networks approach shows that virtually all older people in the community are linked into informal support networks.

In our sample, only six people appear to be bereft of supportive ties.[1] The average network contained nearly seven people, and almost half contained five to eight. One particularly gregarious man identified 21 people, but very large or small networks (more than 12 or less than 3) together accounted for only 14 per cent of the respondents. In all, 6013 people were identified as network members, and the breakdown of these by relationship to respondents is shown in Figure 3.1.

Figure 3.1   Relationship of network members to respondents (percentage) (n = 6013)

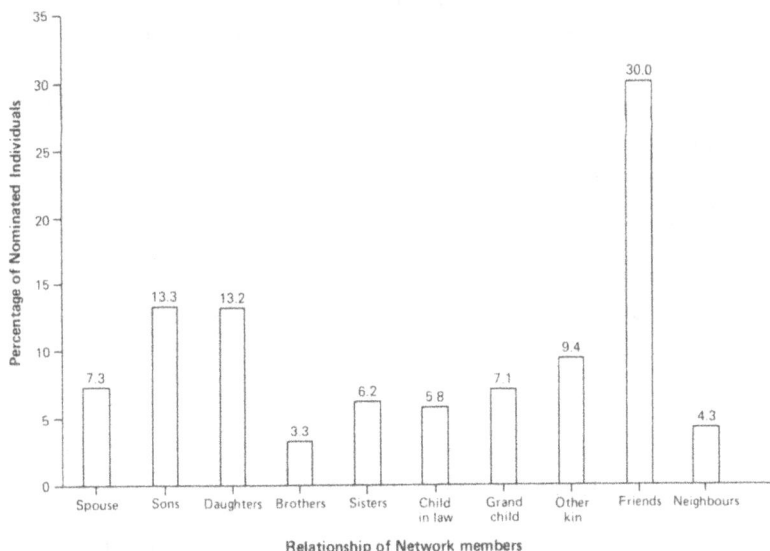

Our findings suggest both the utility of the networks approach and also some of the substantial limits of studies which use purely demographic measures as indicators of social support. Eighty seven per cent of the bonds are with non-household members, confirmation of the limits of co-residence as a primary measure of social integration. Nor are close family members always found in the support networks. While the 910 respondents report having a total of 2914 immediate relatives (spouses, siblings, children, and parents), a significant proportion—25 per cent—of these people were not viewed as exchanging any support with our respondents. In short, family and household structure are best understood as indications of potential rather than actual support.

In a similar vein, our results show the limitation of traditional social gerontological preoccupation with parent-child bonds. Of course, such bonds do provide the basis for intense attachment and both expressive and instrumental support (factors that we deal with in later chapters). Also, where parent-child bonds are active, secondary ties (to grandchildren, children-in-law etc.) become possible. Nonetheless, while ties to daughters, sons and friends are the only types of ties found in half or more of networks, parent-child ties comprise only a quarter of all network ties (Fig. 3.2). Furthermore, this is true despite the attrition of ties to age peers expected in an older population. Overall, as Fig. 3.2 shows, nearly two-thirds of the bonds are with family members, 30 per cent with friends, 5 per cent with neighbours.

Figure 3.2 Percentage of networks containing particular relationships (n = 901)

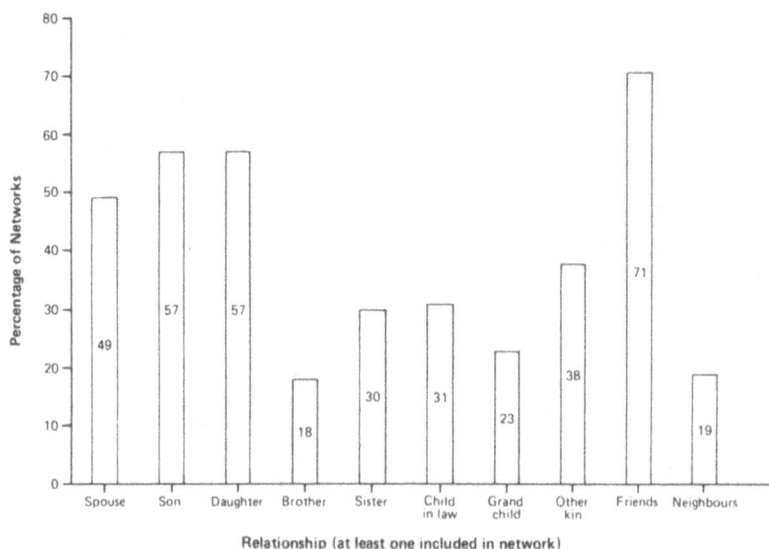

In very simple terms, then, a 'typical' network has about three close relatives, one more distant relative, two friends and a neighbour or other person. But averages conceal wide variations, not merely in the network size but also in composition. For example, close kin were absent from 12 per cent of the networks, yet comprised half or more of the network members for nearly a third of respondents. Similarly, nearly a third named no friends, but 19 per cent had a majority of friends in their networks. To the extent that certain kinds of support are usually provided through particular relationships (Litwak, 1985), these variations in network structure imply that a reasonable number of older people face the prospect of either negotiating alternatives or of doing without certain types of support.

There are several explanations for why many older people appear to exchange support through a limited range of relationships. One is the restriction of our attention to relatively important and easily identifiable kinds of support. For example, we exclude friendly chats with neighbours unless they involve a deeper emotional significance. Other explanations are the wide variability of family structure (See Chapter 2), and the attrition of convoys of support (Kahn and Antonucci, 1981) over the several decades of a typical old age. Finally, even if potential support remains available, the ability to draw upon it can be eroded by declining mobility and exchange power.

To explore the possible erosion of support, respondents were asked if they had 'lost contact with anyone very close' over the last five years. While recall undoubtedly is incomplete, 57 per cent of all respondents said they had lost close bonds. In total, 840 people were mentioned (this compares to the 6013 current network members mentioned). While some of the losses were from the previous and younger generations, 80 per cent of them were likely to be of the same generation. The most common losses were of friends (41 per cent), followed by brothers and sisters (each 12 per cent), siblings-in-law (8 per cent), husbands (7 per cent), and wives (2 per cent). In four-fifths of all cases (and almost every case for family ties) the reason given for such losses was the death of the other person. In explaining losses of more distant kin and non-family, residential mobility (16 per cent) and a variety of other reasons—including ill health, institutionalisation, and disputes—also emerge as important. These losses of close bonds present older people with major adjustments, a topic taken up in Chapter 7. They emphasise the importance of facilitating older people's abilities to maintain continuing bonds and develop new ones. Overall, the results emphasise the vulnerability of age peer ties, and the permanency of close family bonds.

The important question that arises from this overview of network size and composition—and to which we turn in later chapters—is not whether informal support networks exist, but whether they respond fully to a diverse range of needs.

Network members

To answer the third of the general questions outlined earlier (Are network members 'like' the respondent?), we measure various kinds of 'homophily'. We calculate the proportion of network members who match respondents in terms of gender, age (measured in ten year intervals), or marital status. For example, in Mrs Brown's case, her friend Evelyn is homophilous in two ways—gender and marital status—but there is an age difference. Her grandson Geoff is not homophilous at all, being of different age, gender and marital status.

The homophily measures are especially useful in showing the potential for expressive support based on similarity. For the members of networks as a whole, homophily is highest in terms of gender (63 per cent), and considerably less regarding marital status (43 per cent) and age (32 per cent). If we measure total homophily, using a score from zero (no similarity) to three (full similarity) we find that homophily is greater for friends (an average of 1.38) than for family (1.07). As we shall see below, the homophily measures are most useful in showing clear differences between the networks of older people in various status groups.

The predominance of family in older people's networks provides the primary explanation for the dispersal of ties across the entire age spectrum. Excluding respondents' spouses, more than half of the network members are in the relatively resource-rich middle ages (30 to 59 years), and these ties are mainly with children and their spouses. The tendency for people to form friendships with age peers, and maintain them with siblings, is reflected in the 36 per cent of bonds held with people who are elderly. Flows of support to or from young adults (under 30) are thus relatively rare, especially considering that many older people have large numbers of grandchildren and even great-grandchildren who potentially feature in these networks. The ties between alternate generations probably are best understood as operating principally through the middle generation in family systems as a whole (Hill, 1970; Troll, et al., 1979).

How complex are the network ties?

This, the last of our general questions, is a difficult one. The simplest way to approach it is to look at the 'multistrandedness' of relationships. The term 'multiplexity' (Boissevain, 1972: 28–32) refers to the diversity of linkages between individuals, and is operationalised here as the proportion of respondent's bonds which involve the provision or receipt of support in a relatively wide range of areas (See Appendix 1). The basic approach is to count the number of areas in which the respondent provides or receives support with each significant other, and then to calculate the proportion of bonds which have high levels of interchange. This provides an indication of the range of support provided through specific relationships, rather than the intensity or the emotional attachment. For example, in Mrs Brown's network, her relationship with her husband Edward scores 11—there are many ways (instrumental and expressive) in which he figures as the source or recipient of supportive activities. Her Aunt Lucy, however, is directly mentioned only twice (once each in the instrumental and expressive networks) and the score here is three. (See Appendix 1.)

The general pattern of multiplexity in our sample is for respondents to have a small core of several complex ties, and a larger fringe of other relationships limited to one or two of our many categories of support. The complexity of relationships is generally highest for spouses, followed by daughters, sons and then other relatives and friends. Nonetheless, there is great variability in respect of multiplexity, both within and between different status groups. Much of the utility of the measure emerges when we wish to describe particular groups of older people, but in addition, a greater understanding can be gained by creating a typology of networks using multiplexity as one axis.

A network typology

In order to bring out differences in types of networks, we constructed a scheme based on size and multiplexity, two of the most important (but relatively uncorrelated) dimensions. The typology is shown in Figure 3.3.

Figure 3.3   Five types of networks (n = 901)

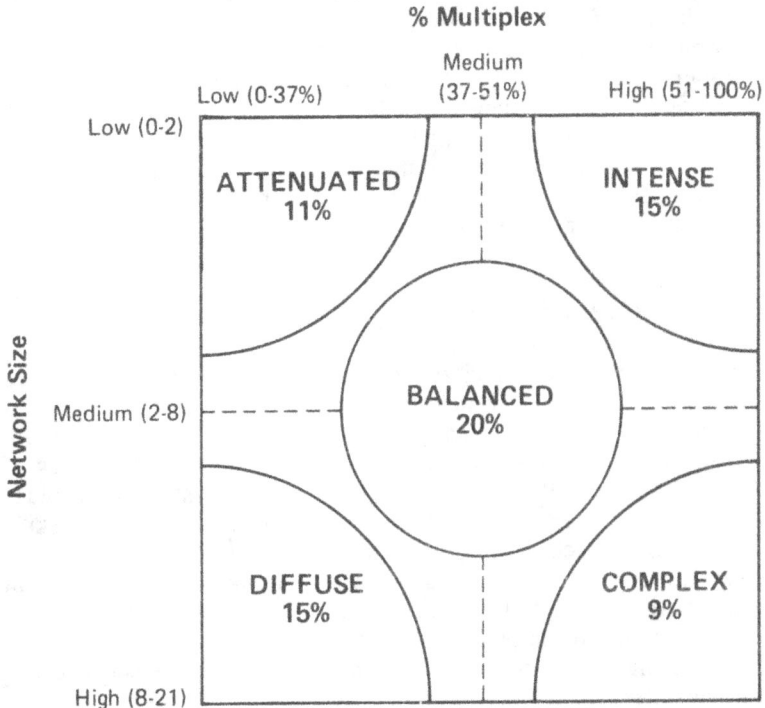

% Multiplex

	Low (0-37%)	Medium (37-51%)	High (51-100%)
Low (0-2)	ATTENUATED 11%		INTENSE 15%
Medium (2-8)		BALANCED 20%	
High (8-21)	DIFFUSE 15%		COMPLEX 9%

Network Size

Note: The unmarked area between the five network types contains the residual cases (30 percent)

The logic in constructing the figure is fairly simple. Cases were allocated to one of the four quadrants depending on whether their levels of multiplexity and network size were comparatively high or low. By separating the corners from the central area, and leaving a 'buffer' of indeterminate residual cases, five clearly-defined types of network were created. Of course, the distinctions are based on the statistical distributions, not on a theoretical argument, and the names are merely intuitively recognisable labels. Thus, the 'balanced type' simply refers to respondents having networks of average size and multiplexity. Nonetheless, the types provide a useful evaluative device.

Mrs Brown's network, for example, is an excellent example of a 'balanced' network, deliberately chosen since this type is relatively common amongst married women. With a network size of eight and a mean multiplexity of 50 per cent, her network falls in the mid-range. Figure 3.3 shows the percentage of each type of network in our sample. As we shall see, these are not equally distributed among different status groups of older people.

To summarise this section briefly, we have developed measures of the size and other features of older people's support networks. Virtually all of our respondents receive or provide at least some informal support, through networks having an average of six to seven members; most network members are family and middle-aged, and, to a great extent, network members are the same gender as the respondent. Typical networks have a core of highly multiplex relations and a periphery of less multiplex relations. These summary measures obscure the great variety in social bonds, a topic which we will now consider more fully.

NETWORK VARIATION

Elderly people in any society vary from cheerful, sociable married women with many kin and friendships through to lonely, isolated unhappy old men—with many points in between. Both individual characteristics, such as personality or social skills, and features of social settings, influence networks. Qualitative studies of older Australians, for example, suggest that personality and social skills have major impacts in structuring networks and actions within them (Russell, 1981; Job, 1984), as do the particular circumstances in which family and friends find themselves. In this chapter our primary concern is for the impact of status positions and life exigencies in predisposing and patterning the negotiation of relationships. Using the network measures outlined, we begin by examining three factors—child bearing, occupational background and disability—which might be expected to be important influences upon networks.

In what follows, we report only statistically significant relationships which hold after controlling for possible confounding variables.

Number of children

The number of children obviously sets limits for some kinds of ties, and our findings show that having more of them does increase the total size of support networks. Another effect of having more descendents, however, is that older people become more selective in the bonds they have with family. For example, parents from larger families rarely mention all of their offspring as exchanging the kinds of support that placed them in the personal network. Similarly, available daughters-in-law are less likely to be taken into support networks when older people have one or more daughters of their own. Yet respondents who have relatively more children do not nominate smaller numbers of friends. This suggests that friendships are important in their own right and are not merely alternatives to close family.

Occupational status

Occupational status also could be expected to have many possible influences on the maintenance of different kinds of bonds. Our findings are restricted to a very limited set of differences—namely that the working classes are likely to have slightly smaller and more kin-dominated networks, a finding consistent with network studies of a variety of age groups (Allan, 1979). The differences result from the middle classes having more friends in addition to close kin, not as alternatives to family. The influence of class is somewhat stronger among women. While the sociability and skills of 'class culture' may provide part of the explanation, it is important to recognise that financial resources have a direct influence on access to transport, and to other resources relevant to participation in 'sociable' activities.

Disability

One might think that having a major disability would precipitate a withdrawal from social networks. Our findings would not support this in terms of network size, where disability apparently has little influence. It is possible, of course, that people whose bonds have been attenuated by disability are no longer in the community—an interpretation suggested by the higher institutionalisation rate of the divorced and never-married older people (See Chapter 2). The main impact of disability found in our community survey, however, is a modest restructuring of the network to include relatively more kin. Friendships are slightly less common among the disabled aged, while various distant kin ties (largely in-laws and other secondary ties) are relatively more common. Again, these effects are more pronounced among women, who less commonly have the 'buffering' influence of a spouse. Our exchange perspective explains the findings in terms of family attachments and obligations which hold despite a reduction of mutuality.

Gender and marital status

Of much greater significance than the three factors we have first examined are gender and marital status. These clearly emerge as the most important influences on network size and composition. Overall, as shown in Figure 3.4, women have slightly but significantly larger networks than do men, and the married respondents also have larger networks than their counterparts who are not married, widowed, divorced or separated.

Figure 3.4   **Relationship of support network members, by gender and marital status of respondent (n = 901)**

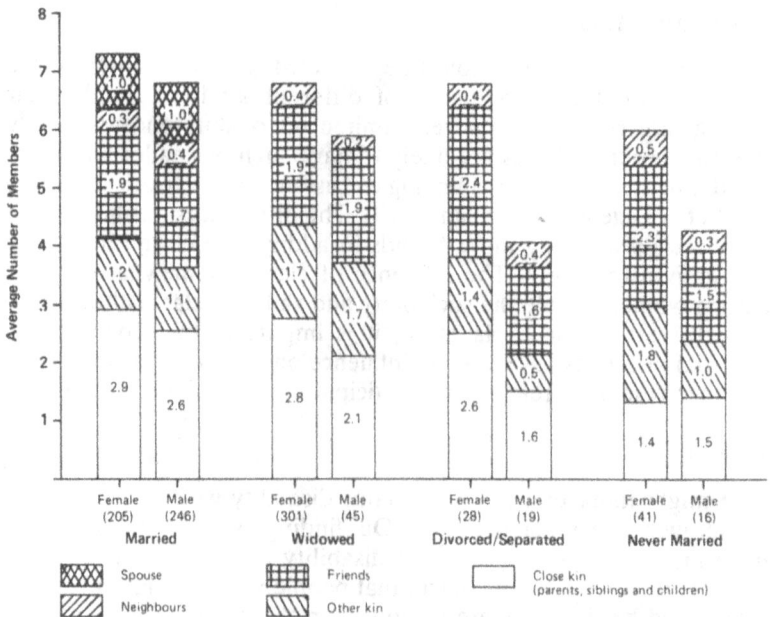

Our findings correspond closely with other studies which show that, across a wide age spectrum, the social networks of women generally are larger those of men (Allan, 1979; D'Abbs, 1982). A partial explanation may be that women are more likely to acknowledge their emotional and instrumental interdependencies

(West and Simmons, 1983). Beyond this, however, women are more active and capable in cultivating interpersonal ties over the entire life course. They take much greater responsibility for activities such as sharing intimacies, remembering birthdays, organising gatherings, and exchanging mutual aid (Adams, 1968; Bengtson, Cuellar and Ragan, 1977). While some of these differences emerge out of lifelong investments in family rather than paid-work (Weitz, 1977), the gender differences in our study persist among women who have held full-time jobs in middle age. The basic explanation, as developed in Job's (1984) study of very old Australians, is the gender conditioning which orients women to a lifelong preoccupation with 'network maintenance'.

Marital status is important because of the consequential sets of ties with descendants and in-laws as well as with the spouse. While marriage could be negatively portrayed as an institution tHat can be destructive for one or both parties (Bernard, 1972; Barrett and Macintosh, 1982), the positive corollary is that it serves to widen support networks.

While gender and marital status each have direct effects on network size, there are also important interrelations. When the two factors are examined jointly it is among the men—not the women—that networks are substantially smaller among the non-married groups. This gender difference is all the more notable because more of the single men have personal resources and family opportunities conducive to maintaining informal bonds.

It is to these questions that we now turn in detail.

Couples

The majority of both sexes enter later life as married people. Only among men, however, are a majority of the aged currently married, and most will remain so to the end of their days. The married generally have more personal resources than other marital status groups (Table 3.1), as well as the largest potential pool of kin ties. Almost all married people of course have co-residents (Table 3.1), the very few exceptions arising when a spouse is away on a visit or in an institution.

Our most important finding is the similarity of the networks of older husbands and wives. Only two differences are worthy of mention. First, slightly more married men have 'intense' networks (Table 3.2), due to a minority who rely heavily on their wives for all kinds of support. Secondly, women maintain more bonds with siblings and friends, and thus have slightly larger networks (Figure 3.3). On balance, however, the gender differences are small. As we saw in the case of Mrs Brown, most bonds are held on a couple basis. Often, wives both provide access to, and maintenance of, sizeable

Table 3.1   Selected characteristics of respondents by marital status and gender (n = 904)

Marital status by gender	Average age (years)	Selected characteristics		Low income*
		Disabled (%)	With co-residents (%)	
Married				
women (205)	66.1	10	98	46
men (246)	68.3	8	97	42
Widowed				
women (301)	73.0	20	37	64
men (45)	72.5	12	30	54
Div/separated				
women (28)	66.9	27	29	67
men (19)	68.0	3	56	41
Never married				
women (44)	71.9	16	53	82
men (16)	67.8	3	40	46

* A 1981 annual income of under $4000 if single or $6000 if married

networks for their husbands. While married men may take a greater part in expressive relations after retirement (Dobson, 1983), informal support is something that men clearly gain more from marriage than do women (Bernard, 1976).

Marriage also provides considerable opportunities for both intra- and inter-generational bonds. The homophily measures illustrate this. On the one hand, the age homophily of couples' relationships is relatively low (35 per cent for wives and 29 per cent for men) due to the availability of children. Of course, this can be important in securing some kinds of instrumental support. On the other hand marital status homophily is high (66 and 69 per cent respectively) reflecting the predominance of marriage, and the opportunities for relating to other couples.

Finally, despite the relatively large size of these networks, our multiplexity measures show only a small tendency for the widespread ties also to be reduced in complexity. Rather, these networks are (typically) both fairly large and constituted of multiplex ties.

Widows

Widowhood is the single most common stage of family life for older women, and the vast majority of women experience it for some period during their old age. Of course, widows generally are much older than the married, and two-thirds of them live alone (Table 3.1). The greater risks associated with advanced age explain why they have relatively high rates of disability and low income. Overall, our results here reflect the status of being a widow more than the social process

Table 3.2 Network types of respondents by marital status and gender (n = 904)

Marital status by gender	Attenuated (small/ low mx)	Intense (small/ hi mx)	Network Types* Diffuse (large/ low mx)	Complex (large/ hi mx)	Balanced (mid/ mid mx)	Residual	Total (percentage)
Married							
women (205)	9	7	16	11	22	35	100
men (246)	12	18	14	11	17	28	100
Widowed							
women (301)	8	16	13	8	23	32	100
men (45)	20	16	16	2	13	33	100
Div/separated							
women (28)	11	18	29	0	18	24	100
men (19)	32	21	5	0	11	31	100
Never married							
women (44)	14	18	16	7	18	27	100
men (16)	38	25	0	0	6	31	100

* See Figure 3.3 and Appendix 2 for definitions of network types.
'Mx' = 'multiplexity'.

of becoming one: 35 per cent of the widows, and 26 per cent of the widowers, lost their spouse four or more years before the survey.

Apart from the absence of a spouse, widowed men and women have networks of a similar size and composition to those of their married counterparts (Figure 3.4). Indeed, especially among widows, there may be a slightly larger number of other bonds. As other studies have found, the reductions of close kin, most commonly due to the death of siblings as well as spouses (and in some cases, sons), are largely offset (in strictly numerical terms) by the emergence of more distant kin in support networks. These differences become more pronounced when we take into account the widow's higher disability rates and greater age—characteristics which tend to reduce opportunities for bonds with others of the same generation.

Notwithstanding the apparent strengthening of more distant ties, later chapters suggest that the primary adjustment in widowhood is the renegotiation of established ties rather than the formation of new ones.

There are relatively few gender differences in the types of network found among the widowed. In contrast to their married counterparts, the widows are as likely as widowers to have 'intense' networks, mainly because some disabled women rely on help from one or a few people (Table 3.2). Proportionally more widowers have 'attenuated' networks, and they also maintain fewer bonds with siblings—an illustration, perhaps, of the lesser capacity of some men to maintain ties once their wives, the previous maintainers, have died. The overall results nonetheless indicate that most widowers are able to maintain the ties developed along with their wives earlier in life. These results match those of various American studies (Troll, et al., 1979) which show that widowers, as well as widows, are unlikely to withdraw from family and friends.

Networks age along with people, and this is shown in the composition of networks of widowed people. Compared to couples, age and gender homophily tends to be lower for widows of both genders, a consequence of the attrition of ties with age peers. And while the widowed have more bonds with other widows than do couples, they remain in a status and marital status homophily that is low. Furthermore, aged widowers, who are even less likely than women to find others in a comparable position, have lower homophily scores than widows, especially in terms of gender (47 versus 65 per cent). While this undoubtedly makes them scarce and valued for certain cross-sex friendships, it may also constrain the development of some kinds of companionate relationships based on gender-related interests.

Divorced or separated

Marital break up is relatively uncommon among the present cohort of older people, with only 5 per cent of our respondents currently divorced or separated. (Another 3 per cent, who were covered in the section on couples, are now married but their last marriage broke up.) The group is too small and diverse to carry out any detailed analysis with respect to such important issues as the timing of the separation, although we can point out that two-thirds of these people were separated or divorced more than four years before the survey. The results nonetheless reveal important gender differences in the maintenance of informal support networks.

Divorced and separated women have networks which are only moderately smaller than those of married and widowed women (Figure 3.4). While bonds with various kin are slightly less numerous, ties with friends and neighbours are among the largest of any of our groups. Another important feature is the relatively large number who have 'diffuse' networks, large ones with few complex ties. It is notable that those who are disabled appear to have considerable support. While a variety of small studies suggest that their social supports are limited (Hennon, 1983), our findings suggest that divorced women are generally able to maintain sizeable networks.

The situation is starkly different in the case of the few men who are divorced or separated and remain in the community during old age. They have nearly as many friends as do their married counterparts and a surprisingly high proportion (56 per cent) have co-residents. But their kin ties are extraordinarily limited and their networks are therefore the smallest of all the groups (See Figure 3.4). Moreover, they are heavily over-represented in the 'attenuated' networks characterised by ties which are weak as well as few in number (Table 3.2). Consistent with the findings of Furstenberg (1981), one has the impression of people whose marital break up has seriously disrupted kin ties, and left them unable or unwilling to reconcile conflict or develop alternative family bonds. Only among divorced men are there any clear patterns of kin ties being lost for any reason other than death. This may explain why so few of the divorced men, as compared to the significant numbers of divorced women, remain in the community while having a serious disability (Table 3.1).

The never-married

The 7 per cent of our sample which never married have developed life trajectories which diverge markedly from those who have been or are married (Neyland and Shadbolt, 1985). The differences are many and substantial: for example, nearly all of the women as well as men have held jobs throughout their earlier adult years and levels of independence and self-sufficiency are relatively high (Gubrium, 1978). Of most direct interest here, they have long been in the position of negotiating bonds as individuals (Penman and Stolk, 1984), with little normative patterning of their relationships. In their later years, they have neither the supports nor the potential loss afforded by having had a spouse.

A sizeable gender difference in informal networks is clear among those who have never become part of a couple. Among the women, a number of exigencies—including closeness to and care of family of origin, death of a fiancé in war or by accident, and the pursuit of careers in a time when they could not be managed along with family life—have led them along the pathways of a minority status throughout adult life. It is notable that never-married women have the lowest retirement incomes of all the marital status groups (Table 3.1).

The most conspicuous feature of these women's networks is the relatively large size (Figure 3.4.), a striking result considering the unavailability of spouses, descendents, and the many other ties normally made accessible through them. They have the least family-oriented of all the women's network's, and the family they do nominate are primarily siblings and their immediate family. Friends and neighbours are also relatively numerous among this group; and women who had held higher status occupations are especially likely to have a larger number of friends (with an average over four). However different the composition of these networks compared to women who have married, the types of networks are remarkably similar. Many never-married women apparently do construct alternatives to the more common intergenerational bonds through children. Over half of them (53 per cent), for example, have co-residents. An interesting example in our survey was a never-married woman who lived with her never-married twin sister. They had taken care of their elderly parents until they died, and then left the parental house to buy their own, and thus had lived together throughout their life.

Considering their rarity among the adult population, the never-married women show a remarkable tendency to gravitate towards people who are similarly situated (the twin sisters being an extreme example). A quarter of their network members are also never-married, a very high level considering the relative ubiquity of marriage: it is a clear cut case of 'like attracts like'. In addition, 45 per cent are of approximately the same age group, and three-quarters are other women. The comparatively high homogeneity probably reflects a measure of exclusion of this minority group, and the many years over which they have had a chance to come together and develop long-term relationships with each other. While these similarities are conducive to exchanges of some kinds of support (particularly expressive support), they increase vulnerability to losses through death and disability, and reduce the pool of people having different skills and more resources (relevant to instrumental support).

The rarity in our sample of men who have never married—especially those who are disabled—is itself a telling indication of their comparative social difficulties. Their chances of even reaching old age are much reduced, and disproportionately large numbers live in institutions, rooming houses, and other kinds of non-private housing beyond the scope of our survey. Those who do remain in the community rival their divorced and separated counterparts in having the smallest networks (Figure 3.4), and they are highly over-represented in the 'attentuated' networks (Table 3.2). While many women apparently do not marry because of competing attachments, their male counterparts tend to be comparative isolates—although 40 per cent do have co-residents. The vulnerability of the men is further highlighted by the finding that nearly three-quarters of their few ties are with people who are elderly themselves.

The never-married respondents, differing as they do from others in several ways, provide a number of particularly interesting case studies which we can contrast with the case of Mrs Brown. Here we chose two cases—one male, one female. They were not chosen because they are statistically typical (although the man is statistically typical in some ways) but because they illustrate a number of themes.

The first case we examined was of a bachelor—Mr O'Leary. As it happens, he was interviewed in depth by Alice Day for an associated study (Day, 1985; Chapter 6 below). Here is how she saw him:

> Never married, 75-year-old Mr O'Leary lives alone. The youngest of seven children (the others all dead) his only kin are three married, but childless, nephews.
>
> Mr O'Leary has a history of institutionalisation. While a young man in his mid-twenties working up country in New Guinea on a river dredge, he 'went troppo . . . a bit—er—light-headed'. He returned to Australia as one of the 'walking wounded sort of thing' and spent at least the next 20 years (he would not give a figure) in a rest home for the mentally unstable. After he left, he got a job as a postman, and managed to accumulate enough superannuation to buy his unit on retirement and live fairly comfortably. A loner, he lived by 'batching and boarding', had made very few friends, and was accustomed to looking after himself, 'I've made my bed now, for instance, for 50 years'. (Day, 1985: 115)

Mr O'Leary's network is a clear example of an attenuated network—small, and low in multiplex ties. It consists of four people—the three nephews and a neighbour-cum-friend Alex (57), another bachelor, who looks in regularly. Mr O'Leary is house-bound, and socially isolated. All the social support he receives is instrumental, and his emotional landscape is effectively a desert.

On the face of it he appears to have adjusted to this, claiming to be satisfied with life, and fairly happy, although the in depth interviews show that there is much deep seated discontent (Day, 1985; 118–119).

The case of Miss White (75) could hardly be more contrasting. An only child, she spent much of her life caring for her parents. She never worked, and lives now off an age pension and some investments left by her parents. A healthy and fairly happy person, Miss White's social life is busy. She goes to meetings of the Church Fellowship, a philanthropic society and the local bowls club and drives her own car.

Miss White's network consists of eight people. Three are kin—her second cousin Louise (56) and husband Ray (58) and an unmarried cousin Florence (75). She sees Louise and Ray about once a month, Florence slightly less often. The other five are all female friends. Alice (56) is married, lives nearby and sees Miss White several times a week. They are very close. Edie (71) is a widow who also lives nearby. She sees Miss White several times a week, although she is not as close as Alice. Both share social activities—visits, outings and so on—with Miss White. Prue (57) married and Mabel (67) another never-married woman, live further away. She sees them less often, but they are emotionally close to her. Finally, there is Ada (68), a married woman who lives nearby, and Miss White is fairly friendly with her, giving her lifts here and there.

Miss White is well-supplied with expressive relationships, both giving and receiving care, and sharing social activities. Unlike Mr O'Leary, her emotional landscape is quite fertile. But she has few sources of instrumental support, relying on paid-help for tasks she cannot manage now and expecting residential care if she were ill in bed for a month.

Mr O'Leary and Miss White illustrate two common themes among older people who have never married. First, their kin ties are very limited: neither of course have any children, Mr O'Leary had lost siblings through the attrition of aging and now, as a consequence, both have kin support entirely with more distant, secondary family (cousins, nephews). Second, the kin ties which they do have are overwhelmingly same sex ties—that is, they have very high gender homophilies. Here the similarity ends. Mr O'Leary is tied to kin via intergenerational bonds, and male-to-male bonds at that. These generate a limited amount of instrumental support, but little else. (We can almost hear the nephews agreeing that they must 'keep an eye on mad old uncle Mick'.) Miss White, however, relies entirely on intragenerational ties—cousins and friends, who are almost all female. In sharp contrast to Mr O'Leary, she has developed numerous friendships, although these too are of the same sex and similar in age. These various ties generate plenty of emotionally rewarding exchanges, but leave her short of instrumental supports. Given that she is reasonably capable and can afford to buy services this lack is not devastating, but she is aware of her vulnerability should she become disabled.

Compared to Mrs Brown, with ties both intra- and intergenerationally, to males and females where a wide range of support and exchanges are generated, neither of these never-married people is as well supplied, although clearly it is Mr O'Leary who is the far more distressed and isolated.

SUMMARY

This chapter has drawn on social networks methodology to portray the informal support groups of older people.

One of the most important findings is that the outlines of support networks are set well before people enter old age. To be born female or male sets in train the gender conditioning which affects abilities to mobilise social support 70 years later. To marry in mid-life is particularly important in enabling men to have supportive relations both with and through their wives in old age. To have children potentially provides both genders with what usually are the most supportive of ties: those grounded in filial obligation and attachment, and which involve people having the resources of middle age and the skills and orientations of both genders. Conversely, divorce can dissolve many of these ties, especially among men. While never-married women often construct alternative support systems, these ties may have less potential for providing or receiving large amounts of instrumental support. Never-married men are even more vulnerable given their marked limitations in forging close informal bonds.

The networks approach is not arbitrarily restricted to any particular kind of relationship, thus presenting a more complete picture of older people's social world. While middle-aged children are particularly important, it is clear that close bonds are developed with a great variety of kinship and other relationships, and the part played by each of these other bonds requires consideration in comparative analyses. Documenting the existence of support networks is but the first step in understanding their strengths and weaknesses, and the lifelong processes which develop and maintain them.

Other major findings are that two of the principal changes in old age, widowhood and disability, have relatively little impact on the overall composition of support networks. The loss of a spouse, for example, is partly offset by the strengthening of other kin ties, and pre-existing relations generally continue among widowed men as well as women. Friendships are the most likely relationships to be dissolved should disability persist, as mutuality and similarities are attenuated, and kin ties become relatively more important. The most notable impact of widowhood and disability, however, is on the renegotiation of ongoing ties. As we will see in later chapters, the kinds, directions, and sources of expressive and instrumental support undergo major changes in these circumstances. These topics, and the social processes which explain them, are considered in the next section of the book.

Part 2

SOCIAL SUPPORT

4

Expressive relations and social support

DIANE GIBSON and STEPHEN MUGFORD

The last chapter, illustrated by the cases of Mrs Brown, Mr O'Leary and Miss White, described how a variety of social statuses are linked to particular network sizes and structures. We saw that various kinds of networks have different potentials for generating expressive and instrumental support. In this chapter, we focus more closely on one part of these findings—the set of expressive relations. We ask not only who provides such support, and which aspect thereof, but also whether the presence or absence of it makes any difference. Our broad answer—and it comes as no surprise when we look back at the case studies in Chapter 3—is that it does make a difference. Those having relatively more expressive support tend to be happier and have higher levels of psychological well-being.

MEASURING EXPRESSIVE SUPPORT

A great deal of attention has been paid in earlier studies to the importance of social contact for the well-being of older people. The results of these studies are mixed. Some find relations between limited aspects of well-being and social interaction, but doubt an overall relationship.[1] Others, including the classic studies of Lowenthal and Haven (1968), Riley and Foner (1968) and Rosow (1967), as well as more recent studies, confirm that a higher level of contact is associated with greater well-being.[2] Some studies report this as an overall association, others restrict it to non-kin ties. A few studies have found that the relationship between amount of contact and morale apply only to friendships, which confirm identity and self worth, as compared to family contact which may be based on obligation and reinforce a demoralising sense of dependency (Lee, 1984).

The research on the association between social contact and morale is generally confined to two basic points. The more general of these is a quantitative point—'more is better'—which says little about qualitative differences. Thus, questions such as whether two totally reliable and helpful friends, who provide support in many ways, are 'better' than a dozen looser and less detailed relationships, tend not to be posed.

The second, more qualitative point, and one debated in detail, is the extent to which having a confidant increases the well-being of people in general (see O'Connor and Brown, 1984, for a critical review and new contribution to this area), and older people in particular (Lowenthal and Haven, 1968; and Moriwaki, 1973). This point is elaborated further by the findings of Strain and Chappell (1982) that having more confidants, especially if they are close kin, is positively associated with well-being. Snow and Crapo (1982) show positive association between emotional bondedness and well-being, and Harel and Noelker (1982) extend this, showing that that exchange of instrumental assistance increases well-being.

Our view was that while the confidant relationship is important, and the level of interaction worth general attention, there was more to expressive social relations than these two factors encompassed. Influenced both by Weiss' (1974) proposed dimensions of expressive support and the McAllister and Fischer (1978) techniques for eliciting relationships, we explored several dimensions of expressive relations. After some early pilot work with the many categories suggested by Weiss (1974), we settled on four basic dimensions: confiding, acceptance, reassurance of worth, and social participation. These were measured by the following procedure. One section of the questionnaire began by asking: 'Is there anyone to whom you feel quite close?'. If the respondent answered 'yes' (or did not know)—and these totalled to 95 per cent of respondents—the interview continued with four detailed questions (each with follow up questions identifying up to six people):

1 Is there someone you confide in about things that are important to you?
2 Is there someone who knows you well as a person and accepts you just as you are?
3 Is there someone who makes you feel needed and appreciated?
4 Is there someone with whom you enjoy common interests, activities or outings?[3]

These were followed by the catch-all question, 'Is there anyone else whom you haven't mentioned who you feel very close to?' Finally respondents were asked which of the people mentioned they felt closest to. The data analysed in this chapter refer to the expressive relations generated by these questions. Of course, these questions, plus others on instrumental support, generate the complete network (Chapter 3), so the two aspects of 'networks' overlap. Based on this subset of the total network we ask a series of questions: What is the membership of the expressive network as a whole? How are the various expressive dimensions met (if they are)? What effects, if any, are there from the expressive relations?

OVERALL MEMBERSHIP

Over three-quarters (77 per cent) of the people included in the full networks of our respondents provided expressive support. Thus, the overall patterns for the expressive network are very similar to those reported on the network as a whole in Chapter 3. To begin with, there are marked variations in size, ranging from no-one to nineteen people: 5 per cent reported nobody; 54 per cent, one to five people; 38 per cent, six to ten people; and a further 3 per cent had eleven or more. As one would expect, given the findings in the previous chapters, the groups which were most likely to be emotional isolates were the various groups of unmarried males. The average expressive network size of 5.1 persons clearly puts to rest any suggestion that older people generally are bereft of emotional and social ties.

Given the high degree of overlap between the full network and the expressive network, and the generally similar profiles, interest centres upon general themes and differences, rather than detailed description.

The first important point is that, irrespective of the gender of respondent, female network members are more likely to feature in expressive bonds than are males. This is particularly visible if we compare sons to daughters, sisters to brothers and so on. The cultural identification of women with emotional support is clear here. Gender is also relevant in that older women have more expressive ties than do men, and are more likely to show same-gender links than the men.

Secondly, consanguineal (blood) kin ties are of more expressive importance than are affinal (in-law) ties. Children are far more often named in expressive networks than children-in-law, and siblings than siblings-in-law. (The point is expanded below in our analysis of availability.) Also, when respondents were asked to nominate the person to whom they were closest, answers were entirely confined to the nuclear families of origin or orientation. Taken together, our first two points show the critical importance of mother to daughter ties in linking the emotional and social life of the generations (Troll et al., 1979).

Thirdly, we find that the influences on expressive bonds of marital status, occupational status and disability are consistent with those reported for total network in Chapter 3. Married people have the largest expressive networks (an average of 5.6 persons), basically because of the inclusion of their spouse. Next largest are the widowed group (4.8), whose lack of a spouse is partly offset by a greater propensity to list other kin and friends. Finally, those who are divorced, separated or never-married—particularly the males among them—have the smallest expressive networks (4.0). They are as likely as the married and widowed groups to have emotional and social links with friends but have noticeably fewer kin ties. There is also little relationship between the size of the expressive network and either occupational status or disability. It is notable that those who do not have many close kin are still able to forge a reasonable number of expressive bonds with friends and more distant kin—and the emotional ties appear to hold even when people are disabled.

Fourthly, when we look at living arrangements and expressive networks, we find a somewhat predictable pattern. Those who live alone generally have smaller expressive networks, because they do not have the spouses who figure so prominently in the lives of married respondents. What is less predictable is that those who live with others besides spouses, such as those in their children's homes, have smaller expressive networks yet again. One possible explanation— that expressive ties are less likely when people are co-residents who are 'too close for comfort'—proves not to be the case. The major explanation is that co-residency usually occurs among very old people, whose increasing age and infirmity has led to depletion of non-resident ties and their world has shrunk towards those in their household.

The number of children has a curvilinear relationship with expressive network size. The proportion reporting small expressive networks of less than three members is highest (24 per cent) for those with none or one child, declines to 12 per cent of the networks of those with two or three children and rises again for those with four or more children. This result bears some examination. The expressive networks of those with two or three children contain a few trusted friends, perhaps a sibling, and the person's children, with each of whom the parent tends to have a fairly intense relationship involving various types of expressive support. The other situations differ from this. On the one hand, for those with no children, the absence of children reduces the number in the expressive network. On the other hand for those with many children, the larger number appears to diffuse the intensity of parent-child relationships, and some (or all) of the children do not appear in the expressive network. In the latter case, family life appears to involve more group activities and ties rather than intense dyadic bonds.

Our final question is whether available close kin feature in the expressive networks of the respondent. The limit of these ties is set, of course, by the availability of various kin; for example, the widowed cannot mention a spouse, nor can the childless include children. Comparative take-up rates, defined as the proportion actually receiving expressive support from various categories of available kin, are essential in examining family support. We are able to examine such rates in respect of daughters, sons, sisters and brothers.[4]

The results are partly what we would expect, and partly a surprise. We are not surprised to find that gender is involved—the take-up rate is slightly higher for available daughters (75 per cent) than sons (66 per cent), and more notably higher for sisters (40 per cent) than brothers (25 per cent). Moreover, same-sex ties are stronger, with greater levels of mother-daughter ties than father-daughter ties, greater levels of sister-sister ties than brother-sister ties, and so on.

Less predictable is the fact that the take-up rates in expressive networks are at a considerably higher level for children (about 70 per cent overall) than for siblings (about 35 per cent overall). This indicates that parent-child ties, although dissimilar in age, are more likely to involve strong emotional bonds than are age-similar ties to siblings. This is clearly one point where age-based similarities are not sufficiently strong to overcome the much more complex and deeper attachments typical of filial bonds.

THE FOUR EXPRESSIVE DIMENSIONS

We turn now to the question of whether respondents have people who provide each of the four expressive dimensions outlined earlier. We have already seen in the case studies in Chapter 3 that individuals in expressive parts of networks may not be linked in all four ways. Miss White, for example, did not confide in her widowed friend Edie, but they were involved in social activities together. In such a case Edie shows up under 'social participation' but not under 'confiding', 'acceptance' or 'reassurance of worth'. Indeed, we would not really expect the majority of expressive contacts to be spread across all four areas, except for spouses and a few very close friendship, parental or sibling ties.

Rather, we would expect that confiding might be more common among very close kin ties (and very selectively between friends), and that reassurance would be mainly limited to kin ties especially younger ones who have been nurtured by respondents. Acceptance and social participation, however, often involve age-based similarities which are more common among friends. After all 'you can choose your friends but you can't choose your relatives', and what more sensible basis for such choice than a general affinity involving acceptance and mutual activity?

In addition to these expectations for relationships, our earlier results suggest that married respondents may be expected to have more expressive dimensions filled than do those who were formerly or never married, and that females would have the dimensions met more often and more widely than males.

In general these expectations prove correct as the findings in Table 4.1 make clear. Of the variety of results in this table, the more obvious concern the impact of gender and marital status. Irrespective of the measures used, women have a broader base of expressive support than men. Furthermore, there is a general trend for the married to be more broadly supported than other groups. For example, the never married men, who are have already shown to be comparatively isolated, score very low on all four dimensions of expressive support. Indeed, the differences in network size between men and women, discussed in Chapter 3, derive largely from the comparative difficulty that men have in forging expressive ties.

There is, however, one set of divergent findings which raise an interesting point about network structures, and the strategies (conscious or unconscious, chosen or socially constrained) employed in network-building and maintenance (Richards, 1985). These results concern the divorced and separated people, especially the women among them. On the one hand, the low average number of expressive bonds for these groups fits our general view of divorce as disrupting and reducing the size of networks. On the other hand, however, the proportions with at least one person for any dimension tell quite a contrasting story. Here levels are very high among the divorced and separated group, indeed for the women extraordinarily high. For example, while 66 per cent of married women have someone with whom they participate socially, the comparable proportion for those who are divorced or separated is 77 per cent for men and 82 per cent for women. Similar findings emerged in the 'reassurance of worth' questions.[5]

What does this mean? Are the results simply an anomaly? With small samples certainty is impossible, but some results suggest an explanation due to the very heavy reliance on only one other person. First, there is an over-representation of attenuated and diffuse networks (see Chapter 3) among this group of respondents. That is, whatever the size, there are few highly multiplex ties reported. Secondly, research in depth by D'Abbs (1983) points to a strategy among some non-married people, especially women, to rely extremely heavily on one 'best friend' for a very large array of supportive interchanges. The strategy is, of course, effective but 'brittle', liable to complete collapse if that relationship is lost. Detailed examination

Table 4.1 Availability of informal ties with the four dimensions of expressive support, by marital status and gender of respondents (n = 904)

Marital status by gender	Dimensions of expressive support							
	Confiding		Acceptance		Reassurance		Social Participation	
	Av. No.*	Pct With Any**	Av. No.*	Pct With Any**	Av. No.*	Pct With Any**	Av. No.*	Pct With Any**
Married								
women (205)	2.0	69	2.4	79	2.4	72	1.6	66
men (246)	1.7	75	2.3	80	2.1	71	1.7	61
Widowed								
women (301)	1.8	75	2.2	77	2.2	72	1.4	61
men (45)	1.6	71	1.9	73	1.2	76	1.0	67
Div/separated								
women (28)	1.5	71	1.9	86	1.8	86	1.1	82
men (19)	1.2	79	1.0	79	1.0	74	0.8	74
Never married								
women (44)	1.5	64	1.9	82	1.3	66	1.4	61
men (16)	0.8	70	1.1	62	0.8	56	0.7	50

* 'Av. No.' is an abbreviation for 'Average Number'

** These figures show the percentage of respondents who have one or more informal bonds providing this kind of expressive support. 'Pct with Any' thus means 'the percentage with anyone' named of some of the questionnaires from this group suggests that this strategy is relatively prevalent in our sample.

These results imply that the divorced or separated women have more homogeneous networks than other groups. They tend to have at least one person who provides all types of emotional support, and to focus heavily on that one. Other marital groups have more heterogeneous networks, due no doubt to a greater variety of circumstances and wider availability of social bonds.

A third finding that emerges from Table 4.1 is the gender difference in the numbers of significant others providing particular dimensions of expressive support.

The findings here are relatively complex, and it is hard not to give a detailed exposition that is extremely difficult for a reader to unravel. Our strategy, therefore, is to present a thumbnail sketch, based on detailed analysis of the results in Table 4.1.

The necessary context for understanding these findings is that gender roles were sharply delineated in Australia when our respondents were in middle age. Men were typically more linked into a world of work relations and mateship, women to a world of 'hearth and home'. Women derived (or were held to derive) great satisfaction from their children, men from their work and extra-familial leisure, and both were thought to derive some satisfaction from marital relations. The relationships maintained by women with adults other than their spouse were thought to be more emotional and expressive than the comparable social ties of their husbands.

Our data tends to fit well with this picture. We have already shown, both earlier in this chapter and in Chapter 3, that the worlds of married men and of married women are different in a variety of network aspects, and that, with the end of marriage (whether by death or by divorce or separation) different patterns of bonds result. The same story emerges here. Beginning with the provision of confidants we find a much clearer difference between men and women (ignoring whether they are married) than between the married and widowed. Thus there is little difference between married women and widows, or married men and widowers, but more women than men have confidants, reflecting the wider expressive ties of women.

When we turn to reassurance of worth we find an interesting pattern. The mean numbers are higher for the married, than the widowed and, within the married group, slightly higher for wives than for husbands. When we turn to the widowed, there are striking sex differences. On the one hand, widows have lost their husbands, but on average this has made little difference to the number of those—principally their children—who regard them as being worthwhile. Widowers, on the other hand, have lost their wives, and clearly in so doing most have lost the one person most likely to reassure them of their worth. For this generation, men derive reassurance more from being husbands than fathers, while women derive it more from motherhood than from being a wife. While children may provide reassurance of worth to both parents when they are together, this support is attenuated notably when fathers are on their own.

A not dissimilar pattern applies for participation. Again the impact of widowhood is greater for men than women, although here the effect is complicated by external demographic realities. The category of widowers includes men who could have lived unusually long, and thus have lost more age and gender peers through death—a process both of losing their wife and also their 'mateship' ties.

The one partial exception to our story of gender difference concerns acceptance. As we noted above, both men and women were thought to derive a common emotional satisfaction from marriage. This commonality emerges clearly in the findings on acceptance, for the married people have a high average number of people who accept them—slightly more than the widowed counterparts, some of whom have lost 'accepting' spouses—and there is little gender difference.

Having looked at these general patterns, we turn now to a more detailed examination of the four dimensions.

Confidants

There is general agreement in the literature that having a confidant is important for people's well-being. We have seen that nearly three-quarters of our respondents do have confidants (Table 4.1). More-over the percentages without a confidant vary only a little by gender and marital status. Thus men and women generally confide in someone even if there is no spouse or child available: alternatives outside the nuclear family are generally available. Confiding is an intimate and important activity, so we are led to ask the question: Who are these people? The answer to this question is shown in Table 4.2.[6]

The spouse is an obvious, although not automatic, choice as a confidant: only 52 per cent of the married say they confide in their spouse. Moreover, only 29 per cent of all the confidants of our married respondents are spouses. One must ask why these propor-tions are so low, given our obvious cultural norm that stresses 'marital communication'. There are a number of possible explana-tions here. The first of these is methodological: for a minority of cases the 'absence' of the spouse here (and in other dimensions) is a form of reporting 'oversight' (See Endnote 4). Second, generational and cohort expectations for marriage behaviour may be quite different. For the present generation of older people 'communication' may be less of a shibboleth both in rhetoric and reality than for younger cohorts. Indeed, more detailed analysis shows that the gender of the significant other is crucial to confiding relationships—the gender gap

Table 4.2 Respondents having particular relationships as confidants, by marital status and gender of respondents (n = 904)

| Marital status by gender | Daughter (%) | Son (%) | Relationship in whom the respondent confides* | | | | |
			Sister (%)	Brother (%)	Other kin (%)	Friend (%)	Neighbour or others (%)
Married							
women (205)	29	21	17	5	19	20	2
men (246)	20	24	5	5	14	13	1
Widowed							
women (301)	38	26	16	3	22	22	5
men (45)	20	29	7	7	19	31	2
Div/separated							
women (28)	29	7	14	0	18	22	14
men (19)	11	21	5	11	5	42	0
Never married							
women (44)	—	—	23	14	14	30	2
men (16)	—	—	13	6	6	25	0

* The figures show the percentage of respondents who have one or more confidants in each kind of relationship. For example, the upper left hand 'cell' shows that 29 per cent of married women confide in one or more daughters

may remain too large for some intimate discussions even among couples who have lived together for 40 or more years. Finally there is a point suggested to us by Lyn Richards—that older people may worry a good deal about their survival or that of their spouse in ways that may inhibit confiding. For example, a woman may not want to burden her husband by confiding her fears about how she will manage after his death. As Simmel (1950) notes, social distance is necessary even in, indeed especially in, intimate social relations.

There is a notable gender difference in the confiding patterns of older couples. Fifty eight per cent of the husbands, as compared to 46 per cent of the wives, say they confide in their spouse. Similarly, spouses comprise 37 per cent of the confidants of the older husbands, as compared to 23 per cent among older wives. Once again, we see that married men are more dependent upon their marriage for expressive support than are married women. Wives are more likely to provide emotional support to their husbands than to receive it in return. They also are more skilled in forging alternate expressive bonds, usually with other women, outside of marriage.

A final finding, which is best illustrated by the married respondents, is the remarkable diversity in confiding relationships. While these people have virtually a full complement of expressive bonds, it is notable that confiding typically is limited to but a few of them. One of the implications is that confiding relationships are largely voluntary and negotiated. Kinship may often be necessary to the relationship, but certainly is not sufficient in itself to ensure it. Personal compatibility is often necessary to bring a family tie to a deeper level of relationship. Another implication is that by restricting one's innermost fears and feelings to but a few trusted people, older people limit the exposure of their vulnerabilities to others who might use the information in ways which act against the perceived interest of the older person.

Turning to the non-married respondents and comparing their confidants with those of the married, interesting differences emerge. The widowed, for example, are generally quite similar to the married, in their patterns of confiding in children, siblings, other kin and friends. There are two small differences. First, the widowed, lacking spouses, tend to confide a little more often in these categories than the married—evidence of a partial substitutability effect. Both widows and widowers confide more often in their children than the married, and the tendency for same sex confiding—widows to daughters and widowers to sons—is the more marked.

The second widowed versus married difference is that widowed men are much more likely to confide in friends than are the married. Only 13 per cent of married men say that they confide in friends compared to 31 per cent for the widowed. Once again there is an apparent substitution effect.

As we have seen in Chapter 3 and earlier in this chapter, the divorced or separated respondents are quite different from either the married or the widowed. In the case of confiding, the difference does not result in a loss of support, but relates to the sources and depth of support. Not surprisingly, the more fragile ties, such as cross-sex ties, seem to break first. For example, while exactly the same proportion (29 per cent) of married women and divorced or separated women have daughter confidants, the former are three times as likely to have son confidants (21 per cent versus 7 per cent). Similarly, with divorced men, ties to daughters are reduced, compared to married men, as are ties to other kin. Both these comparisons speak of network loss. Conversely, the proportion of divorced men who confide in friends is the highest (42 per cent) of any group by far, and over three times the rate for married men. Here we see another substitution process at work. And, of course, friendship being more 'discretionary' than kinship, it is not surprising that, with divorced people, the substitution operates more with friends than kin. Friends, after all, can (even if with difficulty) be replaced, but kin cannot.

Finally, the never-marrieds again show some degree of isolation—especially the men (with an average of less than one confidant). The women maintain relatively more confiding ties to siblings and to friends, but not really enough to substitute for the lack of ties to spouse or children. Insofar as never-married men name any specific persons as confidants they rely heavily on their friends (55 per cent of all named confidants). The more important point is that only a quarter of these men confide even in friends.[7]

If we step back and consider confiding patterns as a whole, several broader patterns become clear. First, while close family usually are the first recourse when available, other relationships can provide this kind of expressive support. Family ties may facilitate confiding, but the permanency and obligation typical of marital and filial bonds does not appear to be necessary for this kind of support which does not make great demands on the provider. Second, while men and women who have been married appear to find alternative confidants in widowhood, the never married—especially the men—appear to have less of either the desire or interpersonal skills to forge these bonds.

Acceptance

The second dimension of expressive relations is the extent to which there are other people who the respondents say accept them as they are. Given a long tradition in the social sciences that stresses the importance of the 'significant other' who serves as a mirror providing self-confirmation (Cooley, 1909; Simmel, 1950; and Goffman, 1961 are among the host of obvious writers), it is surprising that so little attention has been paid to this factor in literature on social support.

This is doubly true for the elderly. Surely to reach the latter stages of one's life and find that no-one accepts you as you are can be very threatening. An inability to find acceptance among significant others could be expected to be among the most damaging of the consequences of ageism, generation gaps and reduced exchange power.

Fortunately for our respondents all but 22 per cent could report someone who accepted them. The mean number of people who accepted each respondent was 2.2—compared to a mean number of confidants of 1.76.

The results, shown in Table 4.3, are all variations on the control theme that acceptance is provided primarily by friends (46 to 61 per cent for the different groups). Friendship is the only bond in which people can select others who are very similar to themselves. It is also notable that friendships are typically between age peers, people who can appreciate the historical experiences which shape individual lives. Friendships which provide acceptance also are based primarily on same-gender ties, further evidence of the noticeable gender gap in the present generation of older people.

Only about one-third of married people listed their spouse—another age peer bond—as a person who accepts them as they are. While the caveats about such reports (noted earlier for confiding) continue to apply, the comparatively lower levels—one-third for acceptance versus about one-half for confiding—must be taken seriously. It is interesting—if depressing—that the end-point of 40 or 50 years of marriage seems to bring so few couples a sense of mutual acceptance. It may be that the accumulation of common experiences points out divergence as much as convergence among partners whose lives have been shaped in very different ways by gender expectations.

Children seem to be more accepting of respondents in the normatively sanctioned situations of marriage and widowhood than of those in the 'deviant' status of divorce. For the latter group very few women and no men listed their children as people who accept them. It is only among never-married men, however, that a relatively high proportion (38 per cent) report that nobody accepts them. Once again, we see the extensive emotional isolation of many of these men.

Reassurance of worth

The third expressive dimension is reassurance of worth. Our previous general comments on acceptance are again relevant here. There is every reason to suppose that this dimension is important to self-image and psychological well-being, especially among elderly people, who are no longer in the workforce or raising children. Overall 72 per cent of respondents said there was someone who provided this dimension; an average of 2.2 persons were named.

Overwhelmingly, reassurance of worth is provided by kin, with

Table 4.3 Respondents having particular relationships providing acceptance, by marital status and gender of respondents (n = 904)

Marital status by gender	Relationship providing acceptance*						
	Daughter (%)	Son (%)	Sister (%)	Brother (%)	Other kin (%)	Friend (%)	Neighbour or others (%)
Married							
women (205)	20	17	15	3	18	48	7
men (246)	16	20	4	7	18	46	4
Widowed							
women (301)	20	18	11	6	26	50	11
men (45)	13	18	2	0	20	42	7
Div/separated							
women (28)	7	4	18	4	14	61	25
men (19)	—	—	5	5	11	48	11
Never Married							
women (44)	—	—	14	7	18	50	7
men (16)	—	—	13	—	13	44	6

* The figures show the percentage of respondents who have one or more persons providing acceptance in each kind of relationship.

Table 4.4 Respondents having particular relationships providing reassurance of worth, by marital status and gender of respondents (n = 904)

Marital status by gender	Relationship providing reassurance of worth*						
	Daughter (%)	Son (%)	Sister (%)	Brother (%)	Other kin (%)	Friend (%)	Neighbour or others (%)
Married							
women (205)	39	29	9	2	27	15	3
men (246)	39	30	2	2	21	14	0
Widowed							
women (301)	38	28	9	3	37	17	1
men (45)	13	13	4	2	26	11	2
Div/separated							
women (28)	32	18	0	4	32	14	0
men (19)	0	16	5	5	16	32	0
Never Married							
women (44)	—	—	20	7	20	36	5
men (16)	—	—	19	0	13	25	6

* The figures show the percentage of respondents who have one or more persons providing reassurance of worth in each kind of relationship.

friends featuring at substantial levels only for the never-married respondents and the divorced or separated men. Within the kin category, much depends upon the gender and marital status of respondent and the significant other. For example, many of the women who are (or have been) married, and the married men, mention their children, although the women are more likely to mention daughters. The currently married—both husbands and wives—mention their spouses in over half the cases.

Brothers are comparatively unimportant as sources of reassurance and this is partially due to their absence for mortality reasons and partially to a factor discussed earlier—namely the low take-up rate of available brothers in the expressive network (only 25 per cent feature at all). Sisters are significant only for the never-married. 'Other kin' are important only for the widowed—where they tend mainly to be grandchildren—and as a more diffuse group of kin for the divorced or separated women.

Here the picture is relatively simple, then. People find reassurance in the most intimate relationship that they entered by choice (marriage), from their offspring, and, in turn, their offspring's offspring. Only the marital dyad, and ties down the lineage, involve relatively permanent ties in which older people would be known for their many past contributions as well as possible present vulnerabilities (Chapter 5). For the never-married, who have no spouse or offspring, or for those whose relations have been disrupted by divorce or separation, such reassurance is provided less often and by fewer people. It is a type of support that finds no easy substitutability for the close kin ties of marriage and parenthood.

Social participation

The final dimension concerns social participation—people with whom the respondent shares common interests, outings and so on.[8] Overall, this is an area of relative paucity compared to the other kinds of expressive support. Over one-third of our aged respondents say there is no-one with whom they share interests and so on, and an average of only 1.48 persons are named per respondent. The explanations are twofold: firstly, social participation requires levels of mobility and other personal resources which are beyond some older people; and secondly, the age peer ties which facilitate social participation can be eroded severely over the years. The large bulk of such social participation is provided by friends. Friends are listed by 31 per cent of the never-married males through to 44 per cent of widowed women (accounting for 62 per cent of the people listed by them). Friends account for over half of the people who provide social participation listings for all except the married. Even there, friends are listed by 43 per cent of married women (compared to the 23 per cent who list their husband), and by 48 per cent of men (compared to the 18 per cent who list their wives). Clearly, the world of the married aged is not one of high integration. Rather for social activity it is far more a question of 'his leisure' and 'her leisure'.

LIFE SATISFACTION

So far we have shown that most, but not all people have someone in whom they can confide, someone who accepts them, someone who reassures them of their worth, and someone with whom they carry out various leisure activities (social participation). We have also suggested that the fulfilment of each of these dimensions of expressive support should increase happiness and well-being. The question, of course, remains whether this argument can be empirically substantiated.

Such a question can be answered, in part, by looking at information about the happiness, life satisfaction, loneliness and other aspects of well-being among our respondents (See Appendix 1 for details of measures).[9] Of course, it is not only network factors, as measured in Chapters 3 and 4, that have an impact on general well-being. Disability, social contacts, and visiting patterns can be important also. We examined a number of measures, asking, in effect, whether there was variation depending upon levels of social integration and network.[10] Controls for disability and for gender were used, although, as we shall see, these had relatively little effect in general.

Social integration and well-being

All four measures of social integration (See Endnote 9) showed considerable variation in themselves. For example, the number of joint-outings reported with non-residents, in the week before interviews, ranged from none—reported by over 60 per cent of our respondents—up to 12, reported by one person. In general, however, there were few significant associations between levels of outings, visits or visitors and any of the well-being measures. These findings are further reinforced by an analysis of the scope and frequency of contact with network members reported elsewhere (Gibson, 1983). Statistically significant associations observed were all in the expected direction—greater social contact was associated with greater well-being—but they were certainly not very large or strong. Examining men and women separately, and looking at those who were disabled, had little effect on this general conclusion.

Quite a different result was obtained, however, when we considered whether individuals had, in the previous month, attended any organisations or clubs. Here the general picture associating social integration with well-being is much clearer. Overall, people who had been to an organisation were less likely to say that they were lonely, and less likely to say that they wanted to see more of people. They were happier and more likely to express general satisfaction with life, and, on a variety of the morale measures, there were statistically significant associations between organisational membership and positive scores. Of 14 measures examined, only 5 failed to show any statistically significant level of association (two of the latter being the general questions about depression and anxieties/worries).[11] The results reinforce the importance of facilitating social participation of older people, although it is notable that few of these visits were to age-specific gatherings such as meetings of senior citizen centres.

Expressive relations and well-being

As we have shown in the previous section, wider aspects of social integration, which are related to but not reducible to networks, have an impact upon the well-being of our respondents. We now turn to the question of whether the size of the expressive network or the extent to which certain expressive dimensions are met are associated with various indicators of well-being.

If the association between social integration and well-being is mainly based upon a quantitative explanation—'more is better'—we should expect that the size of the expressive network would predict levels of well-being. In fact, expressive network size was not significantly related to any of the various measures of well-being. The picture is not substantially altered by controlling either for gender or disability. In short, nothing very constructive emerges from attempting to use network size as an explanation or predictor of well-being.

What then of the various dimensions of expressive relations? The picture here is a little less complex, although at first glance not entirely convincing. For most of the variables used to measure well-being, the presence or absence of persons for each dimension shows little association in any direction with any measure.

One very clear exception emerges, however, and that is the question concerning general happiness. This was phrased as follows: Taking all things together, how would you say things are these days? Would you say that you're ... very happy/fairly happy/not too happy/unhappy?

The results are shown in Table 4.5.

For all four dimensions of expressive support there is a significant association with happiness. Clearly then, it is possible to argue that the overall level of happiness of our respondents is affected by having confidants, people who accept them and so on.[12] Those with such contacts are somewhere between twice and four times as likely to

Table 4.5 Happiness by availability of informal ties providing each of four dimensions of expressive support (n = 888)

Perceived happiness	Expressive dimensions							
	Confiding		Acceptance		Reassurance		Social Participation	
	Yes (734)	No (154)	Yes (789)	No (99)	Yes (722)	No (166)	Yes (650)	No (238)
Very	32	17	32	10	33	17	34	18
Fairly	60	71	61	74	61	68	60	68
Not too	6	10	6	11	5	13	5	11
Unhappy	2	2	1	6	1	3	1	3
Total (percentage)	100	100	100	100	100	100	100	100

report themselves 'very happy' as those without them.

The 'happiness' item is, of course, only one variable. Although the result is unambiguous one must ask whether it is theoretically important. According to George and Bearon (1980) the measure is important for such analysis. Unlike more complex measures that may reflect complex personality traits and processes, the happiness item measures current mood, is relatively sensitive to changes in circumstance and hence is a good measure for assessing impacts of subtle kinds of social support. Thus these results support the argument, generally well-accepted in the literature, that confidants are important, but goes further and illustrates that the other three dimensions we have described are also of considerable importance. Indeed, as shown in Table 4.5, acceptance may be more vital to happiness than having a confidant, a poignant illustration of the difficulties of those, such as some of our never-married men, who said they had people they could confide in, but did not have someone who accepted them.

It is, of course, possible to go further into this question of well-being and expressive relations. To do this we developed a simple score, ranging from zero (for those who had no expressive support) through to four (for those who had mentioned someone for each of the four dimensions).

When this variable is related to measures of well-being a fairly striking picture emerges. For a considerable number of these measures there are clear associations between the number of dimensions where people were available and the level of well-being.[13] With the exception of the desire to see more of people (which will be discussed below) these associations are strong and statistically significant. For example, as the number of dimensions increases, respondents are much less likely to say that they are lonely, much less likely to say that they are often sad, and much less likely to perceive life as getting worse as they get older. They are more likely to see life as worth living, do not 'take things hard' as often, and are much more likely to be happy and satisfied with life. Controls for gender and disability do not alter this picture.

The variable that shows the strongest effect again is the simple and robust one—happiness. The relevant information is shown in Table 4.6. As may be clearly seen, those with people mentioned for three or four dimensions are far more likely than others to be 'very happy' and far less likely to be 'not too happy' or 'unhappy'.

Table 4.6   Happiness by number of expressive dimensions met by informal ties (n = 888)

Perceived happiness	Number of expressive dimensions met by informal ties*				
	None (39)	One (31)	Two (84)	Three (240)	Four (494)
Very	5	19	14	24	37
Fairly	78	53	73	68	57
Not too	15	16	12	7	4
Unhappy	2	13	2	1	1
Total (percentage)	100	100	100	100	100

* The overall table has a significant chi square test (p < 0.001)

It was noted earlier that there was one exception to the direct relationship between the breadth of expressive support and well being—the desire to see more of people. For those who have at least some expressive bonds, having more of the dimensions fulfilled increases the proportion who say that they see enough of others. Those who have no-one close on any dimension, however, in general do not express a desire for more contact. It seems sensible to view such people as 'loners' whose relative isolation is partly achieved through choice rather than imposed by necessity (although, of course, part of the response could be 'putting a brave face on it').[14]

The broad conclusion suggested by this analysis is that both subjective and objective aspects of expressive support are important. But the overall quality of support (whether it encompass the full range of expressive relations) is of greater significance than the number of supporters (size of expressive network). Our findings are encouraging, but by no means definitive. This reinforces the importance of carrying out further research on the topic.

SUMMARY

This chapter has examined the expressive network generated by asking respondents who they felt close to on each of four dimensions—confiding, acceptance, reassurance of worth, and social participation. We have shown that the size and composition of the network varies among our respondents, particularly by their gender and marital status. The size and membership of the network, however, turns out not to be terribly interesting. While it varies in relation to factors such as household arrangement and number of children, it is not of itself very useful in explaining happiness or other aspects of psychological well-being.

However, other measures of social integration, plus the breadth of expressive support are closely related to well being. Each expressive dimension contributes to happiness and to most other aspects of well being, but having more of the four expressive dimensions met is especially important.

Other more detailed findings are also of interest. First, we find that even in the absence of certain types of close kin (such as parents, spouses or children) most respondents are able to form expressive bonds. This indicates that a substitutability effect is at work even in these intimate areas of life. Such substitutability often operates by drawing in more distant kin (cousins, nephews or nieces and so on) rather than non-kin. Of course, such kin are limited in number and may be inaccessible either geographically or socially. There are thus limits to the kin substitution, and for some people, when one kind of tie is lost, it may not be possible to forge alternatives.

Linked to this is a second interesting point. It is clear that these expressive bonds are not an obligatory aspect of kinship ties. Both the inclusion of 'distant' relatives in some networks, and the exclusion of 'close' relatives in others, points to the voluntaristic and negotiated aspects of these ties. This emerges clearly in the case of the married aged. Typically such people have quite a wide range of potential ties—to spouse, to children, to siblings and so on. Rarely, however, are all these activated in their expressive network, even though some others (friends, more distant kin) are.

A third point that flows from this is that a greater range of potential ties facilitates a process of selection and diffusion. Not all children, for example, are included as important for expressive ties. The selectivity process, no doubt is connected to complex questions of gender roles. Perhaps a mother feels more comfortable about confiding in her daughter(s) than her son(s), and more comfortable about one daughter than others. In part it may also reflect diffusion. With a large family one may not confide in one particular child but in children generally.

Finally, the voluntaristic and negotiated character of such ties probably explains, in part, why so few respondents entirely lack them. Declining exchange power in purely material and instrumental ways is less likely to undermine the potential for mutual confiding (for example), and it is encouraging to find that the majority of our sample are indeed well provided with these important ties. Of those who are largely devoid of expressive ties, most notably many never-married men, a significant number are more aptly characterised as being lifelong isolates than being desolate in old age.

5

Intergenerational exchange

HAL KENDIG

In this chapter, we turn to an examination of the instrumental tasks of daily living. We ask whether respondents are independent, and how and to what extent they negotiate support in these areas. Taken as a whole, the findings clearly debunk some popular misconceptions: most older people are found to be independent and contributing, and the small minority who are dependent generally rely on family rather than community or institutional services. Filial ties are examined particularly closely, because they involve complex patterns of instrumental as well as expressive interdependence over the entire life course. We also pay close attention to gender skills, and sources of support when children and spouses are not available. The 'currency' of instrumental exchanges, which may involve substantial dependence on one or two people, is shown to contrast sharply with the many expressive interdependencies explored in Chapter 4.

The case studies presented in Chapter 3, illustrate many of these themes. Mrs Brown and her husband, for example, have a clear gender division of household labour, are completely independent from family support from outside the household, and use paid services for a few tasks such as gardening. While Mrs Brown is aware that her daughter would help if she were ill or widowed, at present the family support flows down the generations to their co-resident daughter. Miss White, a healthy woman who never married, also is highly independent, relying only a little upon paid-help, and she contributes substantially to others by providing transport for friends and extensive volunteer work with the Red Cross and her church. Mr O'Leary, who is housebound as well as never-married, relies on nephews for shopping and errands, and otherwise neither receives nor provides support. Perhaps the most revealing point is that Mrs Brown could rely on family if she were ill in bed for a month, while the two never-married respondents would expect to enter an institution.

The chapter begins by examining expectations for support, and the earlier as well as present contributions made by older people. These aspects of life-long development set the context in which support may be received in the later years. Levels and kinds of assistance are shown to vary markedly depending on the circumstances of the older person and their relationships with the providers. Finally, the consequences of instrumental dependencies are assessed for both recipients and providers. Throughout the analysis, we consider many kinds of assistance covered in the main survey: these include household tasks, transport, personal care, and financial help, asking about past and present contributions as well as support received. The measures are detailed in Appendix 1.

ATTITUDES AND EXPECTATIONS

The provision of instrumental support is influenced strongly by the perceptions and expectations which people bring to their relationships. Attitudinal information on such a complex topic has obvious limitations: people can provide socially acceptable or wishful answers, especially for situations which they never have experienced or hope to avoid. Personal views also vary widely between individuals and families (Carter, 1985: Chapter 6). An understanding of orientations remains valuable, however, in indicating some of the general rules and currency by which relationships are actively constructed and evolve (Hagestad, 1981). In this section, we draw on attitudinal information to show how older people and their children are predisposed towards interpersonal exchanges.

Everyone who enters old age brings along a lifelong accumulation of orientations and expectations. Kuypers and Bengtson (1983) highlight the tension between the goals of autonomy and continuity on the one hand, and the avoidance of social breakdown on the other. The first side of their observation, the strong belief in self-reliance, is given some quantitative support in the main survey: four-fifths of the respondents agree that: 'When the going gets tough, people should rely on themselves'. More convincing is the evidence from qualitative studies of older Australians, all of which found a fierce determination to maintain as much independence as possible (Job, 1984; Pollitt, 1977; Russell, 1981). The overwhelming message from Day's very old respondents, for example, was: 'Tell them we can manage' (Day, 1985). Whether interpreted from a developmental (Erickson, 1977) or exchange (Dowd, 1980) perspective, it is clear that older people actively maintain their 'ego integrity' by resisting support which cannot be reciprocated.

For those who become disabled, the wish to remain independent comes into direct conflict with the avoidance of social breakdown. Our survey respondents were confronted with this dilemma by the following question:

> When older people can no longer manage on their own, do you think most want to . . .
> 1 'stay at home with outside help'   (67 per cent)
> 2 'move in with children'   (8 per cent)
> 3 'move to a home for the aged' or   (18 per cent)
> 4 'to a nursing home'   (7 per cent)

Even in these difficult circumstances, respondents generally would wish to stay at home, thus maintaining a substantial measure of autonomy and independence. Living with children is decidedly unpopular. Older people are disposed to concede as little as possible in the face of mounting dependency.

There is mixed support for the principle of filial responsibility. Fifty eight per cent of our respondents do agree that 'Older people should be able to depend on their children for the help they need'. This view is not universally held, however, and very few respondents say they agree with it 'very' strongly. It also conflicts with the very strong values of self reliance and independent living. Nor is it clear that the belief in filial responsibility reflects a preference for family support rather than paid-help or social services.

Carter's (1985) study of 17 of the younger relatives of our older respondents provides an indication of views from the other side in negotiating intergenerational support. She found that the younger relatives subscribed more strongly than their older relatives to the norms of family support. Nearly all disagreed with the proposition that older people should be self reliant (as phrased above), all agreed with our statement measuring family obligation, and nearly all nominated family as the appropriate carers for old people who are ill in bed for a month. But when forced to consider the appropriate response if their older relative were to have a serious and long-term disability, most became distinctly uncomfortable—Carter reports many 'long pauses' and 'cleared throats'. Fifteen of the seventeen were very reluctant to consider co-residency in these circumstances; residential care was seen as the only alternative because 'the generations do not mix under the same roof', and personal care is 'a nursing job for the professionals'. The one person who wished to take on such responsibilities, if necessary, added the following twist: 'But still, when it's my time, I'm going to have myself booked in! I don't want my kids to feel they should look after me!'

Survey research from the United States confirms Carter's findings on the strength (if not the limits) of a sense of filial responsibility among younger relatives (Bengtson and Treas, 1980; Brody, Johnsen, Fulcomer and Lang, 1983; Brody, Johnsen and Fulcomer, 1984). The Brody study is especially important because it compares the attitudes of three generations of women within the same lineages. It also uses the questions which served as the model for (and yielded very similar results to) those in our survey.

This study shows that the middle and younger generations are most likely to view support as a matter of obligation, rather than exchange, and they are much less accepting of services and paid help as alternatives to family support for aged parents. Other studies also suggest that obligation, more than affection or reciprocity, motivates the provision of substantial, one-way support (Bengtson and De Terre, 1980; Morris and Sherwood, 1984; Kinnear and Graycar, 1984). The generational views reflect different perspectives on intergenerational exchange: obligation underlies the provision of support in mid-life, while a sense of reciprocity for past contributions may increase the acceptability of receiving it in old age.

The middle generation, however, also remains subject to the conflicting demands of other responsibilities. Marriage and childbearing bring commitments which become a stronger priority than care for an aged parent (Streib, 1965). Among all generations of women, unmarried and childless women are expected to provide more support for aged parents (Brody, Johnson, Fulcomer and Lang, 1983). Expectations between the generations are found to diverge sharply, however, with respect to the responsibilities of women who work (ibid.). While all generations believe in rearranging family life to care for parents, only among the older generation does a majority believe that married women should give up employment to do so.

The strength of obligations in filial bonds is seldom found in other relationships. The study by Brody, Johnson and Fulcomer, (1984) found only weak expectations for support from other relatives, friends, and neighbours. Older people were especially reluctant about drawing on these sources for unreciprocated support. These relationships do not have firm norms to order complex intergenerational arrangements, and are very susceptible to disruption. Only family bonds have strong normative pressure to keep in touch, which makes it hard for needs to be ignored, or for the relationship to drift away in times of difficulty.

As compared to the qualified acceptance by older people of informal support, belief in the right to government services is extraordinarily high. Eighty four per cent of the survey respondents agree that: 'People who need help with cooking and housework should have government services'. While some perceive a stigma in becoming a 'welfare client' (Day and Harley, 1985) many older people see services as an effective way to avoid 'becoming a burden' on family (Pollitt, 1977). Nearly half of our respondents go so far as to agree that 'services can take the place of family care' and a similar proportion agree that 'I would rather have help from a paid worker than from family and friends'.

The variation in these attitudes and expectations appears to stem primarily from lifelong orientations towards informal support. Never-married women and men consistently show the strongest beliefs in self reliance, and more frequently accept and prefer paid-help and services than family care. Divorced men, but not women, display similar views. At the other extreme, widowed women, especially those with relatively more children, have the least sense of self reliance and are most favourably disposed towards family care. It is notable that these attitudes remain virtually unchanged when disability is taken into account. As with the findings on expressive support in Chapter 4, the patterns accord more closely with lifelong investments than exigencies in old age.

In summary, the norms of family life organise complex patterns of reciprocity within lineages over the life course (James, et al., 1984; Sussman, 1976). Filial exchanges are facilitated by the long time span, and lack of person specificity, in the accountability between successive generations. Nearly all of the survey respondents agree that 'One of the good things about having family help is that you get a chance to help them back'.

CONTRIBUTIONS

Over the course of the lifecycle, the usual pattern is for people to be heavy beneficiaries in childhood, heavy providers in middle age, and (to widely varying degrees) net recipients again in advanced old age. Sussman (1976) argues that contributions made by parents to their children earlier in life amount to an 'implicit bargain' in securing support in old age; inheritance can be explicitly used in the same way (Sussman, Cates, and Smith, 1970; Day, 1985). The more important point, however, is that the life-long balance sheet is nearly always tipped in favour of ascending generations. Support flows primarily from parents to children, and the 'debt' usually is repaid only as children become parents themselves (Rosenmayr, 1978, cited in Hagestad, 1981).

The survey results confirm older people's mid-life contributions flowing down the lineage. Well over 80 per cent of our respondents had raised children of their own. Moreover, the majority had provided financial assistance to a child after leaving home (Kendig and Rowland, 1983). An important contemporary example is assistance in buying a first home. This is but one indication of how parents serve as a primary source of support even after children have reached adulthood.

Our respondents were as likely to have had a parent survive into old age as they were to have had children of their own. In sharp contrast to the assistance provided to children, only about a third of our respondents had lived with an aged parent, or provided substantial care to one of them, for a year or more (Kendig, 1984c). Part of the answer lies in the tendency for responsibility to fall on but one of several children in the typically large families of that generation. More importantly, the majority of the past generation of older people, like the present one, had remained substantially independent for all but the final months of their lives. Once again, we find evidence of the predominant flow of aid down the generations.

Intergenerational support is structured by both gender and marital status. Women usually take primary responsibility for child-rearing, and they outnumber men by a five-to-one margin among the carers of the past generation of aged parents (ibid.). While the never-married are final links on the chains of support down the lineage, they are nearly three times as likely as their counterparts who have married, to have provided substantial care to a parent in the past. Women who never married emerge as the one group in which a majority had cared in a major way for a parent in the past generation of older people.

One of the many widespread misconceptions is that informal contributions end when people enter old age. Our findings, however, show that older people are more likely to be providers than recipients of many kinds of support (Kendig, 1985). In the case of co-residency with children, the majority of these households are headed by older people who own the home. Most of their children have yet to leave home; some (especially sons) have returned to parents after divorce or another disruption to their lives; and a few have handicaps which have left them in their parents' charge since birth. In these diverse kinds of shared households, it is usually the child who benefits more in the distribution of housing costs and domestic tasks.

The provision of financial support is the most conspicuous area where responsibility now rests with nuclear families and the public sector rather than the extended family. Even when one considers modest amounts of financial help—gifts or loans worth $200 or more over the past year—informal assistance is rarely provided (Kendig and Rowland, 1983). When it does occur, it is overwhelmingly between the aged and their children, and the aged are twice as likely to be providers (12 per cent) as recipients (6 per cent). Higher occupational status substantially increases the proportions having made financial gifts to children, both recently and earlier in life. As with the patterns of household formation, our findings on financial flows are very similar to those found in a variety of American studies (Bengtson and Treas, 1980; Troll, et al., 1979).

Turning to assistance with tasks of daily living, one again finds that older people make substantial contributions. In addition to doing domestic work for co-residents, nearly half of the Sydney respondents have recently provided instrumental aid to someone beyond their own household (Kendig, 1985). The most common of these are childminding, usually grandmothers minding grandchildren, and transport assistance, predominantly given by men to older friends (Table 5.1). The other contributions also follow traditional gender skills, and the most substantial ones are provided to family. The contributions range from minor assistance associated with joint social activity, through to full-time child care or primary aid to someone who is housebound. In many instances, older people may consider the contributions as opportunities rather than obligations. One of the daughters-in-law of our respondents, perhaps justifying her good fortune, remarked that: 'He'd be most offended if we asked somebody else first [to do the baby sitting]' (Carter, 1985).

Nor are older people's contributions made only through the informal sector. Our Sydney survey, and another of the State of Victoria (ABS, 1983c), show that a quarter of older people serve as volunteers. The Victorian study found that the aged are more likely than younger people to be contributing to social services, particularly those for children and old people, and they also work substantially longer hours. Never-married women, who we found had few opportunities to help family in old age, were especially likely to serve as volunteers.

Finally, the calculation of intergenerational exchange must' take inheritances into account. The vast majority of older Australians are now leaving fully unencumbered homes as a final legacy to their children (Kendig, 1984a,b). Their unwillingness to use this capital themselves, and their great resistance to inheritance tax, underscores the compelling urge to further the opportunities of children.

HOUSEHOLDS AND INSTRUMENTAL SUPPORT

Most older individuals and couples are highly independent, receiving assistance in an average of only two of the eight basic tasks of daily living. Typical examples would be occasional and supplementary informal aid or paid-help with less essential activities such as gardening, minor home repairs, and transport. In many cases, informal assistance results from a sharing of household duties, joint-activities, or modest interdependencies—all of which are common among many capable people in all age groups. The one-fourth of older people who receive assistance in most areas of daily living is counterbalanced by a nearly equal proportion who are entirely self-sufficient (Kendig, 1983a).

Whether instrumental support is provided from within or beyond the household depends largely on the demands of the particular task

Table 5.1 Respondents' provision of various kinds of instrumental assistance to non-household members (n = 940)

Number of respondents	Kinds of informal support provided over the last month*					Kinds of informal support provided over the last six months*			Any informal support
	Child minding	Transport	Shopping	House work	Meal prepn	Pers. care	Min. house repairs	Gardening	
	(%)	(%)	(%)	(%)	(%)	(%)	(%)	(%)	(%)
Total (940)	29	19	7	4	3	6	4	3	45
Men (365)	24	31	4	1	1	3	9	5	50
Women (575)	32	12	9	6	4	8	1	2	41

* The figures show the percentage of respondents who have provided each kind of assistance to non-household members. For example, the upper left hand cell shows that 29 per cent of all respondents had minded a child for a non-household member over the last month

under question (Kendig, 1985b; Litwak, 1985). Those tasks which are provided at more frequent intervals, such as meals preparation and personal care, lie at one end of the continuum: even excluding spouses, three-fourths of the providers in these areas are co-residents. At the other end of the continuum are transport (12 per cent co-resident) and minor dwelling repairs (27 per cent), widespread but usually less urgent needs. Other tasks such as housekeeping and shopping are equally likely to be provided within or to the household. The demands of providing the more intense support are the primary explanation for the formation of joint households as disabilities increase and are sustained (Chapter 2).

Couples

The extensive interdependence between older spouses explains their very high levels of independence from outside assistance (Figure 5.1). While there is some American evidence for less separation of domestic tasks among older couples (Troll, et al., 1979; Dobson, 1983), we found a strong and traditional division of household labour.

Figure 5.1   Amounts of instrumental assistance received, by living arrangement and disability of respondent (n = 901)

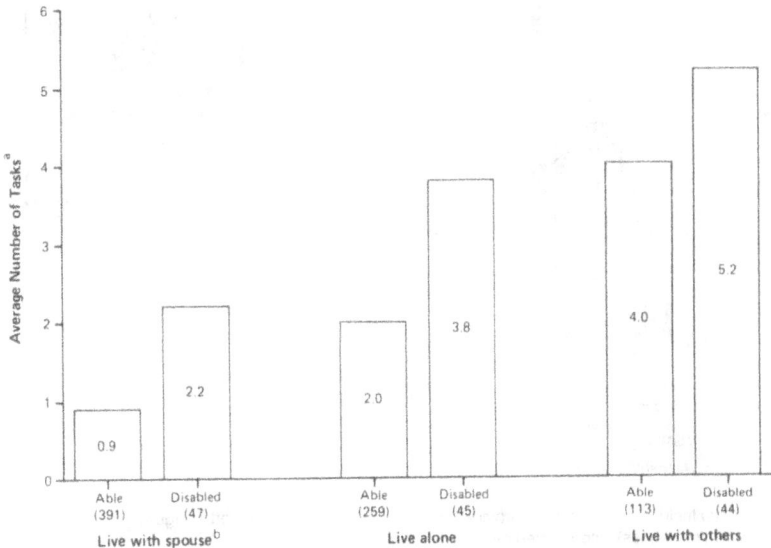

Notes: (a) The amount of assistance is measured by the number of tasks with which assistance is received from any source besides a spouse. Tasks include transport, gardening, minor house repairs, shopping or errands, housekeeping, meal preparation, and personal care (See Appendix 1). (b) Includes a small number of respondents having other co-residents in addition to a spouse

Wives handle most domestic duties within the home, and husbands deal with dwelling repairs, gardening and do the driving for their wives as well as themselves (Kendig, 1983c). Shopping and errands are the only tasks in which there is a substantial proportion of couples who share primary responsibilities.

A lifetime of gender conditioning and habit can present major adjustment difficulties should a spouse become disabled. When the husband is disabled, there apparently is relatively little re-allocation of responsibilities between the spouses: most of his needs continue to be met by the traditional division of labour (ibid.). Wives also are nearly always the sole carers when husbands require intimate care with bathing, dressing, and toiletting. But very few wives are able to take over responsibility for traditionally male tasks which can no longer be carried out by the husband. Disability of the husband usually precipitates the use of support with these jobs which are provided relatively easily from beyond the household (Figure 5.2).

Figure 5.2　Size and location of instrumental support network, by living arrangement and disability of respondent (n = 901)

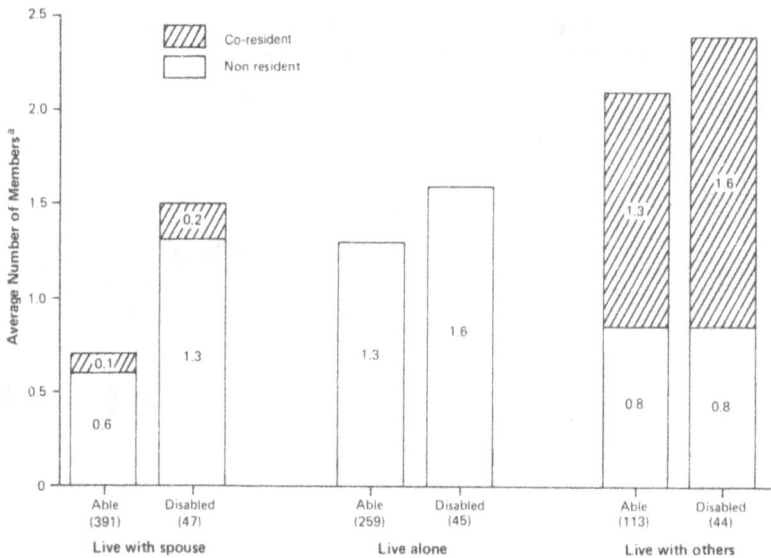

Note: (a) Includes only informal providers of assistance with tasks listed in Figure 5.1 and excludes tasks completed by spouses

The disability of a wife, however, appears to bring about a substantial renegotiation of domestic tasks. In these circumstances, the men usually have primary responsibility for shopping, errands and housework. Husbands are also the most common providers when wives require personal care. Yet half of the disabled wives still have primary responsibility for meals preparation, albeit with supplementary help from spouses. While husbands may not be very well-equipped to take over the traditionally female tasks, it is more difficult to provide these kinds of assistance from outside the household. It also may be resisted because of the substantial intrusion into the couple's independence and privacy.

Living alone

In contrast to the independence of older couples, those who live alone draw more substantially on outside support (Figure 5.1). Three-fourths of them have informal support, primarily through the modified extended family. The balance between independence and dependency depends largely on the personal histories by which these people came to live on their own.

Gender-related skills with instrumental tasks become most important when people live alone. Among the few men who are in this situation, at least three-fourths are independent in each of the basic tasks, including meals preparation and housekeeping. By comparison, three-fourths of the women have assistance with transport and house and garden upkeep (Kendig, 1983b). These findings hold when one takes into account possibly confounding influences such as the proportions who are disabled, have at sometime been married, or are institutionalised. As with the older couples, we have evidence that, when necessary, men apparently do learn many traditionally 'female' tasks, at least to a minimal level. Traditionally 'male' skills are more difficult to acquire, especially if the need to learn them arises late in life, but support with them also is more readily available.

This interpretation is given added weight when we consider the marital history of older women living alone. Those who have never married are in most, but not all respects, as independent as widowers and never-married men. Their greater independence, as compared to widows, remains when disability is taken into account. Never-married women presumably had to cope on their own with the traditionally 'male' tasks in mid-life, and in any event do not have sons or other descendants who could provide support with them in old age. As compared to women who have been married, they are more likely to use public transport or drive, but car ownership remains lower than for all categories of men. Relatively more never-married women also are able to avoid dependency in these areas by living in centrally located home units, or in flats which they do not maintain themselves. While the never-married may have fewer alternatives to self reliance, they also appear better equipped to manage on their own.

The vulnerability of those living alone becomes apparent when needs are more intense. Five of the 45 disabled people in these circumstances do not have any informal support—a very precarious position no matter what one's living skills may be. Most of them, however, receive very high levels of support (Figure 5.1), usually from only one or two people (Figure 5.2). This situation also has substantial risks because it can be very difficult to sustain on an ongoing basis. Overall, nearly half of those who live alone say they could not expect any informal assistance support if they were ill in bed for a month.

Joint-households

When older people live with others besides a spouse, they typically receive high levels of support (Figure 5.1). Those who are able are highly interdependent with their co-residents, while those who are disabled are seldom responsible for many of the domestic tasks. Whatever the balance of exchange between the household members, instrumental support is facilitated by the close proximity and economies of scale.

Of the many ways of forming joint-households, three distinct patterns emerge. First, there is co-residence with a sibling (5 per cent of the total sample) or a friend (4 per cent). In these circumstances, one typically finds two women who have lived together for companionship over a period of several decades or more. Most of them never married and are reasonably healthy. While they display many of the interdependencies found among married couples, they rely much more on assistance with traditionally 'male' tasks.

The second pattern, living with an unmarried child (3 per cent), also tends to be a long-term and mutually advantageous arrangement. In this case, one usually finds an older widow who takes on primary or sole responsibility for most domestic duties. The contributions of the older women usually remain sizeable even when she is disabled.

Finally, there is the notably different pattern found in co-residency with a child and his or her family (5 per cent). These arrangements are by comparison relatively short-term, with the typical period being for five to ten years. The press of constraints in bringing the generations together is indicated by the high proportions who are disabled (nearly half) or on low incomes (nearly all). While these older people usually do some of the domestic tasks, especially childminding if grandchildren are there, the contributions are limited in scope and nearly always supplementary. Assistance from outside the household is very uncommon in these circumstances.

PROVIDERS OF SUPPORT

The substantial self-reliance of most older people enables them to maintain their close bonds primarily in the social and expressive domains. While total networks include an average of nearly seven members, instrumental networks average only 1.8 people—this includes spouses and others with whom older people share domestic responsibilities. Even among those who are disabled, instrumental support networks contain an average of 2.2 people. In other words, responsibilities for providing instrumental support typically rest with only a few people, and increasing needs are usually met by this same small group rather than spread more widely in support networks.

The providers of instrumental support are thus a very distinctive and limited subset of the overall personal support networks. Even if one excludes spouses, family make up three-fourths of the membership of instrumental networks; this compares to 64 per cent for expressive networks. Another difference is that instrumental support is more often forthcoming from people (again excluding spouses) who are not elderly themselves (81 per cent); cross-gender relationships, from younger men to older women, provide nearly all of the informal support with gardening and home upkeep. While expressive support tends to be grounded in similarities between the parties, instrumental support virtually requires that the provider have skills and resources which are beyond the capabilities of the recipients and others similar to them. A notable strength of kinship bonds is that they can overcome lack of direct reciprocity in a relationship and bind together people having dissimilar statuses. We will now consider some key questions, posed in Chapter 2, regarding the kinds of assistance provided through particular informal and formal bonds.

Adult Children

Our findings clearly confirm those from the United States (Troll, et al., 1979; Brubaker, 1983) and Britain (Hunt, 1978) showing the centrality of sons and daughters in providing instrumental support. Apart from spouses, adult children are the single most numerous of the various providers, and are especially important with the more demanding and important tasks of daily living (Table 5.2). As a broad generalisation, the considerable resources of the middle-generation—combined with filial attachment, obligation, and lifelong patterns of exchange—provide the basis for substantial assistance in old age.

A focus exclusively on instrumental support from children runs the risk of obscuring two wider points that put filial support into perspective. First, a variety of other relationships, albeit many arising through children, collectively outnumber children in instrumental support networks. A number of older parents, as well as the fifth of older people who are childless, negotiate at least some informal support from other sources. Second, filial bonds are maintained

Table 5.2 Providers of informal assistance by area of assistance (n = 1113)

Source of support	Area of assistance [a, b]							
	Transport (620)	Home upkeep (413)	Gardening (223)	Shopping/ errands (309)	House-keeping (173)	Meals prepn (59)	Assist when ill (98)	All areas of assist[c] (1113)
Son	16	44	29	12	9	6	16	22
Daughter	22	7	15	40	40	38	42	19
Son-in-law	4	16	10	2	1	1	0	7
Daughter-in-law	5	1	4	12	10	14	12	5
Brother	1	3	4	4	4	2	4	2
Sister	2	1	5	6	12	12	6	3
Grandchild	4	6	15	4	2	4	1	6
Other family	10	9	9	10	10	10	5	10
Friend	34	8	8	9	10	11	10	21
Neighbour	2	5	1	1	2	2	4	5
Total percentage	100	100	100	100	100	100	100	100

Notes: (a) All columns are calculated as a percentage of the total providers. Some respondents had multiple providers while others had none. Excluding spouses, the 904 respondents had a total of 1113 providers of instrumental support

(b) See Appendix 1 for definitions of kinds of assistance

(c) The cases in each area of assistance do not sum to the total because many individuals' assistance is in more than one area largely in social and expressive terms (Figure 5.3); only a quarter of the sons and daughters of our respondents provide any instrumental assistance. Most filial bonds are characterised by emotional and social ties which have the potential to deliver instrumental support if the need arises.

Figure 5.3 Percentage of instrumental and total networks containing particular relationships (n = 901)

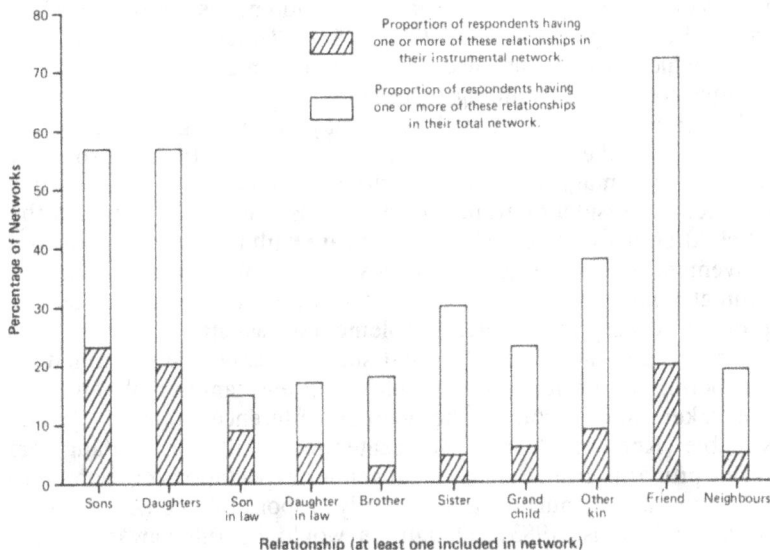

The mobilisation of support from children depends more on the level of need than on family size. It is received by only a quarter of those who are able and married, as compared to four-fifths of disabled widows. Having more children increases by only a slight margin the chances of receiving some filial aid: only children tend to live closer to aged parents and are much more likely to provide care (Kendig, 1983a,c). Within large families, one child usually is designated as, or by default becomes, the primary carer.

The obligatory and normative explanation for filial support is given added weight by two important findings. First, the strength of expressive bonds with children bears virtually no relationship to the instrumental support received from them. Affection has a part in providing care but a sense of obligation appears to be the more decisive motivation (Horowitz and Shindelman, 1981; Jarrett, 1985). Similarly, aged parents have nearly always made intergenerational contributions in the past, but our study found that past financial support to children, or care of one's own parents, had no impact on receiving filial support in old age (Kendig, 1984c). Only in the case of divorced older men is there any systematic indication of the norms of filial obligation being attentuated—findings that parallel those on expressive support in Chapter 4.

Contrary to most popular conceptions, sons are slightly more likely than daughters to be providing at least some assistance to an elderly parent (Figure 5.3). One reason is that more of them live with a parent, and contribute at least a modicum of effort to various household tasks. The more important one is that most recipients are widows living alone, and their most common needs are with gardening and minor home upkeep (Table 5.3). These traditionally male tasks, which in most instances were formerly met by able husbands, seldom are very demanding or urgent.

Daughters, however, are the mainstay in assisting with the more demanding and essential tasks (Table 5.2). They outnumber sons, by a five to one margin, in meeting the household responsibility for a disabled, co-resident parent. Daughters also number eighteen of the 21 children in our study who provide care with bathing, dressing and movement within the home. Moreover, these figures tend to under-estimate the importance of daughters, who are especially likely to provide primary rather than supplementary assistance.

The gender inequalities in filial support cannot be explained by competing responsibilities to employment and families. When these are taken into account, the gender differences remain equally sizeable (Kendig, 1983a). The greater responsibilities of daughters result primarily from the powerful gender expectations on women to meet household, nurturing and family responsibilities (Burns, Bottomly and Jools, 1983). Daughters would be fully aware of the sizeable inter-generational payments which their mothers had made (and were prepared to make if necessary) to various relatives earlier in life. Notwithstanding massive social change over the past generation, revocation of the implied contract would bring women into conflict with values which are deeply entrenched within, and reinforced by, extended family and broader social circles.

The filial expectations on women are so strong that they usually hold firm even when demanding commitments are maintained in other areas of life (Kendig, 1983a). If we look at the provision of substantial support—primary responsibility for the shopping, housekeeping, or meals of a disabled parent—we find that never-married women are especially likely to provide such high levels of assistance. However, most families today do not include these recruits who were so important in the past. Two-thirds of the women who provide substantial support to our respondents are married, and nearly half have children at home. While a United States study (Cicirelli, 1983) suggests that divorced children provide slightly less support to aged parents, we found that divorce is likely to increase the provision of support, mainly through co-residency.

There are very few differences in the support provided by married women who are housewives and those who work full-time (ibid.). The one exception is personal care, and half of the women who provide such high levels of care have left the workforce in order to do so (Kinnear and Graycar, 1984). As with a similar United States study (Stoller, 1983), we find that support for an aged parent typically emerges as an addition to other family responsibilities, and can take precedence over employment.

The impact of social class on filial support varies sharply depending on which actors one considers. If one focuses on older parents, their income or occupational background has little impact on whether or not they receive some filial support, but it substantially increases the likelihood of co-residency with a child. When our attention is directed to daughters, the occupational background of themselves or their husbands makes no difference in patterns of support. Yet when we turn to sons, we find that 37 per cent of those having a high status occupation, as compared to 14 per cent of those in low status jobs, are providing instrumental assistance to an aged parent (Kendig, 1983a). These differences are more pronounced when parents are disabled, and they apply in terms of the intensity as well as the incidence of support.

Both financial resources and attitudes toward caring may explain the greater contributions of sons in more advantaged occupations. First, our survey found that older people are more likely to turn to sons than daughters for financial support, and co-residency is a primary means of providing it. Sons in higher status occupations are more likely to have the commodious housing which eases the stresses of multigenerational living, and they are better positioned to meet the financial costs. The pattern fits the 'noblesse oblige' by which resources can be redistributed between the generations (Hill, 1970). A second possibility, which may combine with the first one, is that upper middle class men may feel closer to their mothers and more appreciative of them (Adams, 1968). Finally, our findings show that some men in more advantaged occupations have a less rigid gender differentiation of parent care, especially with more traditionally 'female' tasks such as shopping and housekeeping.

Overall, blood ties emerge as more powerful than gender roles as influences on the provision of support. Consistent with our findings on expressive support, children-in-law of either sex are much less likely than natural children to be providing instrumental assistance (Table 5.2). Yet two important gender differences do remain. First, more sons-in-law than daughters-in-law provide some support, main-ly because they provide supplementary help to wives caring for aged parents. They are the one group of people who often provide instrumental support without having any close expressive bonds (Figure 5.3). Second, when older parents turn to the families of married sons, the daughters-in-law provide most of the assistance with the more demanding tasks. More detailed analyses show that daughters-in-law serve principally as first reserves who are enlisted when daughters and unmarried sons are not available (Kendig, 1983a).

Other Relatives

Most older people know of dozens or more people to whom they are related by blood or marriage. Yet even when these other ties are included in support networks as a whole, they rarely involve the provision of any instrumental support (Figure 5.3). As noted in Chapter 1, these relationships seldom evince the complex patterns of interdependency found in marital and filial ties.

Notwithstanding the low 'take-up' rate of these other relatives, collectively they make up nearly a fifth of the members of instrumental support networks. The most important of these supports involves co-residence with a sister. But the more common kinds of assistance are with gardening by grandsons (some respondents insisted on saying they were paid modest sums), or a sharing of household tasks by grandchildren of both sexes in multigenerational households. To the extent that generalisations can be made of this diverse group, one finds that close blood ties, such as siblings, are more forthcoming than more distant or in-law relations; the kinds of assistance provided are ordered by gender and generation (nieces provide kinds of assistance similar to daughters); and much of the instrumental support is through closer kin ties such as children (grandchildren assisting parents).

To a limited extent, other relatives can serve as alternatives for the unavailability of children. For example, nearly a third of the childless elderly have some support from other relatives besides spouses, as compared to only 16 per cent of older people with children. One example would be a niece or nephew who provides a modest amount of assistance to a woman who never married. In many cases, this kind of help is forthcoming through strong expressive ties to a sibling (Johnson and Catalano, 1981). It also can evolve out of a lifelong relationship which takes on some of the emotional and obligatory qualities of a filial bond (Townsend, 1963). But with the exception of sisters, the various other kin typically assist with the more important tasks only as supplements, rather than as alternatives, to primary care by a spouse or child.

Friends and neighbours

Friends may rival children in terms of their numbers in networks as a whole, but these bonds are overwhelmingly expressive and companionate (Figure 5.3). Only with transport, a less demanding task, are friends very frequently found among providers of instrumental support (Table 5.2). Moreover, support from non-kin is not appreciably more common among older people who are disabled. Taken as a whole, the findings suggest that the mutuality inherent in friendships cannot withstand a markedly unequal flow of instrumental support.

Substantial support is occasionally found, however, in some friendships between single women, especially those who have never married and live together. These women apparently have renegotiated their original expressive bonds to include a considerable measure of instrumental interdependency. But once again, the emphasis is on mutuality: relatively few of the women in these arrangements are disabled.

Neighbours are insignificant in terms of tasks considered in our study. But neighbours make up more than half of the people who would be expected to notice and come to investigate if an older person living alone were not up and about. Accessibility is the notable strength of the neighbour bond, and it is clear that it can enhance older people's sense of security without involving any burden or obligation. Neighbours are probably especially important with modest assistance not addressed in our study: borrowing tools, carrying groceries up stairs, and looking after homes and pets while the occupant is away (Litwak, 1985).

Support from friends and neighbours is slightly more likely to be forthcoming for childless older people (30 per cent) than for those with children (21 per cent) (Kendig, 1983c). This adds to the evidence that some childless older people have developed stronger bonds with non-relatives. Yet the support usually remains limited and seldom serves as an alternative to the more substantial help available from close family.

Formal support

Paid or social services have far greater potential in meeting instrumental than expressive needs. Love, companionship, and respect are difficult, if not impossible, to receive from someone who is simply 'doing their job'. Many instrumental tasks, however, can be met equally effectively (in some cases more so) by organisations having resources and skills beyond those of informal networks (Litwak, 1985; Kendig, 1986b). Notwithstanding their considerable potential, only a quarter of our respondents have some kind of paid-help, and only 7 per cent use any community services. While older people generally are able to negotiate informal support, they are relatively powerless to mobilise the public funding necessary for widespread use of paid or community services.

Privately paid services offer the attractive prospect of assistance without obligation or burden. Those which are most commonly used are taxis (20 per cent); tradespeople, gardeners, and landlords (12 per cent each); and housekeepers (7 per cent) (Kendig, 1983c). These services are used more frequently by those who are disabled or childless, which suggests they can serve as limited alternatives to family support. Most users, however, are able people who have the incomes required to pay for them as conveniences. Unmet needs are most likely to arise in these areas where paid-help can be important, and an inability to pay is the single most common reason given for not having needed support. A further limitation is that private, paid-help requires high levels of trust and accountability when the worker enters the home of a vulnerable older person.

Use of community services is remarkably rare: a modest 7 per cent of our respondents have meals on wheels, home housekeeping, or visiting nurses (ibid.). Those who have only informal assistance in these areas generally say they do not use services because they are not known, or are thought to be too difficult to obtain—a preference for informal support is seldom mentioned. There are high levels of ignorance about services among our respondents (Gibson, 1984) and their families (Carter, 1985). The situation is even more limited with the tasks which loom especially large for older women. With the exception of residents in public housing, virtually no public or voluntary services are received with home upkeep and gardening; specialised transport services are virtually nonexistent.

The vast majority of those who use community services are disabled and living without spouses. Those who are childless, however, do not make disproportionate use of them, because considerable informal support—usually available only from children—is also required to keep seriously disabled people in the community. They thus appear to provide 'shared functions' with family (Litwak, 1965), rather than alternatives when family are unavailable (Cantor, 1979). The typical client of meals or housekeeping services has but one service as a modest complement to primary support through modified extended families. Only visiting nurses provide much support to older people living with a child, which is virtually the only alternative to institutional care for those who are severely disabled. We also found little evidence of family serving as 'managers' of formal care in the community (Shanas and Sussman, 1977), as most people were referred to services by medical practitioners and professionals (Gibson, 1984).

The comparative importance of formal and informal providers can be gauged by examining sources of support with the relatively major tasks: shopping and errands, housekeeping, meals preparation, and personal care. Nearly three-fourths of the able aged are fully independent in all these areas, and those who do have assistance rely nearly entirely on the informal sector. Among the disabled older people, nearly three-fourths have some informal support, and the minority who have paid-help (15 per cent) or community services (24 per cent) nearly always have informal support as well.

OUTCOMES

Before arriving at any overly optimistic conclusions about informal support, we must consider two important qualifications. First, our community survey must be put into perspective by considering how the lack of support can precipitate institutionalisation. Second, sizeable social costs can fall on both the providers and recipients of informal support.

The rates of institutionalisation among older people provide one of the clearest indications of the limitations of community care. If alternatives to marital and filial support were fully available, institutionalisation rates would vary only by various indicators of need. But if we take women aged 75 or older, thus providing a crude control for levels of disability, the proportions who live in institutions are doubled among the widowed as compared to those now married, and more than trebled among the never-married (Kendig and Rowland, 1983). While a variety of informal sources may meet many modest needs, only spouses and daughters are likely to provide alternatives to institutionalisation. Moreover, a breakdown of co-resident care from these sources is usually involved with entry into an institution (Gibson and Rowland, 1984). It has been estimated that up to a quarter of the older people in institutions would be more appropriately cared for in the community (Doobov, 1980; Philips, 1981).

Our community survey provides a different view of the same processes. Limited informal support, not remarkably good health, presumably explains why only two of the 37 never-married or divorced men in our survey were disabled. Available informal support also shows a marked tendency to fall off when intense needs persist. While 82 per cent of our respondents expected to have informal support if ill in bed for a week, only 67 per cent expected it to be maintained for a month. An incapacity lasting months or years would tip the balance much further towards institutional care.

Even when community support is available, there is a substantial risk that the difficulties are transferred to the carer. Older spouses, for example, have only limited resources by which to meet the vows to provide full support 'in sickness or in health ... until death do us part'. One of the difficulties is that the breakdown in mutuality and (in the case of husband carers) major role-reversals can lead to major stresses in the formerly close relationship (Cantor, 1983). Meeting all needs within the small and vulnerable marital dyad—a tendency which is most pronounced among those who are childless (Johnson and Catalano, 1981)—can also lead to spouses becoming 'hidden patients' themselves (Fengler and Goodrich, 1979). After controlling for health and gender of the respondent, we found that having a disabled spouse was associated with significantly lower morale, a higher incidence of depression and anxiety, and reduced social participation outside the home. We also confirm that childless couples, whose lifelong ties and dependencies are very much a closed system, apparently are at greatest risk in these respects, because they have the smallest instrumental support networks of all the marital groups.

When an adult child takes a dependent parent into the home, substantial social costs can be incurred both personally and in the broader social networks (Cantor, 1983; Nissel, 1984; Steinmetz and Amsden, 1983). An Australian study shows that a sizeable toll can be exacted on the carer in terms of emotional stress, family tension, reduced leisure, and forced departure from the workforce (Kinnear and Graycar, 1984). Relatively few of these 'women in the middle' (Brody, 1981) were found to have any supplementary support from siblings, and 90 per cent of them say that family relationships have deteriorated as a result. Care of a disabled mother—often the person who had long served to bind the extended family together (Carter, 1985)—can precipitate painful and irreparable rifts among close relations.

The social costs in caring for older people fall very unequally on family members. In contrast to childbearing, the other significant flow of family support over the life cycle, only a minority of people ever provide a substantial amount of care for an aged parent, or receive it themselves. Providing care to the aged is a 'contingent risk', which lacks the predictability and choice which has become characteristic of childbearing in modern times (Kendig, 1984c). While men typically turn to their sisters and wives to support aged mothers, and to their wives in their own old age, women are at much greater risk of being a provider in mid-life, and of not having sufficient support in old age. The never-married, while not rearing children in mid-life, are major providers of care to parents in mid-life and lack comparable support in their own old age. Indeed, some older women never married because they were preoccupied in early adulthood by the responsibilities of caring for a disabled relative.

One of the most important and neglected consequences of family support is the psychological impact on the older recipient. Given older people's lifelong commitment to their children—a part of themselves which will live on after death—it can be very painful to burden them. From an exchange point of view, receiving substantial and unreciprocated support, provided out of a sense of obligation, can erode self-respect, and undermine the expressive mutuality uppermost in older people's minds. In these circumstances, the older person may face the dilemma of either refusing needed and available help (Day, 1985), or 'paying' in the currency of compliance and approbation (Sussman, 1976), with subsequent demoralisation (Dowd, 1980).

To test some of these hypotheses, we can take a close look at older widows and widowers, including only those who have one to four children. We then examine the complex ways in which family life and personal well-being are influenced by living arrangements and disability. We are concerned with comparative differences between the groups: it should be stressed that overall levels of well-being and family satisfaction are reasonably high in all these situations. While the sample sizes are too small in some instances to establish statistical significance, the findings are wholly consistent with the predictions of exchange theory.

First, there are the differences associated with living arrangements. Those who live only with a child report the highest levels of morale, satisfaction with family life, and sense of devotion by their children. As noted earlier in the chapter, these older people tend to have interdependent relationships with their co-resident child and make substantial contributions to household duties; there is no potential for conflict with in-laws or grandchildren in the home. People who live alone, who we noted earlier have substantial support from beyond the household, have relatively lower scores in terms of all three measures. Those who live with a child and his or her family—thus violating the preference for residential separation of nuclear families—tend to have the lowest morale. By a statistically significant margin, they also have the lowest levels of satisfaction with family life and the least sense of devotion by their children. The comparative position of the three living arrangements groups remain unchanged when disability and gender are taken into account.

When we examine the impact of disability, a number of striking patterns emerge. As one would expect, disabled widows and widowers have lower morale irrespective of their living arrangements. Among those who live alone, disability involves substantial increases of support from non-resident kin, but has no apparent impact on satisfaction with family life or sense of devotion by their children. However, among those who live with a child, or a child and family, both measures of family life are notably lower for those who are disabled. The findings strongly suggest that the quality of family life deteriorates when large amounts of instrumental support are provided on a co-resident basis.

Exchange theory would predict that depression can be caused by the breakdown of autonomy or independence. Among widows and widowers who live alone, the proportion who say they have been severely depressed over the last year remains at 28 per cent, irrespective of disability. These people retain a substantial measure of autonomy and are in a position to refuse help which is not thought to be necessary (Weihl, 1977). But among those who live with a child and family there is a notable difference in rates of depression: 28 per cent for those who are able versus 50 per cent for those who are disabled. The difference is even more pronounced, 5 per cent versus 62 per cent respectively, when the respondent lives only with a child. This last finding most clearly portrays how interdependency can enhance morale while dependency can be demoralising. An American study (Dunkle, 1983) has also shown that making contributions in joint-households increases morale; the demoralisation of dependent joint-living was found to lessen as people apparently adjusted to the situation over time.

There were very few instances in our study of anyone besides a spouse or child providing high levels of support to a disabled older person. Cantor (1983) found that care from more distant relatives and friends generated less stress and conflict, but she did not take into account the much higher levels of support provided by close kin. Another study shows that regular dependence on friends for transport assistance has a perceptible and independent effect in reducing morale (Baur and Okun, 1983). Johnson and Catalano (1981), and the research reported in Chapter 8, found that more distant kin resent providing even small amounts of assistance in securing care. The lack of very much support from friends and more distant relatives, as found in our study, may be partly explained by older people's reluctance to accept the demoralising consequences.

Community services do not appear to involve the inequities or social costs found with informal support. Potentially, they could be provided to all who need them, and the costs fall on the public at large. Nor did use of services have any identifiable impact on the morale of our respondents. Tobin and Kulys (1980) report American findings that use of services can increase morale.

Nor is there any evidence that receiving services has any adverse effect on family relationships. Contrary to the concern voiced by some commentators (Morris and Sherwood, 1984), we found that services replace self-help rather than family support, and complement continuing support from family. As with a recent Canadian study (Chappell, 1985), we found no significant differences between comparable service users and non-users in terms of family contact, satisfaction, or support.[2] Although no Australian research has carefully tested their impact, it seems likely that services provide a modest measure of relief for older people and their carers. If they could help disabled people to remain in their own homes, without unduly burdening informal carers, the result could well be an improvement of family relationships.

SUMMARY

Family, and the norms and emotional ties which underlie it, provide the primary arena in which informal assistance is exchanged over the life course. Most older people, especially the couples among them, are highly independent and receive little instrumental support. Adult children, the primary beneficiaries of older people's earlier and continuing contributions, in turn are the primary providers of assistance should parents become widowed and disabled. While the modified extended family is the most common source of assistance, co-residency is the only practical way to provide large amounts of sustained support.

Network size has very little bearing on instrumental support: the key factor is having a spouse or a daughter. While other informal bonds frequently provide small amounts of aid, they rarely evince the depth of commitment required to serve as viable alternatives in providing large amounts of unreciprocated support. The never-married may be more self-reliant, principally because their lifelong skills are less limited by gender conditioning, but their close bonds provide only modest levels of support which seldom meet intense and persistent needs.

Reliance on informal networks to assist disabled older people has a number of adverse consequences. The risks of not receiving care in old age, or of having to provide it in mid-life, fall disproportionately on women, especially those who never marry. Caring for a disabled person can be stressful and restrictive for daughters and spouses. For the recipient of care, dependency in a multigenerational household can be demoralising and erode family bonds. While community services potentially could limit these problems, their availability is far too limited to have any major impact.

6

Changes in caregiving across generations: perceptions of people aged 75 years and over

ALICE T. DAY

Like the other women I talked to in interviews with persons 75 years and over,[1] Mrs Perkins spoke of her mother with deep affection and admiration. She and the others recalled their mothers as strong, devoted, hard-working and self-sacrificing. Comparing her mother then with her daughter now, Mrs Perkins felt that mothering had changed markedly since she was a girl. It was not that young mothers of today were any less caring, but there were more things now to distract them, and they were less singleminded in their devotion to their children.

> I think the mothers of my generation were devoted mothers or something—they never went to shows, they never went to trips, they never went overseas, never went to any of those things that people do now (Mrs Perkins).

This chapter explores changes in caregiving across the generations as seen through the eyes of those with some eight decades of family relations behind them. These perceptions clearly affected the kind of care older people in this study felt they could expect from their own children. They saw their children as busier and having less time to give to people outside their immediate families. As Mrs Andrews, 82, a widow in poor health living with a divorced son explained:

> I wouldn't like to think other people have to look after me—though they'd do it for me—because everybody has their own family and their own ways and they haven't really time to give to other people.

The chapter begins by explaining the life history approach employed in conducting in-depth, semistructured interviews with 23 people who were selected for follow-up study from the Project's Sydney survey. While a full report of the findings is reported in Day (1985), this chapter draws primarily on the case studies of four respondents in order to illustrate the complexity and diversity in intergenerational care giving. Life profiles are presented describing current circumstances, past experiences with care giving, family networks, expectations about future care and the major themes illustrated by the story of each individual. The conclusion looks at the broader influences of early life experiences and social change on people's expectations for care in later life.

LIFE STORIES

Looking at older people as members of families and social networks is more complex and difficult than looking at older people as isolated individuals without significant ties extending beyond the household (Wellman and Hall, 1984; Streib, 1983; Day, 1986 forthcoming). However, it is also more realistic. At all stages in the life cycle, there are close connections between individual life events and family life histories (Hareven, 1982).

In tracing the connections between individual events and family histories, collecting life stories is a useful complement to the more structured approach of larger social surveys (Johnson, 1976; Bertaux, 1981; Job, 1984; Day, 1985). The life stories of older people that form the basis of this chapter were told in follow-up interviews with ten men and thirteen women who participated in the larger survey described earlier in the book. Appendix 2 presents more detail on the selection of respondents and their characteristics as identified in the previous survey. The interviews were conducted and taped in the older people's homes from April to June 1982, some five to six months following the initial survey. The old people were asked to review their lives, recalling important events and family memories from childhood to the present time. Finally, they were asked to anticipate the future by thinking about the part family would play in arrangements for their possible long-term care in the future.

While the life story method necessarily relies on memory and retrospective interpretation of past events, the purpose is not to get people to recall the precise facts, but to describe how they felt and what was important to them (Bulter, 1968; Johnson, 1976; Bertaux, 1981). Why, for example, does an older person prefer the support of one child over another? Why do some older people with close ties with several sons and daughters choose to go into a nursing home rather than accept their children's offers to live with them? Why do older wives looking after infirm spouses refuse to leave their husbands' sides? What makes some adult children 'unavailable' in the eyes of an older parent? These are all questions arising from actual situations found among older people in the Sydney survey. Going back to visit them a second time—using a less structured, more open-ended approach—provided the opportunity to discover more detail about their relations with their families, and their feelings about receiving help now that they were facing the prospect of deteriorating fitness and diminished capacity to remain autonomous.

CAREGIVING THEMES

A major theme that emerged in these older people's life stories was their perception of discontinuities in their past and present experiences with caregiving. Change in the quality of mothering mentioned earlier is an important example, but there were many others. These feelings of—what I have called—discontinuity were manifested in two main ways: first, in the older people's descriptions of changes in their own lives and the social setting in which they lived; and second, in their perceptions of their children's and grandchildren's way of life, as compared with what they remembered of their own childhoods and early adult years. Both these types of seeing the present as disconnected with the past throw light on older people's current expectations about support from their families, and differences between the older and younger generations' attitudes toward giving and receiving care.

Children's entitlement to a 'full life' is another theme that recurred. In discussing their feelings about family care, above all, the men and women I talked to saw their children (and particularly daughters and daughters-in-law) as taken up with their own affairs. They wanted to spare the younger generation the additional burden of responsibility for an ageing dependent. Thus, Mrs Perkins, whose daughter was seriously ill and could not have provided support even if her mother had been badly in need of help, exclaimed:

> The last thing I want is to be dependent on my daughter—even if she was well. I think you should be entitled to your full life.

LIFE STORY PROFILES

To see how these themes arise in the context of older people's particular life situations, I have selected for more detailed discussion three women and one man whom old age has placed in quite different circumstances. These four were chosen because their family networks and support arrangements illustrate different types of social interaction and different degrees of caregiving intensity—from keeping in touch by telephone and occasional visiting to sharing a common household.

While three of the four are migrants, which may accentuate

perceptions of generational change, the Australian-born revealed a similar sense of discontinuity between the generations. Appendix 2 presents information on the network characteristics of these four respondents as identified in the earlier quantitative survey. The profiles presented here are glimpses only of people with eight decades behind them of interacting with family networks—in good times and in bad. The interviews tapped their feelings and circumstances on a particular day at a particular moment in their lives. Because the follow-up approach was more on the order of 'guided conversations' (Job, 1984) than a schedule of set, predesigned questions, to some extent each person's life story illustrates different themes according to personal and social situations, and individual interests and priorities.

Reflecting the different balance of work and family over their life course, for example, men and women tended to place different emphases on these spheres of social activity. However, there were a number of exceptions among the 23 respondents. Four men who had provided intensive personal care for very ill women (three wives and one sister) talked a great deal about what caregiving had meant to them. Five women who had held paid jobs dwelt at length on the rewards and frustrations of their working lives.

No attempt has been made here to cover the range of situations represented. For example, the follow-up interviews included three childless persons and one never-married. None of these is discussed here, although their expectations about family support are, of course, quite different and they tend to be more vulnerable to institutiona-lisation than are those who are married and/or the parents of living children (See Chapter 2). Nevertheless, the four profiles in this chapter enable us to compare older people who differ by sex, sense of fitness, marital status, family structure, and the flow of past events into the present as factors determining attitudes towards family care.

Mrs Lindsay

Aged 78, Mrs Lindsay suffers from major physical disabilities in-cluding glaucoma and what she describes as 'black-outs' and 'mini-strokes' that leave her in a semi-coma. Poor eyesight and unpre-dictable seizures have made her fearful to go out on her own or cross the street.

Yet despite these major vulnerabilities, Mrs Lindsay is the primary caregiver for a completely dependent husband who has frequent black-outs himself. She and her infirm husband still live in their own house, purchased ten years ago. Though an only son lives 'over the road' and keeps in close touch and their daughter-in-law helps with shopping, the only help Mrs Lindsay receives with housework is fortnightly cleaning supplied by a Home Help Service.

Mr Lindsay has been unwell and dependent for many years. His first attack occurred over nine years ago. For the past four years Mrs Lindsay has remained close by him almost without a break. She describes coming home one day four years ago:

> And he would see me coming off the bus, and he used to open the door, and the door wasn't opened, and I thought, 'That's funny'. And he was unconscious on the floor with the radiator about that far, and he had been like that for an hour or so.

After this episode, Mrs Lindsay gave away her position as treasurer of a charitable organisation, stopped going to all meetings and conferences, and virtually ceased going out. Now she feels she cannot leave her husband alone:

> If he's outside and I don't hear him or see him I have to go look, because I've found him under a tree, and I've found him out on the front lawn. He fell getting out of the bath one day.

Tending her husband full-time has required some adjustment on Mrs Lindsay's part:

> At first I used to feel as if I was a prisoner—not going out. But I got used to it. When I wake in the morning I think, 'Another day. What am I going to do today?' But the day goes and I'm going all the time.

Past experience with caregiving

Mrs Lindsay has always been an active person and before marriage held a full-time paid job for twenty years. Money has been an important consideration in her choices. Her mother was widowed in her mid-fifties and with only a small pension counted on Mrs Lindsay (the older by six years of two daughters) to help with financial support. Though she loved school and got high grades, Mrs Lindsay left early and got a position in the Public Service. During World War II she was chosen to 'take over a man's job'. 'I worked with about six men, but we were all friends, you know. It was a lovely time'.

A major change in Mrs Lindsay's life came at age 38 when she married and moved away from her mother's house. At that time, under a law (revoked only in 1966) that married women could not be employed in the Public Service, she was obliged to give up her job: 'I didn't like leaving really because it was so interesting'. Her son was born by Caesarian section three years after her marriage, and then began what she describes as 'the hardest part of my life'. Her mother who had been living with her unmarried sister developed cancer of the bowel, and needed attention day and night. Because it was wartime and her sister, who had a good job could not get leave, her mother came to live with her. At that time the baby was only three months old and Mrs Lindsay was recovering from what in those days was regarded as a very serious operation. She had no home help services, no telephone and the neighbours on either side were elderly. During the last six weeks of her mother's life, her sister came to live with her and looked after the dying woman at night. Recalling the strain of tending to a terminally-ill mother and a little baby 'who cried all day because he didn't get enough attention', Mrs Lindsay still expresses pain and guilt, especially when she sees how 'my two grandchildren are made a fuss of all the time'.

Family networks

Mrs Lindsay's pool of kin is quite small. When she was nine years old her parents migrated from England to Australia leaving behind grandparents, aunts, uncles and cousins about whom Mrs Lindsay has many fond and vivid memories. With her mother's and father's deaths, and her younger unmarried sister's decision to stay on when she went on a visit to England twelve years ago, Mrs Lindsay's ties with her family of origin have become even more attenuated. Now her only close kin are her son, daughter-in-law and two grandchildren. Because she married in her late thirties and her son also married when he was nearly 40, Mrs Lindsay's grandchildren are still school age. This fact, in combination with the devastating experience of caring for her own mother at home, has made Mrs Lindsay adamant about not living with her son:

> If anything happens to my husband, I will stay here as long as I possibly could. But I feel this way about that sort of thing. I'm old and, well, if it is unpleasant you have just got to put up with it, that's all . . . I mean there is nothing else.

Expectations about future care

The core of Mrs Lindsay's relation with her son is summed up in a phrase she used herself to describe her outlook on the prospect of death: 'I have always been organised and I like to know what is going on'. This has meant talking with her son and daughter-in-law about what will happen when she and Mr Lindsay 'have gone': 'We talk about it. They are going to come and live here when we've gone. Oh, my husband knows that'. Though she talks to her son about her 'social remains' (Minichiello, 1982)—anticipating what her family will do with the house after her death—Mrs Lindsay is ambiguous about arrangements for her future care. Because she has a spouse who is infirm, she has not moved to reserve a place for herself in a nursing home. To do so would constitute a concrete sign that one day one of them will be alone without the other. While she can accept the inevitability of Mr Lindsay's death, and the picture of herself living on in the house without him, she cannot tolerate the picture of him alone without her to protect him. Again, past experience plays a part: Mr Lindsay spent some time in a nursing home when Mrs Lindsay was in hospital briefly herself recovering from a heart attack:

> And he has a horror of nursing homes . . . I hope I live longer than my husband, because of his dread of nursing homes.

Major themes

This slice of Mrs Lindsay's story illustrates two themes of major importance to planning for the aged: the impact of providing support on the older caregiver, and the unsettling effects of discontinuity in women's employment and family life.

The attitudes of other people in this study who were looking after a less fit partner were similar to Mrs Lindsay's. Protection had become a treasured habit and the less dependent person came to feel indispensable. This suggests that living together as a couple may be a source of vulnerability for the old because it fosters a wait-and-see orientation toward future custodial care. Decisions that need to be made to ensure that one has a hand in the arrangements one prefers may be deferred until one partner dies—a time when the other partner may be too frail to make his or her wants prevail. While it is usually wives who are involved in this predicament, the four men I spoke to who provided primary care for infirm women appeared to feel similarly protective and said they hoped they would outlive their more dependent half (Day, 1985).

A second major thread running through Mrs Lindsay's story was the disturbance in her life caused by her early retirement from a job she loved, to become· a full-time wife and mother. Her situation highlights not only the expectation that a woman's primary responsibility is to family work, but also how this expectation is reinforced by social policy. Demographic trends suggest that even more women may become caught in such role discontinuities in the future. The increase in life span which is associated with increasing numbers of the very old and infirm (See Chapter 2) is intersecting with a growing tendency for governments to recommend shifting more of the burden of care into the 'community' (House of Representatives Standing Committee on Expenditure, 1982). As Mrs Lindsay's story shows, we may be moving into a time when there are three stages to women's caregiving cycle: children, infirm parents, husbands. In the absence of changes in expectations, such as that the often gruelling care of a spouse or parent is the 'natural responsibility' of a wife or child (Finch and Groves, 1980)—and in the absence of a major public commitment to increase services that provide respite to the carer— such a trend can only lead to more women risking their own health and peace of mind to shoulder the increasing burden of personal support.

Mrs Smart

At age 83, Mrs Smart is strong, fit and spends more time outside her small, but comfortable two-bedroom unit than at home. Widowed five years and living alone, unlike Mrs Lindsay, her activities are directed outwards rather than inwards. Married at 19 (19 years earlier than Mrs Lindsay), Mrs Smart and her family have been fruitful and multiplied. She is proud to claim two sons, two daughters and eighteen great-grandchildren. Although Mrs Smart says she is lonely sometimes and often misses her husband 'of a night', she has made a good adjustment to widowhood. Good health and her husband's service pension enable her to get out of the house, go on outings with her friends, and make frequent visits to her numerous relatives. She plays bowls regularly and enjoys the theatre and films.

Past experiences with caregiving

The youngest of nine, Mrs Smart admits to being pampered and was the one woman I spoke to who said her family did not want her to work before marriage. However, as usual with women in their age group, 'work', meant paid employment, not unpaid caregiving. Mrs Smart's brothers and sisters gave her pocket money to stay home to help their mother: 'We treated her like a Queen, my Mother. We didn't think she should ever have to do any hard work'.

In Mrs Smart's young adult days, her family helped each other by the more fortunate opening their homes to the less fortunate. She and Mr Smart lived with his parents until they could move into their own house. During the Great Depression, Mrs Smart and her husband harboured for eighteen months a sister whose husband was out of work. Each of Mrs Smart's four children stayed on at home after marriage until they had a good start. Now, Mrs Smart says her children no longer need that kind of help and she, in turn, is reluctant to ask for anything from them:

> But all my family are very comfortably off, very well off. So that, you know, they would give me anything. But I'm very independent. I don't want anything. But, I mean, if I did I wouldn't ask.

The child Mrs Smart feels closest to is her youngest, her 'baby':

> She was 50 a fortnight ago, and we are like sisters. Every morning she rings me and she'll be over here a couple of times a week.

Not just by chance, this closest daughter is also the one who, with her two small boys lived with Mrs Smart for six years while both their husbands were busy in the service:

> Then she went and I missed her terribly and the grandchildren. Well, those two grandsons—they are very close to me.

Family networks

Mrs Smart illustrates one of the many 'family themes' (Carter, 1985) that evolve in families over the years as arrangements for keeping in touch and meeting each other's needs. The attention that she and her siblings lavished on their mother is such a theme, or 'family curren- cy'. Mrs Smart sees consideration for the female head of house as a tradition passed on down the family to her:

> I know my mother-in-law used to say she'd never known any family to
> look after their mother so much as what we did. Yes, we were very,
> very proud of that and my family do the same.

Mrs Smart comes from a line of long-lived relatives and this seems to have raised her own aspirations for longevity. Her mother and father celebrated their diamond anniversary together. Her mother's mother was 96 when she died and two of her older sisters were 88 and 86. The one remaining sibling, aged 95, lives in a nursing home, and 'goes to the RSL every Wednesday to play the poker machines'.

Expectations about future care

For Mrs Smart, an important aspect of having had close ties with many very old people has been the development, on the one hand, of a strong positive attitude toward nursing homes, and, on the other, a firm resolution never to move in with her children. Much of her interview was taken up with instances she knew of where older people had moved in with their children and then moved out because of bad blood or inconvenience. Though she says she gets along wonderfully well with her children, she insists she never wants to live with them.

Not constrained (as was Mrs Lindsay) by the uncertainty of a failing partner's prospects, and favourably disposed to nursing homes by past experience, Mrs Smart has gone to visit two nursing homes with her two daughters, and 'done everything—they all know and they are all pleased'. Moreover, she says she is confident that a few years down the road, she will adjust well to the challenge of living with other elderly people:

> I'm very easy to get along with. So, of course, you know, when I come
> to it—I'll have to cross bridges then.

Major themes

Marital status, level of fitness, and size and composition of family network are major factors differentiating Mrs Smart's situation from Mrs Lindsay's. A widow in good physical and mental health, and with a large circle of friends, and close relatives spanning four generations, Mrs Smart can avoid depending too heavily on any one or two family members. Instead she is able to spread the responsibility for sharing intimacy and support among a variety of kin and friends, and thus retain the independence from her family she so strongly desires.

Given a history of apparently amicable shared households, it is all the more striking that Mrs Smart has put herself down for a nursing home. Only 11 per cent of the people 75 years and over in the Sydney survey chose this option as the one they thought most older people would prefer. Mrs Smart's choice seems a direct outcome of her extensive personal experience of intergenerational living, and her perception that the costs of caring for an older person at home are too high to risk—in terms of autonomy for the dependent person and the preservation of good family relations (Carter, 1985). Personality is clearly a factor here, too. Mrs Smart says she got through the terrible experience of her husband's death by relying on the solace of friends (widows in her age group) and her own refusal to give up the fight. Thus, while she is the first to acknowledge the importance of family support, being the pampered youngest of a large family may have given her the social skills and confidence to think that she can withstand the depersonalising effects of institutionalisation, as she firmly believes many of her relatives have already done before her.

Mr Sherman

At 76, a retired business man, Mr Sherman is a refugee born in a Middle Eastern country. His Australian-born wife is seven years his junior. Although he smoked heavily and coughed during the interview, Mr Sherman declared he was in excellent health, and didn't feel his age. His wife is also apparently quite fit. However, although they have their own home unit in a pleasant neighbourhood, Mr Sherman said he hated retiring from his job and claimed that he and his wife never went out any more and had to keep a tight watch on their budget. Mr Sherman reads news magazines and is active in his building's co-operative society. He says he no longer goes with his mates to the RSL, but most of the time stays home quietly with his wife.

Past experiences with caregiving

A prominent feature of Mr Sherman's story is his experience of uprooting twice to move to a different country: first in the 1920s when he and his family fled to Israel to escape the political storm they saw brewing in their region; and next at the outbreak of World War II to join his Australian fiancé in Sydney. They met when she was on a working holiday, became engaged, and when hostilities escalated, decided to move to Australia. Both of these moves involved the struggle to find work and to find a new niche. They have also had a powerful influence on Mr Sherman's relations as a son, husband and father and affected his attitudes toward planning for his future care.

When Mr Sherman migrated to Australia as a young man, he broke a centuries-old tradition in caregiving:

> You see we have got a certain tradition—as the youngest boy in the family and with my two brothers away, I had to be with my parents— look after them.

He specified that the kind of help that he was expected to provide was financial. His mother and sisters provided the personal care that his father who was arthritic needed in his later years. When he left for Australia, Mr Sherman said it was hard to convince his parents that it was the right thing to do: 'I've got my future, and so they accept it, but they took it very hard'.

Family networks

Mr Sherman had three brothers and three sisters in his family. It seems probable that he would not have been able to leave when he did had not two of his sisters and one brother remained behind to carry on the tradition of intergenerational care. Mr Sherman said he was on close terms with the third sister who was now living in Sydney.

Mr Sherman skimmed very lightly over relations with his own son. He said simply, 'I'm very close to him—they come here for dinner quite a lot'. His son is doing very well in his own business and did not need financial help from his parents:

> I feel that I am always there to give advice to my son and so forth, but he doesn't need it. He doesn't approach me about it—so we leave it at that. I don't want to interfere.

So far as grandchildren are concerned, Mr Sherman says, 'I am counting the minutes'. However, his son was married only two years ago, his daughter-in-law has a job, and both are saving up to build a house, so Mr Sherman does not feel that grandparenthood is imminent.

Expectations about future care

Breaks in the continuity of Mr Sherman's life have made him sceptical about the efficacy of planning for the future. He expresses strongly the feeling that old age is inevitable and the future uncertain:

> What future? I'll be 77 next birthday so it's a matter of time. Whether I live to 82 or 84 or 90—I'll be old that's one thing and you can't escape that.

Unlike Mrs Lindsay and Mrs Smart, Mr Sherman has not talked to his son about arrangements for his future care. The tradition of joint-households in his background makes him reject nursing homes as institutions that reflect a weakening of familial bonds. But at the same time having a son who is only recently married, is building a house, and has not yet started on his own family makes the notion of living with his children in the foreseeable future seem quite out of the question. Nevertheless, in the event that he had to have help he would choose to live with family rather than go to an institution.

Major themes

Family tradition, family structure, and a life punctuated by beginnings and endings have made Mr Sherman uncertain about arrangements for his own future care. He is reluctant to review both his break with the traditions of his ancestors or to peer into the crystal ball. His network of close relatives in Australia is small. He has no daughter and his one son has a life of his own and apparently does not seek the advice of a father, born in a different country and brought up in a different tradition. Besides, Mr Sherman thinks of himself as still relatively young and vigorous, and he has a wife ten years his junior who is there to look after him. Mr Sherman says his philosophy is to live for today and not think about tomorrow. He has never known anyone personally in a nursing home, but given the tradition of his homeland does not believe in them, anyway:

> Of course, if it comes to a critical stage, well, I say, 'There is no option. They can go [to a nursing home]'. But otherwise, there is a way where you can avoid it—help from the daughter, the son-in-law and everything. They can always help.

He did not say whether he felt the same obligations applied to a son and daughter-in-law. (Others in this study, however, said they would be reluctant to turn to a daughter-in-law for the kind of personal care they would ask of a daughter.)

Mrs Kramer

Though Mrs Kramer, 82 years old, widowed 20 years, reported her health as 'good', she admitted to being depressed, said she quite often has time on her hands and that the worst thing about being over 65 was 'Can't do what you wish to do'. She was one of three people in the follow-up study who lived in the same house with an adult child (a married daughter, son-in-law, and two grandchildren). Perhaps in the early days of living with her daughter, Mrs Kramer had helped with housework and child care. She did not talk about this period in her life. Now she said she was contributing little to the household and could think of no one who made her feel needed and appreciated:

> Well, I can't do nothing now . . . I would like to be in the garden, but they have two dogs—there is no room for me . . .

Past experiences with caregiving

Before migrating to Australia from Europe 22 years ago, Mrs Kramer had devoted herself full-time to looking after her husband and children and had not worked outside the home since her marriage as a teenager. Arriving in Australia, she and her husband moved in with their oldest son who was unmarried and owned a 'big house and big garden' on the outskirts of Sydney. Mrs Kramer had established a place for herself cooking and keeping house for the two men. The pleasant equilibrium of this arrangement was shattered when two years later her husband died and not long afterwards her son suffered a massive stroke one evening while watching television and died a few hours later in the ambulance. Mrs Kramer's whole life changed literally overnight. A latecomer to Australia with a poor command of English and no close ties other than her family, she had no other alternative but to move in with her oldest daughter. Her status changed overnight from mother running a household for an unmarried son to mother living in a working daughter's home—a daughter 'caught in the middle' (Brody, 1981) between the demands of a job, rearing two children, and looking after an ageing parent.

Family networks

Mrs Kramer and her husband came to Australia in the 1960s to join two sons and two daughters who had already come ahead. Other members of her family were widely dispersed—a daughter and sister still lived in Europe and several more distant relatives in Asia and South America. Mrs Kramer had difficulties with her eyesight, but said she spent a lot of time corresponding with her relatives overseas. She talked vaguely about the pros and cons of returning to her homeland, but it seemed more fantasy than a genuine option. On the earlier survey, she said that the person she felt closest to was her other daughter who was unmarried, and working, but visited frequently and took her on outings. Both Mrs Kramer and the daughter she was living with appeared to take it for granted that having her there was a permanent arrangement. We did not speak of what might happen in the future if she should require more extensive personal care.

Major themes

Much of Mrs Kramer's life story consisted of her experiences as a European national, moving from country to country with five children, trying to escape war, and its assault on working life and family relations. Moving from place to place and being responsible for a large family had reduced her opportunities to acquire the personal and social resources that might have contributed to her independence in later life. As it was, of all those I talked to Mrs Kramer seemed the least autonomous. From what she told me of her life, this situation stemmed from a combination of circumstances among the most important of which were the migration to Australia at age 60, difficulties with English, isolation from others on her son's property, and uncertain health which now made her dependent on her daughter's care and prevented her from initiating activities outside the family circle. Once the mother of a large family, now she was living with people who met all of her needs and left her with none of the challenges of managing on her own. She described no meaningful activities either inside or outside the family, and implied that to preserve the family peace she kept her opinions about her grandchildren to herself. However, she commented that children in Australia seemed to be brought up with very different standards from those used to rear the young in her country—in her day.

OVERVIEW AND CONCLUSIONS

This last section integrates some of the main themes about families and caregiving revealed in the life story material.

The four life stories presented here make clear that individual life course events are inseparable from family life cycle events. In the lives of older people in this study, the timing and nature of major life transitions—leaving school, entering a first job, getting married, becoming a parent, retiring from full-time employment, and withdrawing from active social involvement—are influenced heavily by the changing life circumstances of the extended family network. Very often, the major changes that the old people described were in some way linked to the changing circumstances of a parent, spouse, child or sibling to whom they were bound by affection or obligation.

These life stories reinforce the crucial importance of gender and marital status in shaping older people's experience with caregiving. As noted in earlier chapters, a basic gender difference affecting the potential for providing care is the greater possibility that women in late life will be in a position either of living alone or of having an older infirm spouse who requires extensive personal care. Throughout life, men's and women's caregiving roles are coloured by differing expectations about their responsibilities for family support, as well as by differing demographic chances for care provision. Mrs Lindsay's and Mr Sherman's life stories illustrate the operation of both these factors. As daughter and son, wife and husband, and mother and father, their lives were shaped by different responsibilities for household tasks and personal care, and by different demographic positions as younger or older children. In the case of conflicting interests involving caregiving, for women responsibility for family is the primary consideration; for men it may be secondary. Mrs Lindsay retired from a job she loved to become a wife, and then withdrew from all outside activities to nurse her ailing husband. While physically weak herself and nursing a small infant, she undertook the care of her dying mother. Mr Sherman abandoned the caregiving tradition of the youngest son and left ailing parents behind to marry and migrate to Australia. Placed in a position of having to provide substantial personal care for a wife or close relative, the four men in this follow-up study responded similarly to women, e.g., retiring from work, and withdrawing from outside activities to devote themselves to full time care. However, the probability that over the life course men will be obliged to do this is much less than it is for their female counterparts.

While we cannot trace the origins of orientations toward future custodial care back through the life course, the life stories contain important clues as to the many different factors that may enter into the making of personal preferences. Mrs Lindsay was ambivalent about what she wanted: on the one hand, she opposed moving in with her son and daughter-in-law because of the shattering time caring for her dying mother at home; on the other, her husband's horror of nursing homes made institutionalisation seem an undesirable alternative. Mrs Smart preferred to go to a nursing home because she had personal knowledge of many instances of family relations jeopardised by care of an older person at home; she did not want to take that risk with her own beloved family. Mr Sherman did not believe in nursing homes because he came from a cultural tradition where home care of aged parents was still the practice as well as the ideal. Mrs Kramer had moved to a new country late in life, making it difficult to meet new people and make friends. Losing first a husband and then the unmarried son for whom she was keeping house, she had little choice but to shelter with a daughter who could look after her daily needs, and with whom she could at least make herself understood.

Discontinuities in giving and receiving care

In preparing this chapter I set out to look at network building over the entire life span. I wanted to explore the processes by which older people may cultivate relationships early in life to which they can turn in later years and claim reciprocal help in kind. What I found was a marked discontinuity between the amount and kind of support these older people had extended to their own parents and children and what they expected to receive in return. While the discontinuities reported in three of the four case studies were heightened by migration, similar patterns were found in the broader study of 23 respondents, a majority of whom were Australian-born (Day, 1985).

Many of the women like Mrs Lindsay had personally cared for aged parents and parents-in-law in their own homes when they were bringing up children of their own. Others like Mrs Smart had opened their homes to sisters and brothers and shared households with married children until the second generation could afford to set up in places of their own. They did this because times were hard—lives were disrupted by war or depression—and they accepted the norm that families should look after their own.

Now times were better. Most of those I spoke to said their children were doing well and did not need financial help or a roof over their heads. On the contrary, a common experience of these older people was that the children wanted to reverse the dependencies and help out their parents, whom they saw as growing older and more vulnerable to accidents and isolation. However, far from using past caregiving to negotiate for help now, most of those I talked to were uneasy about the obligations that their adult children felt toward them. They saw themselves beginning to need the very kinds of help they had given so much themselves in the past, and wanted to avoid as long as possible the sense of being less needed and useful.

Faced with the prospect of having to depend on intensive help from others, only two of the 23 people interviewed in the follow-up study were looking to children as the sources of that assistance. These were Mrs Perkins whose daughter was ill and not available to provide even the emotional support her mother yearned for, and Mrs Kramer whose need for instrumental help had reached a point of no return. The others—despite in some cases, severe infirmities—did not regard themselves as frail and firmly asserted, 'I do not need more help at the moment' (Day, 1983). Although five of the thirteen women and one of the ten men expected eventually to live with their children, for all but one of these the decision seemed as much succumbing to the pressure of their children's insistence as something they really wanted to do. Perhaps the women, because of their experiences looking after ill parents at home, viewed moving in with a son or daughter as almost synonymous with dependency.

Attitudes toward providing support

In vigorously rejecting premature dependence on their children, the older people in this study reflect a pervasive tendency found among the aged in industrial societies today: they look to their children to provide emotional support, but prefer not to aproach them for financial assistance or help with routine daily activities. Only as a last resort—in the face of serious illness, or major disability combined with inability to pay for private services or to obtain suitable community aid—will these respondents, as a rule, jeopardise their children's 'full life' by placing their own needs first.

An increasing body of research testifies that the old expect less help from their adult children than their children say they are prepared to give (Shanas, 1979; Nusberg, 1984; Lee, 1984; Brody, Johnsen and Fulcomer, 1984). Research also demonstrates, however, that when an older person is unable to manage independently at home, by far the major share of assistance is provided by family members and, among these providers, that wives and daughters take the primary responsibility for long-term comprehensive care at home (See Chapter 5). Moreover, wives and daughters provide such care often at substantial cost to their own health and family stability (Kinnear & Graycar, 1982; Kinnear & Rossiter, 1983; Fengler & Goodrich, 1979).

This discrepancy between the kind of help older people say they prefer and the kind of help they actually receive when they can no longer manage on their own challenges many stereotypes about the current bases of instrumental support for older people. It also raises important questions about the effects of contemporary social and demographic change on the flow of support between future aged populations and their family providers. What kinds of services will future old persons need and expect? Whom will they prefer to provide these services? Are the expectations and preferences changing among successively younger generations, and how will such trends as the greater extent and duration of women's participation in the labour force and the rising expectations of women for a fulfilling life following the childbearing years affect the capacities and willingness of wives and daughters to provide comprehensive help at home (even if at great personal cost)?

The perception of discontinuities in caregiving that figures so prominently in these older people's life stories suggests that both nurturing roles and expectations about support are subject to change along two dimensions: over an individual's life course, and between different age cohorts. This finding should at once be a spur to longitudinal research on intergenerational attitudes toward care of the aged, and a check on the tendency to make assumptions about the needs of future aged populations—and the availability of close relatives to meet those needs—on the basis of the family networks and support systems found among people of advanced age today.

Part 3

TRANSITIONS

7

Retirement and widowhood transitions

JOHN McCALLUM

Widowhood, retirement and institutionalisation are three major role transitions that commonly occur in old age (George, 1980:11). These role transitions are essential elements in the process of social ageing—with retirement being the socially defined entry to late life. The nature of these transitions is considerably influenced by the social context in which they occur. The primary purpose of this chapter will be to document the nature of these major late life transitions as they occur in Australian society. Transitions are not only individual experiences but, as well, network changes. The important contribution made here is the analysis of late life transitions as both individual and network events in the context of Australian society.

Both popular and academic studies of late life transitions have tended to view these changes as events in a negative process of inevitable decline into old age. Social gerontologists have written about the 'disengagement' (Cumming and Henry, 1961:14–15) of older people and the 'roleless roles' of retirement (Rosow, 1977:11) and widowhood (Hiltz, 1978). The second purpose of this chapter will be to subject such views to critical analysis using the data from the Project Survey. Such negative views will probably become less popular as we accommodate to the realities of an ageing society. Retirement is the most positive of these life changes but even here favourable public attitudes are a recent development. Widowhood is obviously a more severe adjustment. However, Day's (1985) interviews of older widows and widowers in our sample found a strong sense of having lived what Facey (1981) describes as 'a fortunate life'. Despite the negative aspects, widowhood can be part of an integrated and happy life. Late life adjustments are typical experiences in the process of building a unique, long life. They are not necessarily more prone to crisis and social withdrawal than is, for example, the change from adolescence to adulthood. They are actually more easily reversed than that life change yet we do not hold general negative views about 'growing up'.

This chapter has two major purposes. Firstly, adding to the overall theme of the book, it documents two of the major changes of late life as both individual and network events. Secondly it criticises negative views about late life changes. Project data are analysed which show that most people successfully adjust to retirement and, eventually, to widowhood. The causes of adjustment problems, for the minority who have them, are analysed but these cannot be generalised to apply to all undergoing such changes. In contrast to retirement and widowhood, institutionalisation is typically associated with physical and mental decline and occupies a relatively brief time span prior to death. This transition is discussed in the following chapter.

DEFINITIONS AND TRANSITION ADJUSTMENT MODEL

'Transition' here refers to major life changes. The concept is defined by (Parkes, 1971:103) as:

> ... those major changes in life space which are lasting in their effects, which take place over a relatively short period of time and which affect large areas of the assumptive world...

Two elements of this definition require explanation. Firstly, 'life space' refers to those parts of an environment with which the self interacts and in relation to which behaviour is organised, for example other persons in one's social network, material possessions, and residential settings. Secondly, when major changes occur in our life space, our assumptions about the world are suddenly no longer useful (Viney, 1980). This initiates a period of dislocation and adjustment which Woodfield and Viney (1984–85) outline as processes of assimilation and accommodation.

Two kinds of personal assumptions about the world will be dealt with here: firstly assumptions based on the knowledge of the actual social and economic resources held by individuals and, secondly, assumptions grounded in perceptions of adequacy of their resources and of the desirability of the particular transition. Transitions, like widowhood and retirement, are changes in one's 'life space' which are permanent, rapid and have major impact. They shatter one's assumptions about the world.

It does seem to defy common sense to class such disparate life events as widowhood, retirement and institutionalisation as belonging together. Yet, in an abstract sense, these events are similar because they involve the breaking and re-making of essential social bonds. Widowhood involves fragmentation of 'intimate, intense, interwoven bonds of family' (Raphael, 1983:3) and, not surprisingly, widowhood is rated the most stressful of all life events in the Social Readjustment Rating Scale of Holmes and Rahe (1967). By contrast retirement rates about half the score and lies in tenth position—two places behind 'being fired from work'. It breaks less crucial 'complex bonds of neighbourhood and workplace' (Raphael, 1983:3). Despite these differences we can define both widowhood and retirement as transitions.

Transitions involve both individual and network adjustment. Individual adjustment, as defined, by George (1980:19), requires two conditions:

> . . . first, the individual meets the demands of the environment; and second, the individual perceives and experiences a sense of general well-being in relation to the environment.

The failure to achieve a new sense of well-being, after say retirement or widowhood, is called maladjustment. The inevitable disruption of transitions as a part of life change must be distinguished from subsequent maladjustment—the failure to meet new demands and re-establish well-being. Erickson (1959:98) sees late life swinging between the polarities of 'integrity' and 'despair'. Integrity is achieved by '. . . the acceptance of one's own and only life cycle . . . as something that had to be, that, by necessity, permitted no substitutions'. Some people do swing in the opposite direction towards despair. However, the causes of such maladjustment can be explained without leaping to the false conclusion that late life transitions are moments in a process of inevitable decline.

The two conditions necessary for adjustment, namely, meeting new environmental demands and experiencing a new level of well-being, can be expanded by the specification of intervening processes in transitions. The model to be used here maps the assumptive world in terms of resources and perceptions. The model begins with major changes in a person's life space, like widowhood and retirement. The two subsequent moments in the expanded adjustment process, dealing with adjustment difficulties and re-establishing personal well-being, are modified by individual resources and perceptions. This model is shown in Figure 7.1.

The model specifies the 'bare bones' of the adjustment process in a way that allows testing with survey data. For the purposes of this model networks are dealt with in a general and limited way as resources. Presumably networks also alter perceptions about the desirability of transitions but this topic is not addressed in this study.

Figure 7.1   A general transition model

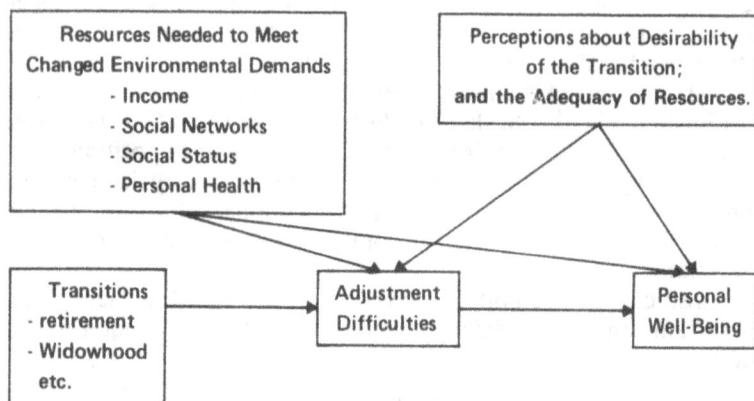

The general model outlined above depicts the challenge of major transitions to the assumptions one holds about the world. It seeks to predict the successful outcome of transitions by variability in these assumptions which are based upon both fact and personal perception.

Patterns of social ageing

Retirement and widowhood are two central events in the process of social ageing. In contrast to biological and psychological ageing, social ageing occurs by passing through socially constructed transitions which can move over time to younger or older chronological ages. At any point in history we are conscious of being early or late for major life transitions like starting schooling, getting married or retiring. Male retirement patterns clearly show how quickly the chronological index for social ageing can change (Burean of Labour Market Research, 1983). In the most recent Australian Bureau of Statistics Survey of the retired (Australian Burean of Statistics, 1983b) the Bureau puts the words 'early' in quotations advisedly:

> ... Of the persons who retired at age 45 years or more 832 000 (64.8 per cent) had retired 'early'—that is at age less than 65 years for males and at age less than 60 years for females.

What has happened is that younger retirement is now normal for Australian men. The probability of working between ages 60 and 64 is less than 50 per cent and beyond age 65 it is less than 10 per cent (Australian Bureau of Statistics, 1981–2). The entry to late life has been lowered relatively in terms of chronological age. Not only has late life been lengthened by the lowering of retirement age but also that lower point of entry has become more absolute. There is now an absolute end to work at retirement (Bureau of Labour Market Research, 1983).

By contrast to the expected and sometimes planned event of retirement, death of a spouse strikes most often 'like a thief in the night'. Widowhood becomes a more common experience with advancing age. Whereas 14 per cent of those aged 60 to 64 years were widowed, some 36 per cent of those aged over 65 had been widowed (Australian Bureau of Statistics, 1983a). Figure 7.2 shows the probability of being widowed or now married in our Project sample, using weighted data. At around age 70 years the probabilities become equal at about 40 per cent and after age 80 years respondents are more likely to be widowed than married.

Figure 7.2   Percentage of persons widowed or married by age (n = 915)

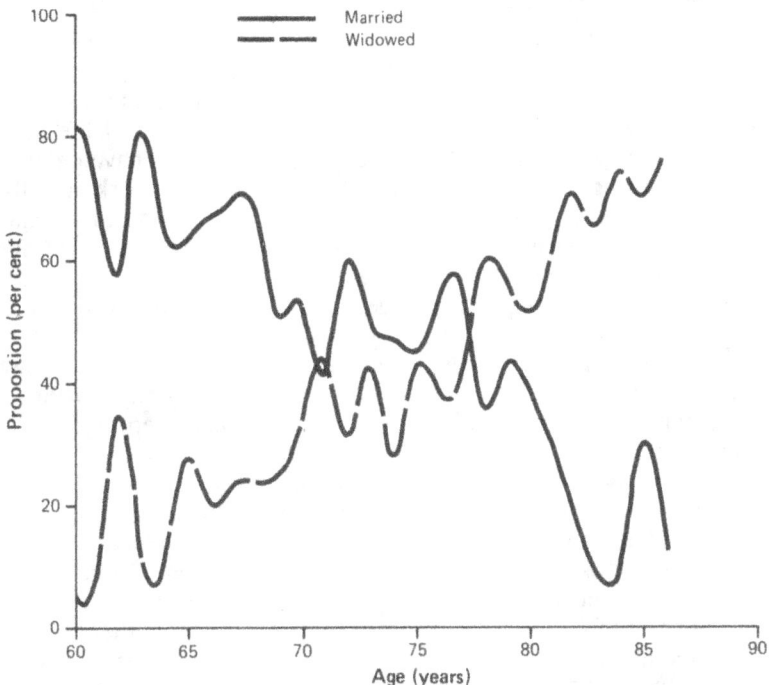

The relative increase in the widowed category is totally dominated by females. Rates of 'widowerhood' never rise above male married rates and our sample included 53 widowers compared to 367 widows. some 10 per cent of the widows and widowers in the sample had remarried but none in the last five years, and 8 of that 10 per cent had remarried 15 or more years prior to the survey in 1981. In Australia during the 1970s widowhood, like retirement, was almost always irreversible. Both these historical facts can change in the 1980s if part-time work becomes legitimate in retirement or if late life remarriage becomes more acceptable.

The 'social' ageing of Australians is characterised by three major transitions prior to death. Retirement, the gateway to social ageing, has been happening earlier than ever in the 1970s. Then the longer the married person survives the greater the likelihood of becoming widowed and, subsequently, living alone or in some joint-household with family. A final major event can be institutionalisation which becomes more likely at very old ages. The terminus of the life career is death. A more detailed examination of transitions begins at the entry to late life, retirement.

The retirement transition

Retirement with some degree of choice, as opposed to the cessation of productive activity due to frailty, is a creation of industrial societies. Only in such affluent societies can families accumulate the resources necessary to provide for an extended period of life as a 'non-producing' consumer. Indeed only those societies have defined such lives as non-productive. Retirement from formal work actually means a full-time day potentially spent in the family and wider social network. To varying degrees the retiree has been a part-time inhabitant of this world so the change need not be extreme. The changes are of three primary types, namely, changing away from work-based friendships, adjusting to a satisfactory activity pattern at home and establishing an adequate level of income without working.

Only 15 per cent of Project respondents regarded adjustment to retirement as difficult and a further 17 per cent reported it as 'somewhat difficult'. It was more often reported as 'difficult' by those aged 60 to 64 years when they retired because relatively more of them are the unhealthy and involuntary retirees. The most frequently mentioned complaints were about financial consequences (25 per cent), missing workmates (23 per cent) and boredom (10 per cent) which are the negative side of the three major adjustment tasks of retirement. Only 16 per cent of Project retirees reported that nothing was good about retirement. These poor adjusters in our survey have been reported on in detail by Braithwaite, Gibson and Bosly-Craft (1985). In reporting general difficulties in adjustment, 32 per cent of men and 34 per cent of women found it 'difficult' or 'somewhat difficult'. Women are more likely to mention 'financial problems' and 'missing workmates' as their first item of retirement difficulty than are men. Men are more likely to mention 'boredom' and to report that 'nothing is good' about retirement. Some 19 per cent of men report 'nothing good' compared to only 12 per cent of women. These results reflect the greater number of affiliative bonds of women compared to men (See Chapters 3 and 4), and the male tendency to be preoccupied with work activity.

The attractions of retirement were slightly different for men than for women. Men, who have no difficulty with adjustment to retirement rated 'leisure', 'sport', 'hobbies', 'absence of timetables' and 'freedom and independence' as the best things about retirement. These were not often rated by poor adjusters. Women, who did not find retirement adjustment difficult rated 'leisure', 'seeing family and friends', 'staying in bed' and 'freedom and independence' as the best things about retirement. Again these items are mentioned by only a few of the women who had difficult adjustments to retirement. It is no surprise to find that 'retirement for leisure' is an attractive life option. There appear to be only a few people who have difficulty with retirement and those who do not have difficulties have a range of enjoyable descriptions of the retirement experience. We can conclude that retirement is, on average, a positive change in one's life.

Factors indicated in the General Transition Model, Figure 7.1, were tested as predictors of adjustment difficulties. The method used here, and in subsequent analyses, is outlined in the endnote. In this case two models were tested, one for 'difficulties' and another for 'not at all difficult'. Three factors predicted, in opposite ways, both difficult and easy adjustment and three more factors were important in one or other model. The predictors are shown in Table 7.1 below:

Table 7.1 Predictors of difficulties in adjustment to retirement (n = 369)

Predictors	Difficulties of the adjustment	
	Difficult[a,b]	Not at all Difficult [a,c]
Duration of retirement	Negative	Positive
Overall health rating	Negative	Positive
Willingness to retire	Nagative	Positive
Adequate income	Negative	Not significant
Owning home	Negative	Not significant
Occupational status	Not significant	Positive

Notes: (a) This question asked 'Would you say your adjustment to retirement was difficult, somewhat difficult, or not at all difficult?' The methods used are outlined in the methodological end note to the chapter

(b) The dependent variable is 'difficult' versus other responses

(c) The dependent variable is 'not at all difficult' versus other responses

The importance of duration comes simply from the fact that it measures how long people have had to get on with the process of adjustment themselves, regardless of levels of resources and amount of help received. This finding supports the claim that late life transitions demonstrate the resilience of older Australians rather than their frailty. Vulnerability, on the other hand, is shown by their health rating. Those in poor health are more likely to have adjustment difficulties than those in good health. Poor health inhibits the management of adjustment by the person undergoing the transition. Physical and mental limitations make it difficult for them to meet new environmental demands. Inadequate income and not owning one's home are argued to indicate the absence of basic resources needed to meet new demands and to re-establish well-being. These two economic factors, however, only predict adjustment difficulties. Once the basic thresholds are crossed, namely by having a home and adequate income, occupational status takes over as the important economic resource in successful adjustment. Higher occupational status prior to retirement is related to higher wealth and income, greater coping skills and to meaningfulness of retirement as a reward for a successful life. The North American retirement experience (Fillenbaum, et al., 1985:92–3) shows a similar threshold effect associated with social security income. The general observation is that low resources lead to environmental pressures which inhibit the individual from getting on with the process of adjustment to retirement.

The willingness to retire variable operates in quite a different way. Applying Woodfield and Viney's (1984, 1985) constructs, 'unwillingness to retire' can be classed as an impermeable construct because it does not allow the inclusion of new experiences and ideas. This variable indicates resistance to the new experiences in retirement, despite the fact that the person could manage adjustment with the resources they have. Consequently willingness to retire predicts successful adjustment and unwillingness predicts difficulties. This perceptual variable along with the resource variables helps us to make sense of the factors underlying retirement adjustment. It seems that general evaluations of adjustment difficulty are reliable indicators of the fact that people do or do not have difficulty because the predictors of difficulties fit an expected pattern. They do not appear to be symptomatic of an inability to express deeper problems with retirement.

There is, as well as individual adjustment, a network adjustment to retirement. Broadly speaking, work organisations adjust to the departure of a member, and the family and social networks adjust to more participation of a member. Friendship networks tend to be diffuse and complex and so provide more options for change or attenuation. This would not hold for confidant relationships which can be carried over from work to retirement. Secondly, the support required from children in coping with retirement is not intensive, often involves pleasant interaction and can be managed from a distance. The major changes and renegotiations of household duties fall upon the retiree and his or her spouse, if the retiree is married.

This might suggest that people married at the time of retirement might find it less difficult to make the adjustment. However, there was no more difficulty experienced by our single retirees compared to those who were married at the time of retirement. Economic studies do show that, where both partners work, they tend to retire together or to change to part-time work at about the same time (Ryan and Williams, 1984). The economic explanation is that retirement is a joint decision of husbands and wives to maximise retirement leisure given sufficient income. The social explanation needs to stress that retirement is an event for the marital dyad not only for each partner alone.

Spouses, as well as retirees, were asked about their difficulties with their spouses' retirement. Most spouses, 72 per cent, found that adjustment to their spouses' retirement was 'not at all difficult'. Some 11 per cent found adjustment 'difficult' and a further 17 per cent 'somewhat difficult'. The worst things about spouses' retirement were 'the spouse being always there' 17 per cent, 'financial' 9 per cent and 51 per cent reported that 'nothing' was difficult. By contrast, the best things about spouses' retirement were reported as 'companionship' 38 per cent, 'joint interests' 14 per cent and 'nothing' 10 per cent. These figures conceal the difficulties of wives with husbands' retirement. Some 88 per cent of men compared to only 65 per cent of women report their spouses retirement as 'not at all difficult'. Men, at 75 per cent, are much more ready to report 'no worst things' about their spouses' retirement than are women at 41 per cent. Wives are more likely to report 'companionship' and 'joint interests' as best things about retirement than are husbands. About one fifth of women report 'the spouse always there' as a worst thing, but males do not report this at all. So the retirement of one's husband has a much greater impact on household arrangements than does the retirement of one's wife. These patterns confirm the results of many studies that paid work is less central to women's identities than is household work which remains as their domain of responsibility. It should also be noted that whilst the potential for positive development of marital bonds in retirement is clear, this process of adjustment is more difficult for women than for men.

The final criterion of adjustment, re-establishing well-being, remains to be investigated. Our crossectional data suggest that, apart from those cases of maladjustment already specified, morale (See Appendix 1) remains at reasonable levels through the retirement experience. This, then, is the final piece of data supporting the claim that retirement is not a crisis prone transition for the majority of people. That is not to say that it is completely stable in its morale consequences. Atchley (1976:64) proposes that retirement has multiple stages, namely, a honeymoon phase, a disenchantment phase, a re-orientation phase, a stability phase and a termination phase. There appears to be some support for variability in the experience of retirement (Ekerdt et al., 1985) at least in terms of 'enthusiasm' and subsequent 'let down' in the first eighteen months of retirement. If we look at the morale of people at different durations of retirement our sample lends support to the phase theory, as shown in Figure 7.3 below:

Figure 7.3   Levels of morale across phases of retirement (n = 323)

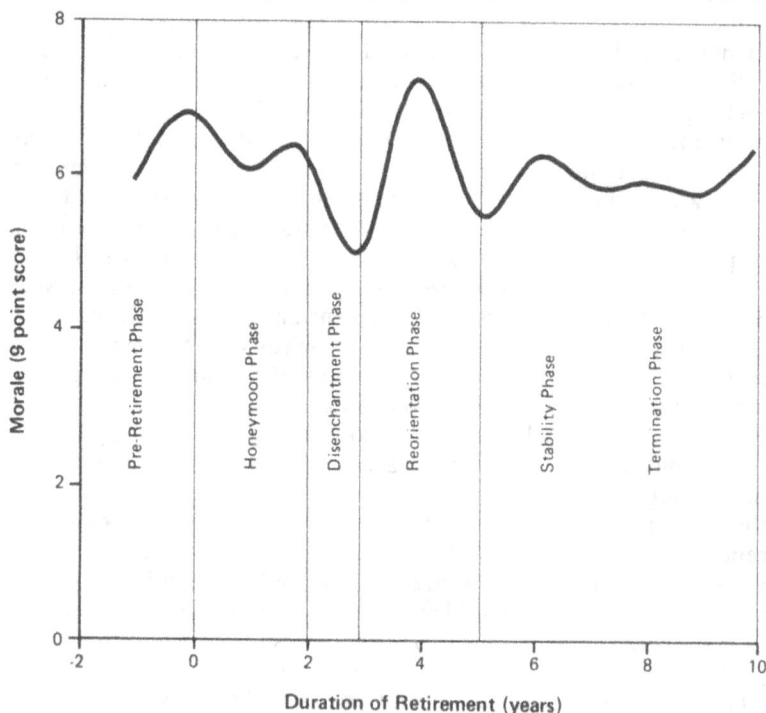

The General Transition Model and arguments find support in Project data but further, more elaborate hypotheses require longitudinal data for substantiation.

Transition to widowhood

Widowhood and retirement are both major transitions which require different levels and types of adjustments. Unlike retirement, widowhood causes severe shock and forces the person to cope with the absolute loss of a life long partner, to learn to live a single life and to take on new activities and responsibilities. The event of widowhood is a network-wide shock. Besides being the loss of a spouse, it is the loss of a parent for a family. Moreover, as Lopata (1979:31) observes widowhood is disruptive to the woman's social network:

> Often the husband's death breaks old ties with many people, his family, his work associates and the voluntary associations she belonged to with him or through him, such as women's auxiliaries of fraternal groups. Friendships must be modified if they depended on couple-companioniate interaction.

But, it should be noted that the network also responds positively to this transition by providing social support as will be shown here.

The immediate impact of widowhood is upon living arrangements. A joint-household becomes a single one. The subsequent options are to live alone, to move to kin or others, or to have them move into the now single household. A clear demonstration of impact of widowhood can be seen in the comparison of the living arrangements of widowed and married respondents:

Table 7.2 Living arrangements of married and widowed respondents (n = 914)

Living arrangements	Marital status	
	Married (498)	Widowed (416)
Lives alone	1.8	61.6
With spouse only	77.7	—
With spouse and other	19.5	—
With siblings	0.2	4.8
With children	0.2	13.8
With children's family	0.2	13.6
With other persons	0.4	5.5
Total percentage	100.0	100.0

Widows and widowers do not differ significantly in their probability of being in any one of the above arrangements. The transition, in terms of living arrangements, is clear. It is from living with spouse (and others), to living alone, or living with children, siblings or others.

Living alone rather than with others was found to have no implications for morale, happiness and satisfaction. It is a preferred choice for many widows rather than a necessity. The methods used here do average out minority opinions and outlying responses which can be seen in qualitative investigations. The predictors of living alone (See Endnote) were owning one's home, not having single children and, for a small number of widows, being still employed. There is a resource limitation on being alone as a preference—one needs to own a home. The availability of single children might also be considered to be a network resource which facilitates remaining in one's home. The joint arrangements between widowed persons and single children are most likely to be an arrangement preferred by both parties rather than arrangements by necessity.

All respondents indicated specific areas as 'the most difficult adjustments to make'. Those most frequently mentioned were 'living alone', 'loneliness', and 'life without spouse'. Difficulties receiving few mentions were 'moving', 'shock'and 'being unused to finances'. The three major difficulties do have specific meanings. If we measure the frequency of responses over duration of widowhood, as in Figure 7.4 below, we see that each has a different importance at different times:

Figure 7.4   Consequences of widowhood, by duration (n = 125)

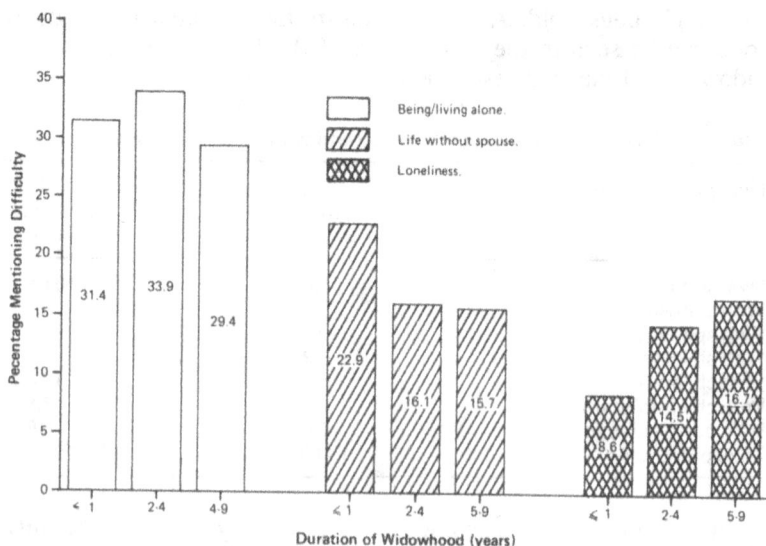

Duration of Widowhood (years)

'Living alone' refers to the practical difficulties of maintaining oneself and one's house after the departure of a co-worker and intimate partner. As we saw in Chapter 5, older widows seldom manage to do traditionally male tasks without help. Consequently the frequency of this difficulty remains consistent in the first ten years of the life phase. By contrast, the impact of having to live without one's spouse is felt most acutely in the first year but less so thereafter. However, in its place one begins to feel lonely. As Raphael (1983:184) observed of widows:

> The first intense experiences of grief center on the absence of the loved partner—the experience of living apart and being separated from him.
> All the woman wants is to have her man back.

Each time this longing for the dead spouse is rebuffed by the reality of his absence, the finality and permanency of widowhood begins to be accepted and the 'longing' is replaced by 'loneliness'—the loss of adult attachment. Loneliness will be accentuated by the loss of peer ties with age (See Chapter 3).

There were only 53 men compared to 367 women in our sample. They specified similar adjustment difficulties with the one exception that males were twice as likely as females to mention 'loneliness' as a difficulty. We know from Chapter 4 that husbands are more dependent than wives on emotional support from their spouse. But gender differences in adjustment to widowhood are complex. Helsing, et al. (1981) report American evidence that males were far more likely to die within ten years of death of spouse than were females and that remarriage improved survival for males but not for females. In our sample of 'survivors' females certainly outnumber men at a rate of seven-to-one. This could be claimed as support for Bernard's (1972) grand thesis that marriage is beneficial to most husbands but not to most wives. Glenn (1975:594) offers a revision of the hypothesis such that women exceed men in both stress and the satisfaction they derive from marriage. The matter is clearly complex and not open to simple solution. Men may be less robust biologically than women and they may need a spouse late in life to provide a reason for living. Day's (1985) interviews report the situations of an older widower:

> With his wife gone and his own activities limited by a weak heart and bad circulation, Mr . . . seems quite ready to depart this life.

Thus despite similarities between widows and widowers in reported difficulties, there are unexplained gender differences in survival rates after the loss of spouses.

The loss of a spouse brings an immediate need for many kinds of support to deal with the difficult tasks of adjustment. This need associated with widowhood is clearly greater than that associated with retirement. Despite the obviousness of the need, some 28 per cent of our sample reported receiving 'no help' with adjustment to widowhood. Three factors were found to predict the likelihood of receiving 'no help' (See Endnote): longer duration of widowhood; smaller size of total support networks; and less personal importance placed on religion. We would expect that the ability to recall assistance received reduces over time, particularly given the shocked state at the time of the widowhood event. The second factor suggests that people draw upon existing supports for help. The importance of religion is more difficult to interpret and could indicate that the widowed person is embedded in stronger and more interdependent networks or that there is a bias against reporting 'no help' amongst the very religious. These perceptual factors show the ambiguity of the 'no help' category.

Those reporting 'no help' are also more likely to report having no difficult adjustments than those receiving help. It would seem, then, that this category covers a number of possible responses, namely:

I didn't need help, I can manage my own adjustment.
It's a relief (probably after long-term care of an ill spouse).
I had no problems worth mentioning.
There was not anyone who could help with my specific needs.

These varieties of interpretation of the answer suggest the need for more detailed qualitative research to identify the complex possibilities connecting receiving 'no help' and having 'no difficulties' with widowhood. Mitchell (1969:31) argues this case, in specific terms for network research:

... questionnaires should play a supportive rather than a major role in the study of more general sociological situations where contents may vary and other characteristics of the network are likely to be significant ...

Having reached the limits of the quantitative data here, the detail and subtlety of qualitative data is now needed to complete the explanation. Fortunately more detailed investigation of the importance of help after the loss of spouse is available from other studies.

The literature shows that support is subject to complex interplays of factors. Bankoff (1983) found the role of social support in adjustment to widowhood depended upon where widows are in the adjustment process, the type of support given, and its source. Walker et al. (1977) report that dense social networks may offer best support at the time of crisis but that less dense networks may better facilitate longer-term adjustments through the bridges they offer to new roles and relationship development. More specifically, Maddison and Walker (1967) report that widows with poor help outcomes perceived themselves as having many more unsatisfied needs in interpersonal exchanges during the bereavement crisis than those with good help outcomes. Poor help outcomes were also associated with interactions perceived as unhelpful because they blocked the widows' expression of feelings. The appropriateness of help is as important as help itself. As Day's (1985) interviews show it is the quality of the relationship between the recipient and the helper that is important. For example, a working daughter who bosses her ageing and widowed father is a very threatening helper.

We have ambiguous evidence in the survey about perceptions of help with adjustment to widowhood but quite clear reports on who actually helped. Those widowed in the nine years prior to the survey, if they reported receiving help, were asked: 'Who helped most (with the adjustment) and what did they do?' The sources of assistance and the matching of helpers and tasks are of interest. Litwak and Kulis (1983) have proposed that a group can optimally manage those tasks which match it in structure'.

They argue, for example, that kinship is motivated by internalised, altruistic feelings and a sense of duty to family. This matches tasks which require time and energy and hence long-term commitments. Other tasks which require common status are typically provided, for example, by another older person or another widow who is likely to be 'a friend'.

Those who reported receiving help were most likely to report being helped by children and other kin. Some respondents reported up to three helpers whilst others reported only one. The helpers are listed in Figure 7.5 below:

Figure 7.5 Relationship of helpers with adjustment to widowhood (n = 186)

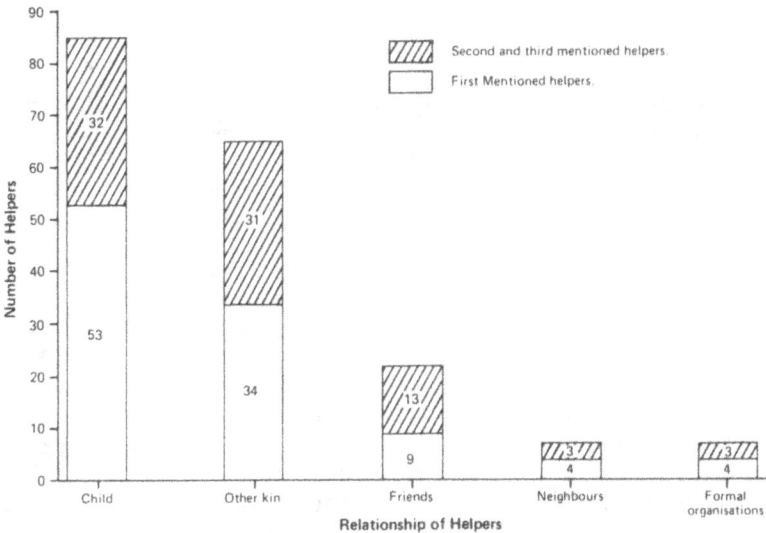

The predominance of family in this figure bears comment. As Rosenman, et al. (1981:20) observe in another Australian study of widowhood:

> The most frequently mentioned resources in both time periods
> (immediately after spouse's death and at interview time) were the
> widow's family, friends and doctor, the family being more frequently
> called upon at time of death, and friends later on.

It is reasonable to assume that our older widows and widowers when asked about help with adjustment to widowhood, refer to the initial crisis and grief and not to the longer-term transition to single status. Consequently our respondents describe the tasks or support in which kin are the appropriate helpers and do not mention those aspects of longer-term adjustment in which friends may be the most likely helpers.

There are few gender differences in the numbers of children providing support with adjustment. Sons are nearly as often mentioned as daughters—20 per cent compared to 25 per cent of all mentions of helpers. Given that we are mostly talking about mothers, we would expect to find strong emotional relationships with sons as well as with daughters (See Chapter 3). Gender differences emerge in the kinds of help reported, as show in Table 7.3:

Table 7.3 Sons and daughters help with adjustment to widowhood (n = 85)

	Kind of help	Sons (38)	Kind of help	Daughters (47)
1st	Emotional support	21.1	Support in general	25.5
2nd	Company	13.2	Stayed short-term	21.3
3rd	Stayed short-term	13.2	Company	19.1
4th	Business advice	7.9	Emotional support	10.6
5th	Financial assistance	7.9	Visits, outings	8.6
	Others	36.7	Others	14.9
	Total percentage	100.0	Total percentage	100.0

Sons may be useful for emotional support but seem to be less important in providing a wide range of support than daughters. Sons provide more of the business and financial advice which husbands previously handled, whilst daughters deal more with the expressive support and housework assistance. As in the earlier chapters, we find that daughters have more diffuse and stronger ties with their mothers. Traditional gender orientations and skills structure the kind of support provided to widowed parents.

Other kin helping is dominated by sisters, with 'in-laws' being less frequent helpers. Their tasks tend to be similar to those of sons and daughters. By contrast, friends and neighbours do not tend to provide help which requires long-term commitment. Friends provide tasks facilitated by commonality of status, such as outings, holidays, whilst neigbours provide limited practical help which requires proximity but low commitment. Overall there is a pattern to which helpers do what tasks, matching those found by Litwak (1985). Clearly widowhood involves many more network interchanges than retirement as close personal bonds respond more actively to the generally negative consequences of widowhood compared to retirement.

As one would expect the immediate consequences of widowhood can be very severe. While no measure of mortality is available in our type of survey, the available data showed no effects of widowhood on current health status nor on health now compared to five years ago.

Nor does the absence of help have any health effects on the 'survivors' in our survey. Where the effects are observed are in the psychological consequences, namely in terms of morale and depression.

As Raphael's review of a large number of studies shows (Raphael, 1983:216–7), most widows and widowers are likely to experience sadness and depressed feelings. Maddison and Viola (1968) found, in their studies of Boston and Sydney widows (under 60 years of age) carried out during the thirteen months after the death, that one in eight subjects had consulted a physician to seek treatment for depression, and as many as two in five had problems with insomnia and nervousness. There is some difficulty in differentiating transient from profound depression which Freud (1917) commented upon in his original distinction between mourning and melancholia. As shown below, respondents felt depression most severely in the first year of widowhood and up to four years afterwards. The initial depression, after widowhood, can be described as transient but those cases which persist long after widowhood are probably cases of profound depression.

Figure 7.6 Severe depression in last year, by duration of widowhood (n = 252)

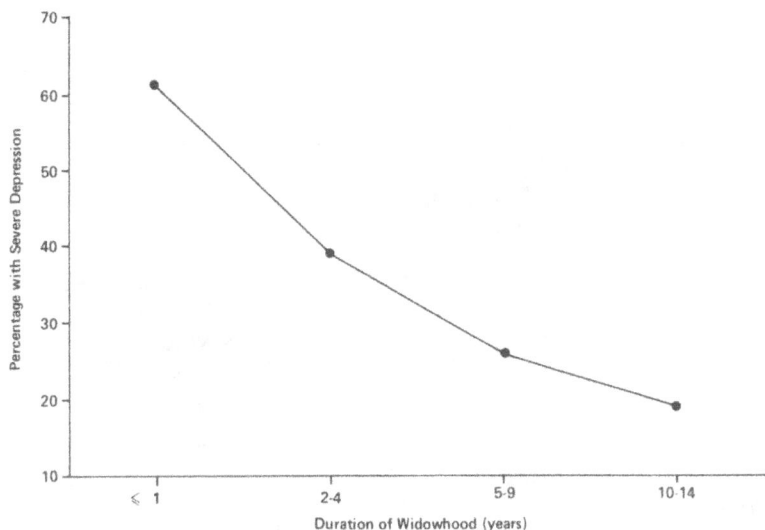

The differences between the peaks at two to four years and ten to fourteen years in morale could indicate phases of re-orientation and stability respectively. However, unlike the retirement phases, these means do not differ significantly on t-tests.

Figure 7.7   Morale by duration of widowhood (n = 223)

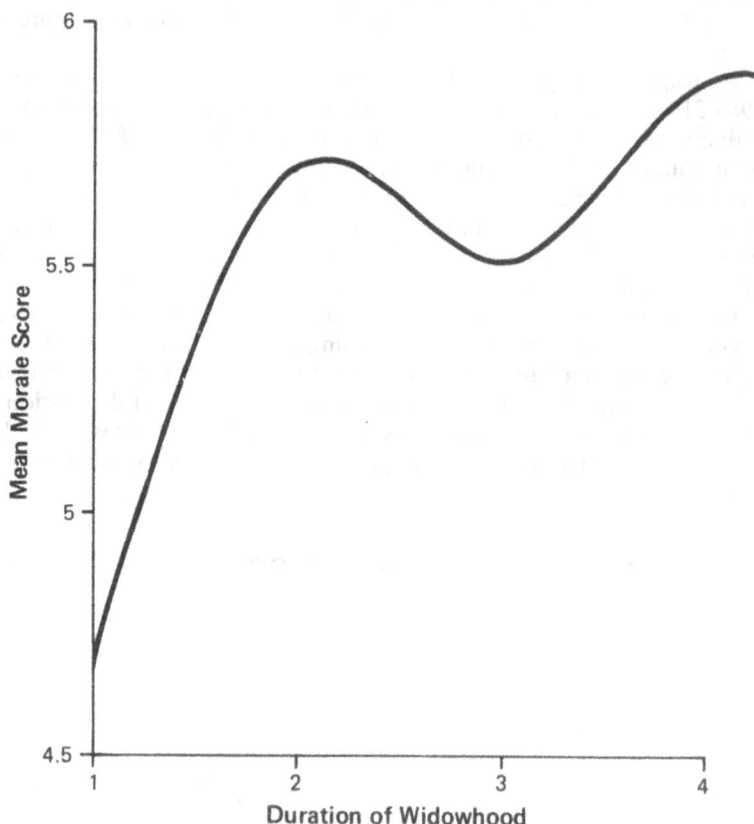

In general some 29 per cent of widows had felt serious depression in the last year compared to 20 per cent of married respondents. The predictors of widows and widowers 'having had severe depression in the last year' (See Endnote) are shown in Table 7.4:

Table 7.4   Predictors of severe depression during adjustment to widowhood (n = 313)

Predictors	Severe depression*
Duration of widowhood	Negative
Overall health rating	Negative
Adequate income	Negative

* This question asked 'In the past year, have you been severely depressed?' See methodological Endnote to the chapter for full description of methods

The duration factor, as in the retirement adjustment case, indicates the length of time which people have had to get on with the process of adjustment. Similarly, the resources, personal health and income, are again important. Where health is poor or income is inadequate resources are low for meeting new environmental demands. The management of adjustment is to that degree hampered by having few resources to call upon. Network support is shown by the other studies reviewed earlier to be important in adjustment, however its effects are too complex to be identified in the measures available here. Our respondents show resilience in the face of this severe life change and manage their adjustment. The absence of desirability or perceptual variables in the final set of predictors, which did appear significant for retirement, is explained from the fact that, for widowhood, there is little variability—most people are unwilling widows or widowers. The general implication of these results is that not even widowhood can be generally regarded as a regressive late life transition. However unattractive the adjustment tasks, it remains as a normal event in a unique and potentially integrated life career.

SUMMARY

In retirement and widowhood we have two contrasting transitions. One, retirement, is predominantly a male experience and the other, widowhood, is predominantly female. Retirement is a working career transition and widowhood is part of the family life cycle. They are changes in separate threads of an individual's life career. Their impact is markedly different. Retirement is normally a positive life change and morale is quite high around the time of retirement. By contrast widowhood has a severe negative impact and morale is restored only after some years of adjustment. Finally widowhood is a shock to a broader network whereas retirement is the primary concern of a marital dyad.

Despite these differences both are clearly transitions in that they are rapid, permanent changes which have major personal and social impacts. Consequently the general process of adjustment can be modelled in a similar way. This model, Figure 7.1, shows that adjustment is affected by resources needed to meet new environmental demands, and perceptions of the desirability of change. These variables, along with the ease or difficulty of transition, affect the re-establishment of a satisfactory level of well-being after a transition experience. Generally our analyses have shown that adjustment proceeds without crisis unless the absence of health and economic resources lead to 'environmental press'—the failure or inability to meet new demands from the environment. The network data and specific adjustment items showed that widowhood and retirement are both individual and network events.

The findings of this chapter show that negative views of late life transitions are groundless. There is little evidence of maladjustment to transitions and we have been able to identify specific predictors of maladjustment. Morale is certainly low in the first year of widowhood but it steadily improves with time. By contrast, early in retirement morale is high and it drops in what we could call the disenchantment phase. A satisfactory level of well-being is achieved by most people even after the most traumatic transition namely widowhood. Thus late life is not, characteristically, a series of disasters and withdrawals. It is not necessarily more crisis prone than any other period of life. With adequate resources people do manage the adjustment process. As more Australians live long lives these transitions are also being experienced as normal, but not necessarily pleasant, life events. Late life transitions can be moments in a 'fortunate life'. We need also to remember that some people lead 'unfortunate lives' which involve serious problems in adjusting to late life transitions.

8

Social processes in entering nursing homes

M.VICTOR MINICHIELLO

In this chapter, we move to another transition, the long-term placement of older people into nursing homes.[1] The chapter uncovers the pathways which aged patients and their next-of-kin have taken to arrive at the doorstep of nursing homes. It explores what lies behind the aggregate statistics and attempts to describe the decision-making process through each individual's own words. The analysis focuses on the active social processes and the subjective meanings individuals construct about their experiences.

In a study that examines the influence that social factors have in this decision-making process, it is important to select patients who were likely to have been admitted predominantly because of social rather than medical reasons. Ninety-two aged residents and their next-of-kin were selected for in depth interview. Eligible respondents were the comparatively less disabled residents as assessed by the professional nursing home staff. It is among this sample that social reasons would be expected to loom large in the decision to seek nursing home care. This represents a subsample of the nursing home population (See Appendix 3) and excludes patients whose admission was necessitated principally because of mental or physical disability.

The chapter begins by presenting cases which typify and illustrate the variety of decision-making situations. Each of the cases is selected to highlight different vulnerabilities found in social support networks when the respondents were living in the community. They illustrate how various social contingencies identified in the previous chapters, such as gender and marital status, predispose entry into nursing homes.[2] The discussion then considers the actions of family members and professionals in admission decisions and the reasons aged persons present to explain their presence in nursing homes.

149

Miss A

The never-married elderly are over-represented in nursing homes: they make up 18 per cent of aged residents living in nursing homes as compared to only 9 per cent of those living outside institutions (1976 Census). Their greater risk of placement is largely a result of the absence of close family support. Many live alone and a crisis often necessitates institutionalisation.

Miss A highlights the vulnerability of the single aged living alone. Miss A is 85 years old. She never married and as an only child, lived with her parents until they died. After the death of her mother, Miss A continued to live in the family home for twelve years. She has no family. Her only cousin died a few years ago, and in recent years, her friends, who are also old, 'stopped calling'.[3] Although she was always courteous to her neighbours, her relationship with them never extended beyond the ceremonial greetings. As people were forgetting her, she was also withdrawing from the community.

Miss A never gave a thought to living in a nursing home. She had never 'been to such a place before'. The circumstances surrounding her application were simple. 'It just happened' and she had very little influence in the decision. Her next-door neighbour noticed that Miss A had not been collecting her milk and mail. (She only received business mail.) Worried that Miss A might have had an accident, the neighbour called the police. They found Miss A locked in the garage, holding a gun in her hand. Frightened of being alone at night, she took refuge in the cold, dirty garage. She was half-dressed and suffering from malnutrition and arthritis. She was rushed to hospital and a social worker was assigned to her case. With no family member to assume responsibility, her fate was determined by 'professionals'. The medical team decided that it was not safe for Miss A to return home and they arranged to transfer her to a nursing home. Upon admission, Miss A required assistance from staff with dressing and bathing. The matron noted that Miss A's overall physical health had improved 'greatly' since moving to the nursing home. At the time of the interview, she was able to bathe and dress herself.

Miss A was not upset about being told to move into a nursing home. She could see no other alternative, nor was one presented to her. She had nursed both of her parents at home until they died. She believes that only the family can assist an aged person to remain at home. This is why she never bothered with community services. 'I am an only one as it happens; that is how I came to be in this home'. The doctor and the social worker were doing 'their duty'. They had given their 'medical orders' and she was following the treatment. Miss A does not, however, enjoy living in a nursing home. She feels that she has lost her rights as a human being. 'I can't even go out to buy stamps'. But what can she do about this? 'Nothing really'. 'Who can she turn to for help?', she asks. Throughout her life, she has had to make the best of her situation. She does not have a 'friend left in the world'; this is why her remaining days will be spent at the nursing home. She told me that she 'can walk out of the nursing home' but feels that there are no caring hands waiting for her to lead her out.

Miss B

Not all never-married aged persons are without assistance from family. Several studies have illustrated that when children or spouses are not available for support, older people will turn to other relatives for assistance with home care (See Chapter 5; also Cantor, 1979). Recent studies, however, point out that the quantity and quality of support from siblings, nieces, nephews, cousins and friends are different from those received from children or spouses (Cantor, 1980; Hoyt and Babchuk, 1983; Johnson and Catalano, 1981). Elderly unmarried people receiving care from their relatives appear to be most vulnerable to dissolving the caregiving relationship, as is illustrated in the case below.

Miss B is 83 years old and, with the help of a younger sister and her sister's son, she had been living on her own for over 20 years. Her sister provided abundant expressive support and her nephew managed her financial affairs, did the house repairs, and took her shopping. During the last three months, her niece helped Miss B once a week with the housework.

Miss B was putting her laundry on the clothes line, fell and fractured her hip. With the help of her neighbour, she called her nephew and was taken to the hospital. Her nephew had been worried about his aunt. He had been discussing with his mother the possibility of placing his aunt in a nursing home. As Miss B was getting older and more forgetful, it was becoming much more difficult for the family to look after her. Miss B's sister was also in her eighties and receiving help from her children. Miss B's family support was dissolving. To relieve himself from some of the responsibility, the nephew arranged to have meals on wheels and home help services assist his aunt.

The nephew wanted her to move into a nursing home and with her accident, his tentative plans were realised. While she was in the hospital, he arranged to have Miss B transferred to the nursing home. Miss B reluctantly agreed. She realised that her sister was not 'well enough' to look after her. And she needed constant care to recover from her accident. When she moved to the nursing home, Miss B received assistance from the nurses with bathing, dressing and going to the toilet. With the aid of a walking stick and physiotheraphy, Miss B recovered from her fracture. The matron described her overall physical health as 'good' and noted that she requires 'very little help' and 'sometimes goes out for a little walk'.

Miss B was terribly upset about going to live in a nursing home 'amongst strangers'. But she had no choice and, after all, she reasoned, it was only for a short while; instead it turned out to be for two years. 'I never thought I'd be here this long. I thought three months would be long enough'. She had hopes of returning to her empty home. 'I've got my own home and it has been empty all this while and I hope to get back to it soon'.

She does not think she belongs in a nursing home. Her nephew disagrees. He realises that he is unable to meet the demands of managing the responsibilities of multiple households. Although he feels 'sad' about her living in a nursing home, he sees no other alternative. He has difficulty managing the daily needs of his own family. Miss B will never return home.

Mr C

As we saw in earlier chapters, divorce can weaken family ties. Mr C is 67 years old and he has been divorced since the early 1960s. He lived on his own. His daughter and son seldom visited him.

His difficulties coping with old age began as soon as he retired. In the absence of family support, he payed a neighbour to do 'the housework'. But he had no company. Feeling lonely and abandoned, he began drinking to escape from his marital failure. Although previously a meticulous person, he seldom cleaned his unit, ate proper meals or worried about his physical appearance. Concerned about his liver pain, he arranged to see his family doctor. The family doctor arranged for a community nurse to visit Mr C weekly. During one of her weekly visits, the community nurse found Mr C 'passed out' on the living room floor. She arranged to have Mr C admitted to the hospital and contacted his son.

Mr C's son never had a close relationship with his father. But seeing his father 'helpless', old and in a hospital bed, he 'began feeling sorry for him'. He decided to do something. But what could he do? And as he thought about it, how much was he prepared to do for his father? The divorce had erased the family bond. His mother and sister did not want to get involved. That left him. But he still carried a lot of resentment towards Mr C. He contacted a social worker. Maybe community services could help maintain his father at home? The social worker did not think so. Even if he was receiving proper meals and help with the housework, chances are that without expressive support, he would return to 'the bottle'. The only safe solution was to place his father in a nursing home. This was not an easy decision; he felt guilty about institutionalising his father. 'Dad was still young; he did not belong in an old folks home'. On the one hand, Mr C's son believes that the family should 'prevent such things from happening'. On the other hand, he was also realistic. Mr C's family existed only in name. He was not prepared to change his life style and have his father live with him. There was only one solution. With the help of the social worker, Mr C was transferred from the hospital into a nursing home. Mr C's 'heavy' drinking habit seriously affected his health. Upon admission, Mr C was fully dependent on the nursing staff. He required help with dressing, bathing, going to the toilet and walking. He still complains about liver pains and has difficulty 'getting around'. The staff worries that he 'may get a hold of a drink'. He is closely 'watched'.

Mr C was very upset about his son's decision. 'I didn't know anything about it. Had nothing to do with it'. He resents living at the nursing home because he was never once asked 'what I wanted'. He is a prisoner. He seldom talks to the 'other inmates' and the staff describe Mr C as a 'difficult and unhappy patient'.

His son visits him more frequently since the move to the nursing home, but his daughter and former wife continue to have no contact. In an attempt to come to terms with the decision to institutionalise his father, Mr C's son told me:

> It was the best solution; the lesser of the two evils. If he continued living alone, he would have killed himself. If he came home with me, he would have destroyed me. I am a bachelor, nothing means more to me than my privacy.

The family was unwilling to offer Mr C the support he needed to remain at home; 'that is why he is in a nursing home'.

Mr and Mrs D

Chapters 5 and 6 have shown that the most reliable source of support when one becomes ill in old age is the marital dyad. Although Mr D's admission was necessitated because of his health problem, the case is selected to show the dilemmas wives face when caring for a sick husband. Mr D is 76 years old and for the last six years he was receiving home care from his 73-year-old wife. He had had a stroke, and although the doctor had suggested that he move into a nursing home, his family agreed that it was 'best to look after him at home'. He was released after spending several months 'getting stronger' in the hospital and rehabilitation unit. The stroke left Mr D partly paralysed. With the help of a community nurse and two adult children, Mrs D looked after him at home for over five years. But gradually, Mrs D felt that she could not provide her husband with the care he needed without 'harming my own health'.

Wives caring for a sick husband are often themselves old, and concerned about their own health or inability to fulfil the role of carer. The psychological burden of providing continuous care was 'finally getting to me'. The community nurse and her two children were 'pressuring' her to institutionalise Mr D. Tired, and at the edge of a physical and mental breakdown, she 'gave in'. She told her husband that she could no longer manage him at home.

Mr D went willingly. He recognised the agony his wife was 'struggling' with. He had often suggested moving into a nursing home but 'she would not listen to me'. He had been waiting for his wife to come to terms with what he had accepted long ago. He had not been happy about his wife 'being miserable because of me—I was a lot of trouble'. He was totally dependent on Mrs D's help. He could not get on and off a chair, in and out of bed, or 'on the pot' without her assistance. All of this 'fuss over me' has created 'a distance between us'.

With the help of her children, Mrs D contacted several nursing homes, and they selected the 'one' they liked. This was not an easy decision for Mrs D. Her devotion to Mr D had kept him out of hospitals and a nursing home. But her back pain was getting worse from lifting him. It had never been easy to look after him: 'always a constant struggle'. She never went out for fear that something would happen to him. Her daughter did all of the shopping and her son managed their financial affairs. The children had become 'worried' that their mother 'would end up in a home before he did'. And although they helped regularly, they had their own families to raise. As Mrs D said, 'how much can you expect?'

The family saw Mr D's situation as a permanent crisis. The only alternative open to the family was to institutionalise Mr D. With the help of a doctor, her children were able to 'convince' Mrs D that 'the time had come'. As they were getting 'more involved with their own lives', the children had become less supportive. Mrs D was left on her own to care for her sick husband. When she began to cry out for help, the nursing home, she was told, was the only alternative. This was not what she wanted, 'but what was I to do?' She feels guilty about her decision. She often cries.

Unlike Mrs D, her husband has no difficulties accepting the decision. He 'knows' he cannot return home. His health prevents him. 'I am here for good; this is the way it has to be'. He prefers the nursing home to living at home. He is able to enjoy his wife's company rather than being worried about being a burden to her. His dependency for instrumental support was altering their relationship. The nursing home would help restore normal interaction between them. He reassures her that 'this is the best way'. His only concern is what will happen to her 'when she is also forced to leave our home'. Mrs D is not thinking about her future needs. She is 'too worried' about what is happening to her husband.

Mr and Mrs E

The marrieds are less likely to turn to family or community services even though both spouses have difficulty in performing the activities of daily living. We often find what Johnson and Catalano (1981) have termed 'social regression' among older married couples, who rely on the marital dyad to meet the demands of a disability. Although Mrs E and her husband were able to maintain an independence from their family, a fragile interdependency was created within the household, placing both of them at risk of institutionalisation when the caregiving relationship collapsed.

Mrs E is 92 years old, and prior to moving to the nursing home, she was living with her frail 95-year-old husband whom she had nursed for the last six years. 'Father was totally dependent on mother for his simplest daily needs'. Although her two daughters helped Mrs E with the housework and cooking 'once a week' and 'the two boys did the other things around the house', it was Mrs E who was solely responsible for bathing, shaving and dressing Mr E.

Mr and Mrs E had never once thought about 'ending up in a nursing home' until the accident. Mrs E got up to go to the toilet during the night, slipped and fell. She screamed for help, but without his wife's assistance, Mr E could not get out of bed or to the phone. Unable to lift herself, Mrs E remained on the floor all night long, with her husband lying helpless in bed, both 'shouting for help'. It was not until a neighbour heard their cry for help some hours later that they were rescued and rushed to the hospital.

Upon arriving at the hospital, they jointly decided to move into a nursing home. They requested that the social worker search for a nursing home that would 'accept us both'. They were emotionally very close to one another. When her husband had a stroke six years ago, Mrs E had moved into the hospital 'to be near him'. This was no time to be separated. She had to go into a hospital to recover from her fall. They were so dependent on one another that 'if one went, then the other went also'. The decision was made even before their children arrived at casualty. Although the children had long felt that their parents should not have been living on their own, 'we never raised the subject of moving into a nursing home'. As with all of their parents' decisions, 'it was going to be theirs'. The nursing home solution seemed 'the obvious choice'. Looking after both parents would have been impossible 'for any of us to handle'; they have their own families and work commitments.

There was very little family discussion, nor the drama of a long and postponed decision. 'They realised their situation and made the decision willingly. And they didn't believe in living with their children or in-laws'. As with many elderly couples, receiving support from their families is defined as a violation of the cultural norm 'we can manage' (Day, 1985). The decision, however, was not without personal troubles. Mrs E blames herself for leaving their home:

I had the fall and I couldn't leave him alone or have him worry my children, so we had to look for a home that would take the two of us and he came with me. It was my fault that we came here really.

When Mrs E recovered from her broken hip, she decided to remain at the nursing home, even though she required no assistance with any of the daily living activities. Her husband's health had deteriorated. Although capable of looking after herself, it would have been too difficult for Mrs E to look after her ill husband. Besides, it was he who now needed nursing home care. He moved into the nursing home for her; she was not going to abandon him.

Although she would rather be living at home, she is quite happy at the nursing home. She accepts that she 'will always be here'. Her husband died a year ago and although her daughters tried to persuade her to move in with the family, Mrs E prefers to live 'in my new home'. She feels close to the other patients; 'I have found a new family'. Her family visits her daily. As she is getting older and frailer, she does not want to become a burden to her children. She recalls the difficulties (and embarrassments) of going to her children's homes for the day:

> I can go to my daughter's place, but I'm on this frame and their homes don't have rails to hold on to like I have here. I went to my daughter's place recently and she had visitors and I wanted to go to the toilet. I felt that I held up to that point quite well. But I don't want to be a nuisance because I can live quite comfortably in a nursing home, where I'm least trouble to anybody. And to go visit them is too much of an effort. I'm now harder to get in and out of the car and there are steps in the front, so we have to go around the back, there are no steps there. I think I'm better to have them visit me.

Mrs E thinks they made a 'wise decision'. She could not have continued to look after her husband for much longer. No one was aware of the physical burden she had carried for the last six years. Mrs E had reached the stage where she required help but because 'all of the family's concern was on father, no one, including mother, realised this until she entered the nursing home and matron pointed it out to us'. Recognising that her independent days are over, she told me, 'when you reach the stage where you feel that you are dependent on other people, the only sensible thing to do is to accept your situation and realise that you have got to be where you are and I've accepted that'. Her health has changed greatly since her admission two years ago. She is fully dependent on staff for bathing and requires assistance with going to the toilet and dressing.

Mrs G

Mrs G is 75 years old. She and Mr G were about to move into a smaller apartment when he suddenly passed away. As they were getting older, the garden and house repairs were becoming less of a leisure pursuit and more of a painful chore. They were talking about settling down in their new home and 'taking things easy'. Mrs G never expected 'anything like this to happen'. With the death of her husband, Mrs G's hopes and dreams of living together for another ten years vanished.

In the midst of a family crisis, her two sons were making simultaneous decisions about their father's funeral plans and Mrs G's living arrangement. Now that she had lost the company of her husband, they were concerned about what would happen to her.

The sons both agreed that she could not live on her own. They reassured each other how she would be 'better off' in a nursing home:

> My father passed away and something had to be done. She couldn't look after herself. She suffers from chronic arthritis and has difficulty getting up and down the stairs. She would have been lonely in the house and frightened of people calling in.

Besides, they were not in a position to look after their mother. The eldest son is a priest and 'I couldn't have her live with me'. The other son is 'always ill' and has a large family of five children to support. 'What other alternatives did we have?' he asked.

Mrs G was not pulled into the nursing home because of her health. The matron described Mrs G's health as 'excellent' and stated that her health is 'better' than most people her age. She requires no assistance from staff and 'often goes out for a walk'. It was her vulnerability as perceived by others that forced her to move. The decision to move into a nursing home was not as important to her as it was to her children. She never thought about it. Upset about her husband's death, she left her fate in the hands of her family. She would have preferred to live alone but 'they had already decided for me'. Even before her sons had approached Mrs G about living in a nursing home, they had already made arrangements for her admission. The eldest son used his influence to admit her to a Catholic nursing home. Mrs G moved in only three days after her husband's death.

Was she upset? 'No, what was I to do?'. In severe shock over losing her husband, she had little time to think about moving into a nursing home. What was more difficult for her at the time was accepting the loss of her beloved 'hubby'. The reality of living in a nursing home came much later. But by then it was too late for her 'to change things'.

Mrs G's house was sold and her furniture divided amongst the family. 'There was nothing else for me to do but to go peacefully'. She has 'settled down' and enjoys the attention she receives from the nursing home staff. Her sons even visit more regularly than when she lived at home. She 'now realises' how wise the move 'really was'. With all the 'crime out there', she figures she is 'safer in here'. But as I was leaving her room, she confessed that she would never have moved 'here if I hadn't lost him'.

Mrs H

Although for the large majority the decision to enter a nursing home is initiated by others, a few residents decide for themselves. Day (1985) has called these people 'planners' and Mrs H illustrates the decision making process that often characterises the planners' pathway into nursing homes.

Mrs H is 84 years old and has been widowed for the last six years. When her husband died her three children suggested that she move in with them. Instead, she decided to live in her home with student boarders, and received support from a distance from her children. They would 'drive her places' and occasionally 'did the odd things around the house'. Mrs H was 'healthy' and did 'things herself'. When she moved to the nursing home, she was able to bathe, dress, go to the toilet, and walk without any difficulty or assistance.

It was her decision to move into a nursing home. 'I suggested it to myself'. Unexpectedly, she announced to her family that she was going to move 'into one of those homes'. 'She never mentioned it before then'. Mrs H is a person 'who makes her own decisions'. Her children 'were not asked' to participate. 'It would not have mattered what we thought'. It was a 'surprise' to the family that she had made inquiries about moving into a nursing home.

But for Mrs H, this was not a sudden decision. She had been anticipating the move since her husband's death and for the past year, she was gauging 'when my time had arrived'. Her children had their own families. 'My daughter has four boys to rear and she did not have the space, my eldest son also has a large family and the other daughter lives in Western Australia'. Equally as important, she was not prepared to change her habits because of someone else's 'house rules'. She portrays herself as an independent person; she would not permit her children to see her 'any other way'.

And why postpone 'the inevitable outcome?' Mrs H was not prepared to wait until she was too old and ill. She thinks that too many old people leave the decision until a crisis forces the family to decide 'for us'. No, Mrs H decided she would make 'the decision for them'.

She 'really was not ill', but like many people of her age, she was suffering from arthritis. She was getting impatient with doing the housework and cooking. She had reached the point where 'life was not as enjoyable'. She did not want to become 'a trouble to others'. With this philosophical outlook, she 'went'.

Unlike the other patients, Mrs H selected the nursing home she liked. When I asked her daughter about the application details, I was told, 'you really have to ask Mother those questions, we knew nothing about it'. Mrs H was 'shopping' for a single room. She lodged several applications and three months later, she received a call informing her of a vacancy. She went out to 'inspect the home', and after a 'good chat with matron', she decided this was going to be her new 'place'.

Does she have any regrets? 'No, my word! It was my wish to get out of my home'. Her arthritis is worse since the move. She cannot imagine how she would have coped at home. Her 'people' could not offer her the care she receives from the nursing home staff. Besides, she told me, 'you cannot count on people to help you all the time'. There is a limit to everything isn't there Vic?'

Mrs H feels much happier since the move. She has new friends and her family 'gives me more time'. Like many widowed persons living alone, she was vulnerable to loneliness. Her children and neighbours never thought there was a need to offer help. People are now expressing some concern over her and she enjoys it. She continues to be socially active and freely goes out of the nursing home for walks. Often she can be found sitting in the park across from the home, talking to young children or enjoying 'a cig'. 'I have no worries about stopping here' for she chose her own station.

Mrs I

Much has been said and written about the sacrifices that families experience to meet the demands of the caregiving role (Fengler and Goodrich, 1979; Zanit, et al., 1980). In the case below, the strain that children experience when caring for an aged parent and its effect on the lives of their family members is discussed.

Mrs I is 92 years old and when her sister died, her two daughters were worried about 'leaving Mum on her own'. They decided to 'take turns in having her live with us'. As their older children had left the family home, they had 'plenty of space'. 'Everything was fine', until Mrs I's health 'began to fail'. She was no longer mobile. Mrs I often needed help to 'do the little things in life'.

Prior to moving into the nursing home, Mrs I was living with her eldest daughter, Pat, and had been alternating between the daughters' homes for the previous eight years. Afraid of leaving her mother alone, Pat seldom left the house. Mother had become 'a constant worry'. She was afraid she would discover that 'Mother had died in the bathtub and that I was the one who would find her'. Obsessed with such thoughts, Pat was constantly 'fussing over' her mother's welfare. 'I was frightened how I would find her each morning'. She often 'checked Mum's room' in the middle of the night. Pat's health was affected by her 'mothering' of Mrs I. She seldom slept at night and was easily agitated.

Her moods were upsetting the rest of the family. Her husband had just retired and was looking forward to enjoying life with his wife. Instead, he found his wife to be 'tied up with Mother'. Although Mrs I 'cleaned her own room', Pat spent a 'lot of time' taking 'Mother to the doctor', helping her with the medication and preparing 'special meals'. But most troublesome 'of all, was that she fussed over her'. She had 'given up' their social life. Each time they went out, she had to arrange for someone 'to look after mother'. Only when a 'babysitter' was found would Pat leave the house.

Fighting for his wife's attention, Pat's husband decided that 'something else had to be arranged'. He had discussed his frustrations with Pat's sister and she was also concerned about the situation. A family meeting was called and the question of putting her in a nursing home was raised. It was not an easy decision; many tears and emotions were displayed. They all loved Mrs I, but the family was not coping. They felt guilty about suggesting to their mother that she move into a nursing home. Had they failed as a family? Why were other families able to manage and not them? Were they too concerned about what could happen to Mrs I? Maybe it was their attitude that was creating the problem, Pat argued. No, the family replied, they had done 'all we could'. She was getting older and so were they. They agreed that 'it was the best thing to do'. The only problem was how 'to break the news to Mum'. They decided to 'scout for a place' and once they 'found a home we thought she would enjoy living in', they would show it to her. They also arranged for the doctor to have a 'chat with her'.

All of the arrangements were made by her two daughters. Mrs I did not choose the nursing home. 'No they chose it for me'. She was not upset about her family's decision. She knew that her children 'were acting out of concern for me'. Besides, she felt 'that things had gotten out of hand. They would not let me go to the toilet on my own; that is no good, is it?'

Mrs I feels that her life has improved since moving to the nursing home. She participates in all of the recreational activities; 'Yes, it is never dull here'. She has many friends at the nursing home and feels less lonely. Her family visits regularly. She feels the bond between them is much stronger. They no longer have to worry about her nor does she feel a burden to them. The chains of the dependency relationship have been broken. 'Everything has turned out for the best'.

Although she required no assistance from the nursing home staff with any of the activities of daily living upon admission, she had a fall and fractured her hip. She is slowly recovering but the accident has left her dependent on staff and a walking frame. She feels 'fortunate' to be living 'in a place' where she is 'looked after'. Her health is not 'going to get any better'.

Social selective process of entering nursing homes

Australian and overseas studies agree that up to one third of elderly patients living in nursing homes have levels of need that could be met in the community (Congress of the United States Congressional Budget Office, 1977; Doobov, 1980). These studies suggest that admission into nursing homes may be influenced by factors other than the health needs of the residents. For these patients, entrance into nursing homes is a socially selective process. The question of who enters nursing homes can only be fully understood by studying the circumstances under which people choose institutional care. Older people and their families differ in the ways they define need, and in their ability to mobilise informal and formal supports in the community or cope with a disability. Two issues emerge from such an analysis: (1) the recognition of a crisis situation (actual and potential—as planners see the latter and take action to avoid the crisis) and (2) the resources available to cope with the situation. The recognition variable is a determinant in the pathway course because for each person a situation will be perceived, evaluated and acted or not acted upon depending on how people define their coping resources. This may help to explain why there are many aged persons in the general population who require a high level of nursing home care but fail to make use of such services, while others with a lesser medical need end up in nursing homes.

Decision-makers

Utilisation of health services must be viewed not only as the result of macro-level processes[4], but also in terms of micro-level processes influencing individual decisions to seek services. In the gerontological literature, the family has been characterised as either a party that has failed to maintain the aged persons at home or assisted them to stay out of institutions. Andersen and Newman's (1973) 'enabling factors' reflect the important role the family can play in obtaining health services. The family is not a minor cast but leading actors in the admission history.

Families caring for an aged relative find themselves in a reversal of long-established dependencies: they are making decisions for their 'aged child'. Not surprisingly, the aged person is often a minor participant in the decision to seek nursing home care. When the 92 patients were asked 'how much of a say did you have in the decision to move in the nursing home?', more than half of the residents stated that they had 'very little' or 'no say at all'. A further 13 per cent mentioned that they felt they had 'some say', while only 34 per cent said they had 'much say'. Few patients had 'ever thought about ending up in a nursing home'. The family member will often inform them that 'they don't think you can manage' and suggest 'taking you to see the doctor'. Patients spoke about the family as a unified front; factions did exist but the disputes and disagreements were kept backstage.[5]

Who are the decision-makers? As shown in Figure 8.1, 49 per cent of the patients mentioned family members, usually a daughter or son, as the person who was most involved in the decision to enter a nursing home. Usually the family has been providing home care to the aged relative and finds the caregiving role too burdensome. They feel that they cannot look forward to a reduction in the daily needs of the older person. The demands of continuous care are creating a disruption in their lives. Hence, the caregivers' evaluation of whether they can manage with daily needs of the older person will do much to influence whether the nursing home path will be taken.

Figure 8.1   Person most involved in the decision to move into a home (percentage) (n = 92)

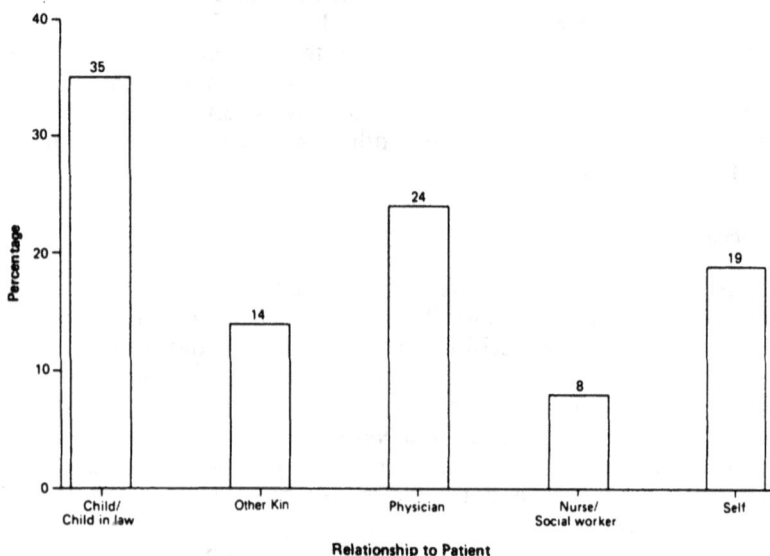

The decision will have involved some kind of discussion with family members other than the aged person. These discussions are held not only for the sake of seeking advice but for also reaching a unanimous decision and confirmation that the person can no longer cope in a community living arrangement. Once this is achieved, the decision to seek professional help is triggered. A medical diagnosis from a professional source is sought to legitimate the entire decision-making process. The aged person may be unaware of these discussions and participate as a third person only after an alienative coalition has been formed between the family and the physician or matrons.

The family will have set up the interview with the physician. The physician records the 'incriminating' evidence about how the family worries 'about mother', her increased forgetfulness, her failure to identify people or remember special occasions, the untidy room, the turned on taps and the resulting emotional strain all this imposes on the family. All of this 'data' is recorded prior to examining the patient. Under pressure from the family to act quickly and decisively, it is inevitable that the doctor's decision is partly influenced by the needs of his 'informants'. This establishes the family as the responsible party to whom information can be divulged, while identifying the aged person as the 'silent patient'. Goffman notes that the patient often feels betrayed by the family as a result of the three-party situation:

> ...upon arrival at the office the prepatient suddenly finds that he and his next-of-relation have not been accorded the same roles, and apparently that a prior understanding between the next-of-relation has been put in operation against him. The professional sees the prepatient alone, in the role of examiner and diagnostician, and then sees the next-of-relation alone, in the role of advisor, while carefully avoiding talking things over seriously with them both together. (1961:137–138)

The doctor may find that the family has already made the decision to institutionalise their aged relative prior to the consultation. He may be asked to play the role of supporting the decision and making the arrangement possible by signing the medical forms:

> I was looking after my mother and not coping at all. She wouldn't listen to anything I suggested so I called the doctor and he made it easier for us by suggesting that she move in a nursing home. We had suggested that she move into a nursing home but hearing him say it made us do something about it. And he looked after all the arrangements.

Although the doctor acts primarily as the family's agent, he has considerable influence in affecting the patient's perception of her situation. Not surprisingly, 24 per cent of the patients said that the doctor made the decision for them. The doctor's involvement is an important force in encouraging the elderly to recognise that they need help. He may find himself giving his patients a 'moral judgement' talk about how much of a burden she has become to her family:

> The doctor explained to me how I was worrying them. He had a little talk with me and he said it would be more sensible to move into a home because the girls would know I'd be well, there would always be somebody here. My granddaughter got the doctor to talk to me ... and he said I was not being fair to Margaret (the patient's daughter) who was working part-time and had two children to look after. And, he said, how was she going to cope with you in the house? What was she to do when she went to work during the day? She would have a nervous breakdown worrying about you! So I just said I would come if he really thought that was the best thing to do.

Patients will use this rhetoric to justify their placement:

> Why did I come here? Because my doctor told me that I had reached a
> certain age and that I would be less trouble to my family here.

For patients already in an institution, such as a hospital, the doctor
may arrange for a 'trans-institutional release', as the use of expensive
hospital resources have to be rationed and some other form of
custodial care is prescribed. Patients have no alternative but to
'follow the order':

> After the operation I went into a convalescent home, and the doctor
> suggested that it would be best if I go into a nursing home where I
> would receive all the attention I needed. I had to go somewhere; what
> was I to do? I could not return home and stay on my own.

Nurses and social workers, who were nominated by 8 per cent of
the patients as the person who was largely responsible for making the
decision, may be providing home help to the older person and
anticipating a decline in health or the failure of existing care
arrangement, suggest transferring patients to nursing homes. Both
social workers and nurses are members of a referral networks system,
and put people in contact with physicians and matrons.

Professional people can also be asked by the aged person to
provide guidance about care alternatives. Less than one-fifth of the
patients said that they decided to move into a nursing home, although
discussion with a family member or physician could have taken place.
Usually such aged persons, like Mrs H, do not want to become a
burden to others or have no family ties and seek the advice of
doctors, social workers or family members to help them with the
administrative details of entering an institution.

'Somewhere to live'

Eligibility for nursing homes benefits is defined in medical terms,
even though for some patients much of the basis for care is social.
Physicians are required to identify physical symptoms to legitimate
the need for 'social care'. Family members may assist in medicalising
the admission process to facilitate the institutionalisation of an aged
person. It lessens their guilt and the social stigma associated with
placing an aged relative into nursing homes because a medical
'excuse' has been 'found'. But how do patients who are not primarily
admitted because of a physical or mental impairment justify using
nursing home care?[6]

Factors other than health accounted for three-quarters of all
reasons cited by patients for moving into a nursing home. Less than a
quarter of residents mentioned a change in their health condition or a
specific health problem as the reason for moving out of their homes.
Yet no patient was admitted without health problems mentioned in

their medical chart. But if the medical file contained very little documentary space for the patient's social admission history, the patient's stories provided many sociological clues linking the admission to a specific personal history. This is not to say that references to health problems were not included in the patient's stories. Patients often talked about 'their backs giving up on us' or the crippling effects of arthritis. But these were 'en passant'. Health problems were not seen as the most important factor for 'ending up in a nursing home'. Health conditions might have been contributing a factor but it was not identified as the driving force steering the admission decision.

Twenty-four per cent of the sample said that they moved out of their homes to 'stop the family from worrying'. The caregivers are providing support at great personal sacrifices, and the help provided to the aged relative is interfering with other obligations. Relatives are 'running themselves down' trying to 'keep two homes'. Or 'J's responsible career and family' is receiving less of her attention because she is too 'busy helping me'. Unable to continue to provide support, the family suggests moving into a nursing home. The aged person typically is 'shocked' by the 'thought of moving'. Many have 'never thought about such a possibility'. But they may have been forced to enter the nursing home by their family and physician. When talking about the reasons for moving, a little less than one-fifth of the patients simply said, 'well my family put me here'. It was family members who drew the older persons's attention to their disabilities:

How I came to be here? The doctor and the family all got together and they said that I definitely could not look after myself. My grandson found this place. I did not know the place even existed. They said 'it is no good you living on your own; you can't carry the shopping with your bad back. So I said, 'oh well, I'll go' and took it in my stride.

People will not use services unless they perceive a need for them. For many older people, the complaint that 'something is wrong' comes from families. For this reason, patients may resent their families 'for ending up in a home'. It was not the aged person's choice. The real 'patient' usually is the family. It was to relieve their worries that 'I went'. But with time, they come to accept their family's point of view. 'I knew it wouldn't have been fair if I had not come; can't ruin her life because of mine'. Accepting that they need 'help', however, occurs only after they have become 'patients'. Residents often shift their stories of why they entered the nursing home, from portraying the move as voluntary when on the waiting list, to protraying the move as coerced by family immediately after entering the nursing home, and to finally accepting their 'fate' after having settled in the nursing home (Tobin and Lieberman, 1976).

As old age manifests itself, many come to believe that 'we can't manage', a story cited by 22 per cent of the patients. The major cue these people use in deciding to seek nursing home care is the disruption of their daily activities. The house has become too 'difficult to manage', the cooking and house cleaning 'too much of an effort' or the person may find it alarming that she can no longer hold a cup of tea without spilling it.

Perhaps frightened that a road accident could cripple them, they seldom go out. For many, this is an attempt 'to stay out of trouble'. But such measures may lead to depression, isolation, and the realisation that they 'are no longer the person they used to be'. Life is not going to get any better. What happens 'when you stop cooking meals for fear that you will forget to turn off the stove, when you stop going to the shop for fear that you will fall in the street, when you stop doing the things you once enjoyed because you think you cannot do them anymore?' Eventually, someone suggests moving into a nursing home because 'you are not eating properly, you are not doing anything with yourself, and people begin to worry about you'. They do not need to be told by others that they 'cannot go on living this way'. They may fight the idea of moving into a nursing home, but one thing is certain, they have lost any hope that they can still 'do' for themselves. 'You have given up on life; the nursing home is the only place that can cope with you'.

Children do try to lessen the burden of old age by helping parents cope with their disabilities and assisting them with the preparation of food, shopping and house repairs (See Chapter 5; also Callahan, et al., 1980; Kendig, Gibson, Rowland and Hemer, 1983). But faced with competing demands, families turn to formal agencies for 'relief' (Dobrof and Litwak, 1979; Schoor, 1980). The family may seek the help of community services until a more permanent care arrangement may be necessary. The older person feels that they are 'a burden' to their families. Frightened of the stories they heard about nursing homes, many wait until the family 'decides that it is time to go'.

A few will anticipate their dependency and make up their 'own mind to go'. Seven per cent of the sample mentioned 'planning ahead' as the most important reason for moving. These planners (Day, 1985) tend to be people who do not have much informal support and come to 'terms' with using nursing home care as a substitute for family support in the community. Others, like Miss E reported above, may wish to maintain their independence from their families. Her daughter says:

> You must understand my mother's character. She is a woman who treasures her independence. It was her decision to move. She made up her own mind and then told the family about coming to the nursing home. She did not want to be a burden to me or my children. She needed a special privacy, which she felt would have been difficult to achieve in a household of six but easier to obtain in a home of ninety strangers.

These planners see moving into a nursing home 'as being loyal' to their family. The reason for moving is simple: 'it is all wrapped up in one—I just didn't want to be a nuisance to my family'. Other qualitative studies have shown that older people feel that the cost of families caring for them at home is too high to risk in terms of autonomy for the aged person and preservation of good family relations (Carter, 1985).

Disruption of living arrangement, such as the death of a spouse or the illness of a caregiver, can force people out of the community and into nursing homes. A decision about whether the surviving aged parent will remain in their own home becomes critical at widowhood. Families feel that people who have been dependent on their spouses for social, financial or emotional support can not manage when the other partner has died. 'Why I got here? My troubles started when my husband died and my children did not want me to be on my own'. The older person is not 'trusted'. The family is distressed about the idea of something 'happening to mother'. 'What would happen to her if she fell and no one was there to help her? This suggests that the decision-making process contains an emotional component, and that decisions often arise in the context of a crisis.

'It's not bad, it's not good'

Whatever the reason for entering nursing homes, negative views are held by both the aged person and their relatives about nursing homes. Institutionalisation usually is seen as being the only alternative, rather than a desirable choice. The images aroused by the words 'nursing home' are particularly anxiety-ridden. When patients were asked to select the one word that best describes how they felt about moving into a nursing home, the most common words that described their emotional feelings were: helplessness, abandonment, horrified and resentful.

Taken by their relatives in the morning and then left alone at the nursing home, the elderly develop feelings of rejection and loneliness (Tobin and Lieberman, 1976). The nursing home contains no memories of the past, only a reminder that they have become one of many patients. Although many come to accept the nursing home 'as my home', a few never get over the shock of being 'cut off' from the community and confined to the walls of the nursing home.

Several of the case studies showed that family members are often disturbed about their decision, as other studies have also documented (Cath, 1972). They realise that an elderly person in a nursing home has few rights and dignities. Their relatives are forced to leave their homes, stripped of their familiar possessions and deprived of normal social life. Permission will have to be obtained from the matron for any activity that deviates from the 'house rules'. The aged residents are civilians with few rights, and the family realises that they have played a role in curbing the patient's former privileges.

The family feels guilty about their part in the admission history and desperately search for ways of 'making it up to her'. They will visit the patient daily and bring gifts. Soon they come to realise that 'their' decision 'was the right move'. They are no longer bound to the strains and demands of the caregiving relationship. 'It is convenient'. In some cases, institutionalisation can result in a strengthening of family ties or renewed closeness (Smith and Bengtson, 1979); this outcome was also evident for some of the people in the present study (Minichiello, in progress). As the nursing home staff is looking after the daily needs of the aged person, the family can concentrate on providing emotional support. For other patients, expressive bonds with family may be weakened, perhaps because of the family's guilt and sadness over the move, the older person's resentment of being pushed out of their home, or their inability to interact with one another in an institutional setting. Whatever the effects of institutionalisation on family relationships, a trap has been set up for both patient and family. Only death can free both parties. For the aged person, waiting to die is what they are living for; death provides an escape from a situation that has only one exit. For the family, the death of the aged relative frees them from their guilt feelings and allows them to reminisce about 'Mother' the way she was prior to admission. Mother will again become the person she was 'rather than like all those poor souls in there'.

9

Ageing, families and social change

HAL KENDIG

Throughout the book we have presented different views on the complex and varied ways in which older Australians act within personal support networks. Our findings have shown that their close ties typically are deep and enduring, extending well beyond the household and immediate family. These webs of social bonds are revealed in two-way interdependencies negotiated in many kinds of emotional and practical currencies. Of the many sources of diversity, the most powerful are the continuing impact of gender and family experiences over virtually the entire life course. Taken as a whole, the findings emphasise that old age is the culmination of long-term investments and orientations, and constitutes a changing position within the ongoing saga of intergenerational relationships.

In this final chapter we interpret more broadly the social forces which structure experiences of ageing. Our concern for older people today is widened by emphasising a further dimension of change: each new cohort of older people face very different social and economic climates in mid-life as well as in old age. Individual actions and backgrounds are bound up in complex interplays with social trends: individuals and their families actively create, as well as passively respond to, social change and ageing.

The chapter begins by demonstrating how the concepts of status and exchange consistently underlie the findings of earlier chapters. An assessment of recent social change then debunks—and attempts to explain—the persistent view that the social position of older people has deteriorated over the past generation. The next section casts an eye toward the less certain future, anticipating the social pressures of an ageing population, and identifying social choices being made today which will influence the well-being of the next cohort of older Australians. Finally, we emphasise that modest improvements of social policies could substantially increase older people's power in negotiating their place within families and other arenas for intergenerational relations. While most older people are well served by their small circles of informal relationships, constructive government policies are required to reinforce these bonds when they are available, and provide viable alternatives as the limits of supports are reached for particular individuals.

OVERVIEW OF FINDINGS

The basic tenet of our study is that ageing is as much a social construction as a biological fact. Social ageing involves a withdrawal, out of choice as well as necessity, from many of the statuses which structure life in middle age. Few older people remain in the workforce, even fewer have dependent children in their home, and most older women have become widowed. The vast majority have also experienced the loss of friends or siblings, and a small minority have made the further transition of moving into an institution. It is important to recognise, however, that many of these changes present opportunities as well as losses. For example, men freed from work demands potentially can develop the often suppressed emotional side of themselves, spouses can spend more time with each other, and widowhood can enable women to develop independent interests which were not possible during married life. The key questions are how people maintain social lives primarily within informal networks, and how they manage the varied transitions in old age.

An exchange perspective emphasises the ways in which waning resources and heightened needs shift the balance in interpersonal relationships (See Chapter 1). Low incomes—a product of fixed retirement ages and stringent government pensions—reduce capabilities to purchase transport and other services, to pursue recreational activities, and to purchase gifts which reinforce emotional ties. These can be the life blood of continued social contact and independence. Substantial amounts of interpersonal dependency are virtually forced on the 15 per cent of older people, most of whom are widows, who are severely disabled. Finally, ageism—the expectation of incompetance based on age alone—exacerbates the difficulties of all older people in relating to a diminishing pool of informal and formal ties. Old age thus can be a time of severely reduced 'exchange power', with consequent risks of dependency, and attenuation of bonds based on mutuality.

It is clear, however, that most older people successfully cope with the demands of age-related vulnerabilities and adjustments. Indeed, relatively few of them are demoralised, depressed, or have many expressive or instrumental needs unmet. Given adequate financial resources and good health, retirement generally involves little stress and is received as a positive opportunity (See Chapter 7). Widowhood typically is a devastating personal loss but again, given adequate resources, a satisfactory equilibrium is re-established with the passage of time. The minority who eventually enter a nursing home, however, usually are extremely vulnerable and become passive recipients of decisions made by family and professionals (See Chapter 8). Yet even in this difficult transition, many become reconciled to their position, and continue strong expressive links to relatives. Notwithstanding the imposition of substantial social constraints, the overall results demonstrate the considerable adaptive capacities of older people and the resiliency of their close bonds.

Informal support is typically drawn from a core of five to eight close bonds in addition to wider circles of acquaintances (See Chapter 3). As with other age groups, the vast majority of these relationships are mutually rewarding for both parties and are entirely expressive or social in nature. Various kin are especially likely to be confidants, and reinforce a sense of personal worth, while friends tend to predominate in providing acceptance and companionship (See Chapter 4). The findings reflect the long-term and deep attachments of some (but by no means all) close kin bonds, as compared to the mutuality and similarities characteristic of friendships. Those who are without spouses or descendents, however, generally are able to maintain alternative expressive bonds through siblings, more distant kin, and more complex friendships. The more general point is that expressive bonds often can be negotiated successfully even when personal resources are limited. The voluntary rather than obligatory nature of these ties accentuates the emotional rewards. Irrespective of the numbers or kinds of close ties, subjective well-being is enhanced when they meet more of the expressive dimensions.

Academic and popular preoccupation with the care of older people contrasts sharply with the high levels of independence among older people. When we take a balanced look at instrumental exchanges, it is clear that many older people—and most married couples—are more likely to be providing than receiving support; the contributions are wide ranging and extensive. Among capable older people, instrumental assistence is usually purchased, or is received as part of two-way interdependencies through informal bonds which remain basically expressive in nature. It is only among the severely disabled aged that we find high levels of instrumental dependencies, and these are met overwhelmingly by co-resident daughters and wives rather than the broader community or government services.

In contrast to the wide range of mutually rewarding expressive bonds, the provision of substantial amounts of unreciprocated care is socially assigned primarily to close female family members, and there are few viable alternatives. Even when this unacknowledged 'welfare sector' is available, the imbalance in the exchange can erode the relationship by demoralising the older recipient and stressing the family provider. In anticipating these adverse consequences, many older people are fiercely determined to resist overtures of assistance for as long as possible (See Chapter 6).

While this summary simplifies our findings, it is clear that family bonds—especially with a spouse and children—are the primary avenue for social integration in old age. As compared to the more limited commitments with friends and distant relatives, close family bonds involve lifelong attachments which structure complex patterns of intergenerational reciprocity (See Chapter 5). It is principally through family that we maintain meaningful and immediate connections to all generations in the life cycle; we look 'up' the lineage in anticipating our own old age, and 'down' to those who will replace us in the ongoing chain of life. Each generation of parents makes a major contribution to children in early and mid-life, and each generation of children in turn has the 'contingent risk' of providing instrumental support should a parent become dependent in old age. Women play a pivotal part in directly providing and receiving intergenerational support, and in the broader 'kin keeping' which nurtures the underlying emotional and obligatory bonds. A notable inequality in these arrangements is the divergence between the mid-life provision of intergenerational support and its receipt in old age, particularly for widowed and never-married women.

It is fitting to conclude this review by emphasising both common patterns and diversity. The basic core of the findings confirms the predominance of the modified extended family in advanced Western countries. The generations typically prefer to and do live apart, while maintaining close social and emotional ties; considerable amounts of instrumental support also can flow between households when necessary. But it would be premature to reject Parson's (1955) view of the nuclear family as the principal unit organising family life. Older couples generally do maintain high levels of independence, turning principally to their spouses in times of difficulty. Middle-aged children typically evince greater commitment to their own dependent children than to the care of a dependent parent. And both the middle and older generations have profound ambivalence over the legitimacy and limitations of providing large amounts of instrumental assistance, especially on a co-resident basis.

Such broad brushed theoretical conclusions obscure the great diversity and inequalities in ageing experiences. The various case studies graphically illustrate how a lifetime's accumulation of individual choices and social impositions are incorporated into the maintenance of viable relationships—or add to the limitations which cruelly prevent some people from meeting their basic needs. We have seen that marital status, for example, is one of the most powerful of the mid-life experiences influencing informal bonds in old age. While individuals may choose not to marry, or to disband a marriage, they do so within firm social constraints. For example, the 'decision' not to marry or have children may be attributable to the reduced opportunities imposed by war or depression, or the cultural assignment of women to care for their parents when they might prefer to begin families of their own. Moreover, whatever one's marital status, the social response—be it the approbation of divorce, the restricted expectations within traditional marriage, or the lack of deep interpersonal commitments outside of immediate family—further constrains individual 'choices' and relationships.

Of the many social constructions in the experience of ageing, gender has emerged as the most powerful in our study of the current generation of older people. On the one hand, we have seen that the lifelong conditioning of men has severely limited their abilities to forge strong expressive bonds. While married men may maintain ties to and through their wives, with ties continuing to others even in the event of widowhood, never-married men tend to be lifelong emotional isolates, and many divorced men have had their family bonds ruptured irreparably. On the other hand, women who came of age during the interwar period have led lives restricted largely to the private world of families and homes. And even here, such basic tasks as driving cars, or looking after the house or financial matters, have remained primarily within the control of their husbands. While both genders can be severely limited by these social expectations, it is women who are overwhelmingly left to negotiate old age on their own.

As compared to marital status and gender, social class has a less apparent effect on informal bonds in old age. The most intimate of family interactions show surprisingly little variation in terms of the social class of older people or their children. But if we widen our concern, we find that a more advantaged class background in mid-life increases older people's abilities to purchase transport and other services, thus maintaining social contact and meeting needs without burdening family; it enables them to make larger financial gifts to children; and it increases access to more desirable forms of residential care. Sons having higher status occupations provide substantially more aid to aged parents. Finally, the enhanced life chances of the middle and upper middle classes are associated with better health, longer life, and higher morale in old age.

All of these social constructions are of course dependent on social and economic conditions prevailing during individuals' lifetimes. In the following sections, we consider the likely impact of social change on ageing and family relations. To the extent that difficulties are social in origin, due to experiences in mid as well as late life, there remains the optimistic prospect that ageing experiences could be improved substantially.

SOCIAL CHANGE

Remarkably little is known about the impact of social change on older people.[1] One view is that modernisation increases the numbers of the aged while at the same time denying them a useful place in a technologically advanced economy—the result is said to be a devalued status and social abandonment (Cowgill and Holmes, 1972). According to Parsons (1955), traditional extended families have been broken apart by demands for an increasingly mobile and educated workforce. In the context of these broader changes, government has been said to be the only institution left to meet the shortfall of support, and has perhaps accelerated the trends by displacing family support (Glazer, 1971). These gloomy interpretations accord well with popular opinion, yet empirical confirmation of the modernisation hypothesis has been limited and contradictory. As Laslett (1984) has argued convincingly, it probably is time to move on from sweeping generalisations, based on idealised views of the past, or inappropriate comparisons between advanced and primitive societies. In this section, we assess more specifically the likely impact of but one generation of past social change on ageing in Australia.

Demographic trends appear to have had little impact in tipping the balance of intergenerational relations over the post-war years (See Chapter 2). The proportion of the population aged 60 or over has been rising only slowly, from 12.4 per cent in 1947 to 14.0 per cent in 1982. (Australian Bureau of Statistics, 1978, 1985.) Since the late 1960s, however, the pace of population ageing has accelerated, principally due to reduced levels of fertility and migration. The potential availability of family actually has been increasing as the current cohort of older people, whose marriage and childbearing prospects were reduced by depression and war, are being succeeded by those who formed the postwar marriage and baby boom (Rowland, 1984). Overall, there is very little evidence that demographic change, in itself, has eroded the position of older people over recent decades.

One of the most dramatic of the economic changes has been the sizeable reduction of workforce participation of older people, particularly over recent years (See Chapter 7). For example, approximately 80 per cent of men aged 60 to 64 were in employment from 1947 to 1966, as compared to 68 per cent in 1976 and 53 per cent in 1981. While the growing numbers of retirees forego the income and social benefits of employment, it is notable that few of them currently have any difficulty with retirement, and their decisions have been facilitated by the financial security provided by improved housing and pension arrangements. Home ownership and public tenancies among older people have increased appreciably over the post-war years (Kendig, 1984a,b). Since the early 1950s, the old age pension rose from a small supplement for a destitute third of the older population, to an indexed payment which provides most of the income for three-fourths of the aged population (Australian Bureau of Statistics, 1982a). The post-war years have also seen the emergence of the virtually free provision of most kinds of medical care for older pensioners of modest means (Sax, 1985). While these improvements may not have fully kept pace with general rises of affluence, the number of older people who are severely deprived financially has been sharply reduced.

It would be easy to overemphasise the impact of changing technology and spatial patterns on the dispersion of close kin. As compared to the United States, Australia has been experiencing considerably less migration between states or from rural to urban areas (Rowland, 1979). The vast majority of people continue to lead virtually their entire lives within their cities of birth, and retirement migration can reunite extended families which have moved apart. While suburbanisation has led many adult children to the increasingly distant urban fringe, most older people continue to live in middle suburbs served by adequate public transport. Moreover, the maintenance of social ties has been facilitated by the widespread availability of telephones; near universal car ownership among middle-aged children and friends; and more convenient and affordable air travel. While changing spatial patterns undoubtedly have attenuated some family ties, improved communication and transport clearly have increased the viability of the modified extended family.

It is against this social backdrop that we can begin to assess recent historical changes in ageing and family relationships. Although household arrangements are poor indicators of family relationships, Chapter 2 showed that multigenerational households have never been the norm in early 20th Century Australia, nor in earlier centuries in Europe. Among the immediate past generation of older Australians (the parents of our survey respondents), only a minority ever lived for a year or more with any of their adult children (Kendig, 1984c). In most instances, co-residency appeared to be occasioned by low income and housing shortages rather than a need for care. The post-war increase in the independent households of older people (Di Iullio, 1976) probably is explained primarily by rising incomes, which have enabled more of them to have the prefered 'intimacy at a distance' from children. In other words, declining co-residency would be viewed as an improvement by most older people.

There is little doubt, however, that family and employment

circumstances of the middle-aged women have made it increasingly difficult for them to provide extensive family care. Recent cohorts have had an increase in competing commitments to spouses and children (Rowland, 1984). Among women aged 45 to 54, census figures show that the proportions who had never married—primary carers of the aged in the past—declined from 13 per cent in 1947 to 4 per cent in 1981. The proportions who are separated or divorced, many of whom face the vulnerabilities of low income and single parenthood, rose from 5 per cent to 9 per cent. Most significant of all, workforce participation among married women in this age group rose dramatically, from 8 per cent to 50 per cent over this relatively brief period of history.

Our cross sectional analyses suggest that the primary impact of these changes would have been to increase the stresses of providing care rather than to reduce its availability. Women's greater responsibilities and opportunities outside the home have yet to be accompanied by much relaxation of social pressures to meet long-established expectations for family support. For example, many adult daughters provide substantial support to an aged parent while raising children or holding down full-time work, and a significant number leave employment in order to care for a parent. The fact remains, however, that full-time employment and providing continuous personal care are incompatible. Some of the costs of change would have emerged in reduced family support for older people.

Accompanying these broad social changes has been the marked development of public policy for older people. Government expenditure on the aged, at the national level alone, increased from 2.7 per cent of the overall economy in 1965–66, to 5.7 per cent in 1982–3 (Advisory Council on Intergovernmental Relations, 1983). Most of the expenditure has been on income support and medical care as discussed above. In addition, subsidies for nursing homes and other residential care increased rapidly in the 1960s, developing an industry which now serves approximately 6 per cent of older people (House of Representatives Standing Committee on Expenditure, 1982). The parallel development of community services has been relatively poorly funded (Brennan, 1982) but still served 7 per cent of the respondents in our survey in Sydney (See Chapter 5). Government clearly has taken on increased responsibility for the support of vulnerable older people.

It seems likely that the growing public contributions have served more to increase the total amount of support for older people than to meet reductions of family support. Families continue to shoulder the major responsibility in the care of disabled older people. Institutions disproportionately serve older people who are bereft of family support, and who would otherwise be neglected, while community services generally supplement and complement family support rather than replace it. The balance of family and public support certainly has shifted most notably in the areas of income security and personal care. This has increased alternatives to the joint-households which can erode family relationships. By relieving some of the pressures of family care, older people are better positioned to maintain expressive ties which are mutually enjoyable, and less tinged by the demoralising consequences of dependency.

One of the most difficult questions pertains to changes in the subjective quality of family relationships over time. The words of our respondents, as reported in Chapters 6 and 8, suggest that perceived difficulties in providing family support result more from the faster pace and multiple commitments of modern life, than from any attenuation of emotional bonds. It also is notable that some older people in the past also may have had substantial dissatisfaction with family life. Hutchinson (1954), whose findings arguably reflect the prevailing nostalgia and perceptions of academics as much as the older people at the time, selected the following quotation to illustrate the attitudes of older women in his Melbourne study conducted more than 30 years ago:

> Everything's fine now. My husband and I are quite independent in our own home. I wouldn't like to have to depend on my family, although I'm sure they would never see us in want. Its very different for parents when they are independent and well, and have a nice home for their children to come to. It's when they are sick and poor and a burden that children are inclined to be neglectful ... There's no home life today. Mothers work and are out all day ... Home life is pathetic today. This business of mothers putting their babies in creches while they go out to work is no good ... Older people wouldn't dare give advice today. The younger people have the money, and they think that's everything. Even the children today are headstrong, self willed, and independent. Years ago children would have never defied their parents. It's all because women are neglecting their homes (Hutchinson, 1954: 27–28).

It remains possible, of course, that intergenerational solidarity has been declining while the personal circumstances of older people have been improving. It seems equally or more likely that the idealised view of the past may emerge, in every generation, out of complex wish fulfilments (Nydegger, 1983), or the confusion of explaining life cycle related losses in terms of historical change (Cohler, 1983). Richards (1985) suggests that guilt and anxiety, induced by comparisons between the immediate stress of the moment and a nostalgic view of the past, are primary forces in reinforcing family commitments among younger people. With the notable exception of migration and women's rising workforce participation, the 'generational discontinuities', as reported in Chapter 6, may well result from the varying life pathways which would be taken by different generations irrespective of social change. The fact remains that marital and filial ties—for those who have them—provide considerable amounts of expressive support to older Australians today. While it seems unlikely that family relationships have deteriorated over the past generation, a reasonably complete understanding of social change and ageing in Australia must await later replication of current studies.

CHOICES AND PRESSURES IN THE FUTURE

The opportunities of older people in the years ahead will be influenced heavily by many social and economic changes which cannot be predicted.[2] Nonetheless, the future generations of older people and their children are already here: their cohort experiences, and trends in ageing, suggest some of the predictable forces which will impinge on the experience of ageing. An appreciation of likely contingencies in the future can assist in developing anticipatory action by individuals as well as governments. As we have shown throughout the book, life trajectories being set by people in mid-life today will have a major bearing on their old age in the future.

As the current population ages and the life span lengthens, the numbers of older people are expected to increase appreciably, from approximately two million in 1982 to more than three million in 2001. The ranks of the retired will be swelled further by the expected continuation of trends toward earlier retirement (Bureau of Labour Market Research, 1983), although the economic dependency is likely to be tempered by relative increases of home owners, superannuants, and couples having had two incomes in middle age. Considerable pressure also will be wrought by the doubling of the population aged 75 or over, especially since age-related disabilities do not appear to be declining along with mortality rates (Rice and Feldman, 1983). In addition to the increasing age diversity, the cultural context of ageing will be widened, as those born in non-English speaking countries increase from 10 to 20 per cent of the older population. Taken as a whole, the findings suggest an increasing distinction between comparatively younger and more capable people, who can make substantial contributions to community and family life, and the very old group who are at considerable risks of dependency on family or government.

The ability and willingness of the public sector to meet a share of the costs of population ageing is by no means clear. On the positive side, the aged will rise very little as a proportion of the total population over the next few decades, and not at all compared to the population in the current working ages (See Chapter 2). The levels of population ageing now found in Europe will not be reached in Australia until the baby boom generation reaches old age 30 years from now. On the negative side, economic stagnation could severely curtail the ability of the public sector to keep abreast of population ageing, let alone to make inroads into the substantial backlog of unmet needs. Judging from the past, economic conditions and political leadership will have a more telling effect than demographic ageing (Social Welfare Policy Secretariat, 1980): the dismal forecasts currently rampant in the press and government could well prove inaccurate should the country come to grips with its economic difficulties.

While public support may follow unpredictable cycles, there is little doubt that most older people will continue to look to spouses and children should they require instrumental support. The demographic outlook is for increasing proportions of people being married in early old age, but for many more widows in the advanced years. It would take a major reversal of life expectancy trends for many husbands to survive as long as their typically younger wives. As the cohort of people imbued with the values of traditional marriages passes, major questions arise concerning the continuation of the virtually unlimited commitment between older spouses. If childless couples become increasingly more common among the baby boom generation, equally important questions emerge regarding the limits of support, and alternatives to filial bonds.

The next few decades will see the emergence of the first generation of older people in which substantial numbers have been divorced in mid-life. Our findings on those who are now divorced show that it is one of the very few family conflicts which can dissolve intergenerational bonds, particularly for the men who are likely to live apart from children and not maintain strong independent bonds on their own. Even when people regain a spouse through remarriage—an option which now is effectively closed for many older women—the parental bond could be diffused among blood ties to children raised by former spouses, and new links to step-children may remain tenuous. It is likely that these major changes in marital patterns will shift the balance of family relationships further towards voluntaristic rather than obligatory bonds. Offsetting these disruptions may be the emergence of a more accepting attitude towards divorce, with new mechanisms for re-integration of family ties.

The development of a full range of living skills, particularly by the many older women who will be living without spouses, could assist in ameliorating the consequences of marital disruption. The next cohort of older women is likely to have many more car drivers among them (Morris, 1981), a trend which may offset some of the disadvantages of ageing in increasingly decentralised suburbs. The more fundamental points are that, for the first time in history, most of the middle years of older women will have been spent in full-time employment and, with the contracting period of childrearing, without children in the home. The implications for self-confidence and integration outside the home, skills in dealing with financial and bureaucratic matters, and power within families—particularly for the middle class women who are leading the way—are likely to be far reaching. But only with the passage of the baby boom generation into old age will there be many older women who will be highly educated, or have experienced many years of independent living earlier in life. It is also notable that this generation has been accustomed to forming group households in young adulthood, and may be more willing to return to these arrangements should they become single in old age.

The demographic potential for filial ties is likely to increase for older people in the future, as the parents of the baby boom reach old age over the next decades, and then declines somewhat as the children of the 1950s themselves reach old age next century (See Chapter 2). If one takes the perspective of a middle-aged child, however, the demands for care of an aged parent are likely to increase as more parents and parents-in-law live to an extended old age. The positive side of the future is that there will be an unprecedented availability of capable older people to provide support to middle-aged children in times of crises, and maintain bonds that provide a sense of family continuity and identity for grandchildren and great-grandchildren. Indeed, the increasing numbers of four and even five generation families will widen opportunities for new forms of family inderdependencies.

There are mixed prospects for the provision of substantial instrumental support by adult children. On the one hand, current trends toward earlier child-launching and retirement will increase the number of adult children who do not have competing family and employment responsibilities. Among the current generation of disabled older people in the community, 10 per cent of their children are themselves aged 60 or over, and the future may well see more support provided by one to another generation of older people. If the current actions of the middle classes can be taken as an indication of social trends, more sons may be providing support to aged parents in the future (See Chapter 5). There may well be a decrease, however, in the willingness of middle-aged daughters to leave employment in order to care for an aged parent. While workforce participation of middle-aged women has been rising only slowly in recent years, substantially more of them will have worked throughout their adult lives (McDonald, 1983), and may be as committed as their husbands to the economic and psychological rewards of employment.

The conversion of potential to actual family support will depend primarily on prevailing social attitudes, as interpreted by individual families. A dominant theme in the literature is that family relationships are becoming increasingly voluntary rather than obligatory, and expressive rather than instrumental (Hagestad, 1981). The next generation of aged parents and adult children probably will be more aware and demanding of institutional and community services. But our research, albeit on the present generation, found that the complex attachments between parents and children usually are resilient and enduring. If it comes to the acid test, the Hobson's 'choice' between family support or neglect, it seems likely that many children generally will continue to provide high levels of support even if the personal costs are substantial. The important caution to this conclusion is that averages can be misleading, and it is likely that many older people in the future—as in the present—will not have significant family support. Even when family are available in demographic terms, a wide variety of personal and social circumstances can intervene in the provision of care (Day, 1985).

A major issue for the future concerns older people's abilities to draw on their increasing assets in order to maintain independence and negotiate care. Rising economic resources should enable more older people to maintain their own households, and make more use of paid-help with household tasks and transport. Moreover, recent years have witnessed the attraction of the middle classes to the burgeoning retirement home industry, a care option which our survey found was generally preferred over living with children. If the stated preferences of a small sample of people currently in middle age can be taken as a guide, retirement homes will be preferred over any other context of care (Carter, 1985). Retirement homes potentially can enable older people to avoid heavy instrumental dependency on children, by drawing on their often substantial assets rather than leaving them as inheritances. Annuity programs, by which older people receive current income rather than leave their assets on death, provide another ˝means by which to realign the balance between family support and inheritance. If family relationships become more voluntary, older people also may directly negotiate support by offering inheritances as explicit inducements for care (Sussman, 1976). Whatever the possible avenues, most older people have financial resources which potentially could be translated into substantial instrumental support.

There also are prospects for greater interpersonal skills among older people in the future. Earlier retirement, higher incomes, and better education will increase the numbers of socially capable people who have extensive ties, particularly with age peers. Age concentrated or segregated living—in home units, retirement homes, and public housing—lessens the potential for intergenerational relations. But it also enables older people to develop their own social worlds in which to keep ageism at bay, nurture friendships with age peers, and construct new expectations for later life (Hochschild, 1973). These possibilities are likely to be enhanced for the large baby boom cohort, which will have had a life-long impact in pressing their particular orientations on society at large. By then, one can hope that social attitudes will have adjusted to the historically new reality of old age as a long and normal stage of life.

In summary, a number of conflicting trends stymie attempts to arrive at any single judgement about the social position of older people in the future. In overall terms, the growth in the number of disabled older widows, and possible attenuation of family support, may be offset by the increasing personal skills and financial resources of older people. Whatever one's views may be on the overall changes, the most important point is that diversity among older people is virtually certain to increase. The obvious consequence is that a wider range of social responses to ageing will be required in the future.

PUBLIC POLICY

The actions of government are arguably the most powerful of the collective means of shaping the experience of ageing. While a full analysis of our research on ageing and public policy is being published separately (Kendig and McCallum, 1986a forthcoming), it is important to emphasise that numerous policies can directly influence the resources and vulnerabilities of older people. A wide range of public actions is required to respond appropriately to the increasing diversity of older people. There is no necessary dichotomy between informal and formal support: effective policies serve primarily to reinforce rather than supplant family relationships.

One of the most neglected topics is the potential for government to counteract the negative stereotypes which undermine the exchange power of 'the' aged. In addition to advocacy for the minority who are dependent, the newly established Commissions and Offices on Ageing can play a major part in increasing public awareness of the independence and contributions of most older people. The development of volunteer programs for older people, such as those now operating in Canada and the United States, are important in their own right and can have a powerful symbolic impact. The misleading belief in inevitable ageing declines can also be confronted directly through preventative health programs and rehabilitation services. Self-care is most accurately viewed as a lifelong process in which many of the most substantial returns are received in the advanced years.

Adequate income support probably is the most important way for policy to increase the independence and choice of older people. Current economic policies impacting on younger people—most notably their employment opportunities, superannuation benefits and access to home ownership—will set the base on which income support policies will be developed next century. Mandatory retirement ages, combined with harsh means tests and tax rates, currently force a withdrawal from employment. While the options for income support will be determined largely by prevailing financial and political circumstances, the increasing economic diversity among older people reinforces the importance of providing more public support to those who lack sufficient private means. It also will be important to recognise that many among the next generation of older people will have had relatively favourable lifetime economic opportunities, with their accumulated resources carrying over into old age. Taxation of capital received through inheritances, and the development of government sponsored annuity programs, provide both collective and individual means for older people to finance more of their own support.

While only a minority of older people ever enter an institution for an extended period of time, demographic change alone will increase the demand for residential care appreciably over the coming decades (See Chapter 2). The current freeze on funding increases for nursing homes, without commensurate increases in other residential and community services, is devolving even more of the already substantial costs of care, from government to families and older people themselves. For many older people—most notably the quarter of very old women today who have never had children—there simply are no viable alternatives to institutional care. Others have difficulties far too intense to be cared for in the community. Desirable initiatives include the development of an improved range and quality of residential facilities. Institutional care also requires close co-ordination with family members, providing periodic respite care for older people receiving support in the community, assisting with moves back to the community, and facilitating ongoing expressive and social ties during and after admission. Vulnerable older residents require services which work with available family in maximising choice and a sense of personal dignity.

The majority of disabled older people are in the community, and only a small minority of them currently receive any services. The explanation lies primarily in the remarkably low levels of resources committed to them. Increased flexibility as well as funding would enable services to better complement family support when it is available, and provide alternatives when appropriate (Kendig, 1986b, forthcoming). Most current services are oriented towards disabled people living alone, and do little to assist the co-resident carers who currently provide the main alternative to institutionalisation. In many instances, support to family carers is more appropriate and effective than directly serving the older person. The improvement and extension of community services would involve very high returns in the choices and quality of life of older people and their families.

Policies are intertwined with family support in a number of ways. While income support is clearly established as a public responsibility, much of the wealth preserved by pension and taxation policies is received in tax free inheritances by beneficiaries: one of the consequences is that inequalities of wealth between lineages are preserved and possibly increased. With the rationale of being a basic health service, nursing homes receive substantial funding for providing intense and specialised support which is considered to be beyond the capabilities of self- and family-care. Community care is the area where policy implicitly assumes that families should carry the primary load. Notwithstanding the rhetoric of politicians, care of older people outside of institutions has yet to be accepted as anything more than a supplementary and minor responsibility of government. The result is a massive but hidden set of social inequalities, with the consequences falling most heavily on women—especially those who have never married or remained childless. Only women are at high risk of bearing the brunt of providing care in mid-life, thus limiting their independence and social advancement, and of being left without community support in old age.

The development of better public policy for older people will require collective action by a number of interest groups. Individuals in need, and those who care for them, are poorly positioned to take any concerted political action. Effective representation will require the inclusion of older people in the concerns of a variety of organisations: unions can act for retired as well as current workers; older women and their carers warrant prominent recognition by the women's movement; and the interests of disabled older people surely deserve close consideration in organisations of capable older activists. The recent mobilisation against the assets test on the pension, with its consequent reduction of the government's electoral strength, is a topical example of the potential political pressure to be applied by older people. The most persuasive argument, however, is that the social position of older people affects virtually everybody, either indirectly through close personal ties, or more directly when the middle-aged eventually become old themselves.

CONCLUSION

Our research has found that most older people are active in strong informal networks through which they provide, as well as receive, a wide range of expressive and instrumental support. While friends and more distant kin figure prominently in many ways, only spouses and daughters are likely to evince the depth of commitment required to provide substantial and unreciprocated aid. Informal bonds in old age evolve out of relationships and living patterns established in mid-life or earlier, with strongly divergent patterns emerging out of gender conditioning, marital experiences and class-based life chances. Ageing and family relationships change over time but there is little basis to suggest that isolation or abandonment have been increasing or will increase in the future. The fact remains, however, that substantial numbers of older people face harsh social circumstances which severely constrain their ability to live satisfactory and full lives. We are keenly aware of the need for further research on the social relationships of older Australians. The circumstances of particular groups—most notably ethnic minorities, Aboriginals, and those suffering from dementia—were beyond the scope of this book but are high priorities for identifying the social context of ageing. Understanding intergenerational relations will require research on ageing from the perspective of younger as well as older people. It will be important to develop studies wich encompass the intertwined fates of several or more family members, and the ebb and flow of their relationships, as the individuals age and historical circumstances change. A range of more applied studies is required to identify the effectiveness of various services and other strategies to provide care. At the same time, there is substantial scope for theoretical work which further develops the conceptual dimensions to findings already at hand.

In conclusion, age is one of the basic divisions in Australian society, and ageing over the entire life course is inextricably bound up with gender, family, and class relations. Of our many research findings, two are particularly worthy of emphasis. First, our evidence clearly contradicts the harmful stereotype of older people as being incapable, dependent, and isolated. Second, the diversity among older people requires attitudes and policies which are sensitive to individuals' preferences and family circumstances. Full recognition of these facts will be essential in demystifying ageing and constructively responding to population ageing in the decades ahead.

Appendix 1

Methodology of the 1981 Survey of the Aged in Sydney

GINA ROACH

The basic outline of the 1981 Survey of the Aged in Sydney was presented in Chapter 1, and the network generating approach was outlined in Chapter 3. In this Appendix, we provide further information on the following aspects of the survey methodology: the interview schedule, sampling and response rates, samples and sample weights, and analytical techniques and measures. More detailed reports are available on the interviewing experience (Gibson and Aitkenhead, 1983) and fieldwork approach and sampling strategy (Rowland, Kendig and Jones, 1984).

Given the virtual absence of any previous survey research on older Australians, our survey had two purposes: first, to establish basic population estimates on the dimensions of social ageing and use of services; and second, to provide information from which to test a number of specific hypotheses on the nature of informal support networks. Limited resources prohibited us from considering a national survey, or extending the sample to a rural as well as an urban area.

The survey was conducted in Sydney from October through December 1981, and a total of 1050 personal interviews with people aged 60 or over were taken. Age 60 was considered an appropriate cut-off point, as it is the pensionable age for women and war veterans, and is important in the timing of retirement. Sydney was chosen primarily because of the size of its aged population—422 000 aged 60 years or over in 1981—and its proximity to Canberra. No more than one interview per dwelling was carried out, to avoid duplication of information likely to be provided by interviewing more than one older person from the same household.

The field force consisted of 30 interviewers, most of whom were

186

women between the ages of 25 and 50 years. Pamela Manley served as fieldwork supervisor, supported by Project staff, and a fieldwork base was made available by the Sample Survey Unit at Sydney University. Strategies adopted to increase quality included three days of training, the use of an area supervisor for every six interviewers, telephone audits, and field and office editing of completed schedules on a daily basis. Questionnaires were again audited during coding.

Interview schedule

The interview schedule was developed over a period of six months during 1981, in conjunction with analysis of existing data, assessment of schedules and questionnaires used in previous studies, and review of Australian and overseas literature. Sections of the questionnaire were developed and tested in the field, on a rolling basis, throughout this period. A full pilot survey of 34 interviews was undertaken prior to development of the final schedule, using field procedures planned for the main survey.

The schedule consisted of primarily structured, precoded questions, interspersed with open ended questions, and a few batteries of questions. While the duration of the interviews varied widely, the average was nearly 90 minutes. Interviewer observations report that 79 per cent of respondents showed no evidence of fatigue, 16 per cent showed 'just a little' and only 5 per cent 'somewhat' or 'a lot' (Gibson and Aitkenhead, 1983). Interviewers' reports of confusion among respondents were equally rare: 83 per cent none; 10 per cent 'a little'; 4 per cent 'some' and 2 per cent, 'definitely, yes'. Incidence of tiring or confusion increased appreciably with age, but still remained relatively low. The main difficulty in tiring was among interviewers, who exerted considerable effort in encouraging respondents to limit their responses to the set format. An indication of acceptability to the respondents was that 88 per cent agreed to have their names recorded for a possible second interview.

Respondents whom the interviewer determined as having difficulty in completing a full schedule, because of physical frailty or communication difficulties, or who were uncooperative, were administered a summary stream of questions limited to essential factual information. In situations where the respondent could not be interviewed personally, even with a summary schedule, because of language difficulties or health problems, a proxy summary interview was attempted with a member of the respondent's immediate family. Summary interviews accounted for 125 out of the 1050 completed interviews, and the average length of a summary interview was 48 minutes (Gibson and Aitkenhead, 1984).

Topic areas

While the design of the schedule reflected the main focus of the survey—identifying and illuminating networks of personal ties and exchange—additional topics included family structure, social inter-action, morale and satisfaction with relationships, health, housing, economic circumstances and retirement. The format of the schedule also provided for differences in individual circumstances of respon-dents. Certain core questions were asked of all respondents, while other questions were limited to appropriate sub-groups, such as the recently widowed and the formerly employed. Subsets of questions on various topics—family circumstances at an early age, care of respondent's parents in old age, knowledge of services, attitudes towards family and care, and daily activities—were less central to the major research questions and were asked randomly of half the res-pondents in each case. This use of sub-samples allowed for a diversity of topics, while not unreasonably extending the duration of the interview.

Matrix

In order to record membership of the networks of the respondent, a matrix was developed, and located in the front of the questionnaire. This matrix, in conjunction with key questions throughout the sche-dule, identified the persons and agencies of importance to each respondent. It consisted of a row of information, as outlined below, on each individual mentioned.

Persons came into the matrix in two ways. Adult co-residents and respondent's children were included in the initial stages of the questionnaire, irrespective of whether or not they were found later to be involved in informal exchange; this made it possible to analyse the characteristics of children who were not involved with their parents, in terms of our various support measures. Other persons, whether kin or non-kin, were added into the matrix as they appeared in questions tapping support to or from the respondent. These questions usually asked the respondent to indicate who were the particular people who performed a function, or received support. Specific examples of these questions include: 'Who mainly looked after you when you were ill?' and 'Which person or organisation do you think would help if you were ill in bed for a week?'

At the time of incorporation into the matrix, each person was assigned an individual person number, by which they could be identified in any subsequent questions. Information was collected not only on the relationship of the person to the respondent, but also the person's age, gender, marital status, location, workforce participa-tion and frequency of contact with the respondent. Additional data on personal contact, contact by letter and telephone, and number of children was also collected for respondent's children; information on children's occupations were recorded elsewhere in the questionnaire. Married persons in the matrix were linked by separate identification numbers. In these various ways, characteristics of these significant persons are made available for analysis.

Thus, if a respondent's son, who was already recorded in the matrix from the initial stages of the schedule, also provided care when the respondent was ill, that son's person number would be recorded in answer to the question on care. This person number could then be transformed into data already collected on the characteristics of the son—his age, marital status and so on—to provide an extra dimension in understanding the provision of such care.

Network-generating questions

As previously mentioned, the matrix was the principal source of information on exchanges of support of different kinds. The questions which generated networks covered current expressive support, current and past instrumental support, and potential instrumental support.

The expressive network, as described in Chapter 4, was calculated from four dimensions: confiding, acceptance, reassurance of worth and common interests. Although the vast majority of respondents had no difficulty with these questions, a small number of people insisted on giving 'global' answers ('I am close to all my family equally'), rather than specifying up to six individuals for each item. Respondents who had already included a large number of people in their networks occasionally appeared reluctant to add more of them in the last of the expressive support questions.

The instrumental network covered questions on many tasks: meals preparation, housekeeping, shopping and errands, transport and personal care (all over the last month); care during illness and after institutionalisation (over the previous six months); and help with gardening and house repairs (over the last year). Information on who performed these tasks was elicited by asking the respondent which person or organisation did most or some of the task. This approach avoided the more threatening question of 'who helps you', which could introduce biases due to quite unwelcome connotations of dependency. Thus, a respondent could answer that he or she performed the task most of the time, while also identifying another person who performed the task some of the time.

While the questions on expressive support were non-directional, the instrumental topics had parallel questions on respondent's contributions: for example 'in the last six months have you looked after anyone who was ill in bed?'. Other questions were asked about current childminding by the respondent, and past financial contributions to adult children.

Additional questions explored potential instrumental support (which person or organisation do you think would help if you were ill in bed for a week, ... for a month?) and those living alone were asked 'if you were not up and about for a few days, who would be most likely to notice and call on you?' The respondent was also asked to indicate to whom they had given gifts over the last year. With regards to financial matters all respondents were asked: 'Who do you think would help if you needed financial advice?' and 'Are there people you could rely on if you needed financial help?'.

The results of our network analyses obviously depend heavily on the scope of the questions which identify significant others. Overall, the wide range of these areas of support—having different require-ments on the providers in terms of commitment, emotional closeness and gender skills—suggests that most of the important areas of support were covered. Some important exceptions, however, are worth noting. First, Day's (1985) follow up qualitative interviews found that grandchildren often were very important to the respon-dents, although relatively few were included in the expressive networks: those who were identified emerged largely through the reassurance of worth questions. Second, with the exception of the question on 'Who would notice and come to help if you were not up and about?', there were no questions which focused on the typically modest kinds of instrumental support most easily provided by neighbours. Third, the lack of questions on informal sources of information on community activities and other matters of special interest to older people—which might be expected to involve friends (Litwak, 1985)—also were not tapped. Finally, no questions were asked about relationships which had negative rather than positive consequences for the respondents, although we expect that these topics would be very difficult to pursue in a relatively brief and structured questionnaire.

A second concern pertains to the reliability of the network measures. The limited evidence from Day's (1985) follow up of 23 respondents six months later, and Carter's (1985) further follow up of some of these same respondents and their families a year later, suggests that the core networks identified by our reasonably stringent measures are relatively stable over time (See Appendix 2). There also seemed to be a good deal of correspondence in the relationships as perceived by the older respondents in Day's study, and the relatives in Carter's study, notwithstanding the time difference. All of these questions are well worth pursuing in further methodological work.

SAMPLING AND RESPONSE RATES

The sampling aimed to identify a representative group of older individuals residing in private housing in the Sydney urban area. This excluded the 8 per cent of persons aged 60 or over living in various kinds of non-private accommodation: institutions (including hostels, nursing homes and hospitals) and boarding and rooming houses. A decision was made to over-sample those aged 75 or over, thus increasing the otherwise small numbers of people who are disabled, widowed, and living with children. This meant that there were sufficient of these rarer cases to permit analysis, and suitable weighting procedures allowed us to correct for this stratification when making population estimates.

A sampling frame was developed from data from the 1976 Census Collection District Summary Files. From this data, 30 census subdivisions were selected, and from each of these subdivisions, two collection districts. The development of the final sample involved two stages—the listing of dwellings in the collection districts and the screening for age of occupants, of a set of dwellings randomly selected from this list. This sampling was designed to give an equal probability of selection to each of the 849 000 private dwellings in Sydney. The census collection districts chosen were neighbouring pairs, which enabled travel costs to be limited, but minimised any potential clustering effects for population estimates. In all, 17 000 dwellings were listed, and of those, 9000 were screened, by means of doorknocking and 'mailback' cards. Full details of sampling and selection procedures can be found in Rowland, Kendig and Jones (1984) and Kendig, Gibson, Rowland and Hemer (1983).

As already noted, the numbers of interviews obtained with very old people were increased by stratifying the sample by age, with the oldest stratum having the highest probability of selection. After initial dwelling selection, 25 per cent of persons aged 60 to 64 were chosen for interview, and 50 per cent of those aged 65 to 74. For those who were aged 75 and over, and who also were the only aged person in their household, the probability of selection was 100 per cent; 50 per cent of this same age group were chosen for interview if they lived with one or more other aged persons.

The 1050 interviews finally obtained represent 75 per cent of persons contacted again after screening, and 69 per cent of the total number of persons selected for interview. Non-contacts, failure to answer the door when the interviewer returned, and broken appointments, accounted for the difference between these two figures, and indicated that only a small number of later non-contacts were implicit refusals. The overall response rate, obtained by assuming that the aged were proportionately represented in dwellings where there were refusals or non-contacts at screening, was estimated at 67 per cent. For those who refused interview, 54 per cent did not state a reason, or the reason was not collected. Approximately 25 per cent were attributed to respondent's state of health; other common reasons were 'not interested' and 'too busy'. Twenty-three refusals were due to lack of co-operation on the part of a relative, or the inability of a potential respondent to respond to the request, because of deafness, dumbness or confusion.

SAMPLES AND SAMPLE WEIGHTS

The final sample consisted of an unweighted number of 1050 interviews, across the various age strata. The potential for sampling error was introduced through the small proportion (0.3 per cent) of persons aged 60 or over in private dwellings in Sydney who were sampled for the survey. For the total sample of 1050 this could be expected to be slight; smaller sub-samples from the full survey might be affected to a greater extent. (For detailed estimation of the effects of this error on smaller samples, see Kendig, Gibson, Rowland and Hemer (1983) Appendix 2.) Principal sources of non-sampling error were the approximately 30 per cent of individuals who refused interview or could not be contacted, and the smaller number who, during interview, did not answer various questions.

While the extent and effect of these sampling and non-sampling errors is often difficult to estimate, a comparison of the weighted data from the survey with 1981 Census data showed a close correspondence with basic demographic characteristics, such as age, sex and

Table A1.1   Survey and census findings on the characteristics of non-institutionalised persons aged 60 or over, Sydney 1981

	Survey			Census[b]
	Unweighted[a] network sample (%)	Unweighted total sample (%)	Weighted total sample (%)	
Age distribution				
60–64	17.2	16.6	32.2	31.2
65–74	46.6	45.0	43.8	46.1
75+	36.2	38.4	23.9	22.7
Sex				
Male	36.0	35.8	38.5	42.6
Female	64.0	64.2	61.5	57.4
Living arrangements				
Alone	33.9	32.7	24.7	23.7
With spouse	48.7	47.0	56.9	54.2
With others	17.4	20.4	18.3	22.1
Total number of cases	904	1050	1050	421890

Notes: (a) As used in Chapters 3 and 4
       (b) Figures for age distribution and sex from 1981 Census; figures for living arrangement from 1976 Census

living arrangement, for the total non-institutionalised population aged 60 or over. Taking into account small sampling variations, the weighted or adjusted sample only slightly underenumerated men, and those older people living with others besides a spouse. This comparison is set out in more detail in Table A1.1.

Table A1.1 also illustrates some of the contrasts which occur with the data in an unadjusted form, that is without any weighting applied. Both the unadjusted total sample, and the unadjusted network sample used in Chapters 3 and 4, showed an under enumeration of those in the 60 to 64 age group, compared with the weighted sample, while the reverse was true for those aged over 75. Similarly, both unadjusted samples gave higher numbers of those older people who live alone, and smaller numbers of those living with a spouse. The unweighted network sample also contained a lower proportion of those living with others, most probably due to the exclusion of summary questionnaires. While the application of sample weights changes the percentages and numbers, the differences are small and do not have any bearing on the direction of the findings.

ANALYTICAL TECHNIQUES AND MEASURES

Many of the measures referred to in previous chapters required the use of the matrix and collected characteristics of matrix members. A brief outline of these measures will serve to illustrate further the importance of the matrix for this survey.

Calculations of network size, whether in overall, expressive or instrumental terms, involved scanning across the appropriate component areas previously mentioned, and counting the number of different matrix members who appeared in any of the areas, by the use of the already assigned person numbers. As each matrix member could appear in a number of different areas of support concurrently, only the first mentioned occurrence of each member's person number was counted, to avoid overenumeration of total numbers. Thus, network size measures the number of individuals providing or receiving support, rather than the amount of times from any source that such support is provided.

In calculating overall network size, and the size of the instrumental network, areas of support from the respondent were included. Overall network size also encompassed the questions on potential support, and financial advice although these components were excluded from specific instrumental and expressive analyses.

A measurement of homophily, developed in Chapter 3, was derived from the characteristics of network members as identified in the matrix. Again, after scanning across support areas, the relevant network members' age, gender and marital status were matched with those characteristics of the respondent. The extent of homophily was determined for each dyadic relationship with network members, as well as for a respondent's network as a whole. For example, homophily for the network was shown by the percentage of network members who were the same gender, age cohort or marital status as the respondents.

The multiplexity measure, also discussed in Chapter 3, was based on a count of the number of support areas in which each matrix member gave to or received support from the respondent. Again, the score was derived by first scanning across areas of support for each individual separately, and assigning a score each time that individual appeared in an area. Non-directional areas of support from the expressive network were assigned a score of '2' towards the total individual multiplexity score (emotional closeness, personal acceptance and common interests) whereas all other areas, including support from as well as to the respondent, scored '1' for each area. After determining each network member's score, ranging from a '1' to a possible '20', a mean multiplexity score was calculated for respondent's entire network. This was done by summing individual scores for all network members and dividing the total by the number of network members.

The construction of the network typology presented in Chapter 3 was based on measures of overall network size and multiplexity (discussed above). Initial analysis of individual multiplexity scores had determined a mean score for spouses of four, and for other network members, a mean score of three. The percentage of the respondents' network who scored at or above this mean multiplexity score was then calculated. Both the percentage mean multiplexity and network size exhibited a wide variation, allowing the formation of a cross-tabulation with a large number of rows and columns (11 × 11). In each case the middle row/column included the median values. Cases were then placed into one of the five named types or the residual area. This was done by allocating cells from each of the four corner zones plus the central area, in such a way as to approximate the stylised diagram shown in Figure 3.3; those cells unallocated formed the residual area.

For this survey, data on current or (for the retired) former occupations was collected for the respondent, spouse, adult children, any other co-residents and spouses of married daughters. Each occupation was coded into appropriate three digit code from the 1971 Census classification (Australian Bureau of Statistics, 1971). These codes were further coded into a 16 point scale (from Broom and Jones, 1969), reflecting high to low prestige rating. For respondents and spouses who were or had been employed, the occupational status of the family unit was determined to be the higher score of the two, from this scale; a similar measure was developed for married daughters. The multivariate analysis in Chapter 7 used this sixteen-point scale, while cross-tabular analysis in other chapters used three hierarchically ordered categories, termed professional or managerial, clerical or skilled and semi or unskilled. The first category took in upper and lower professionals, graziers, managers, self-employed shop proprietors, and other farmers; the second category, clerical and related workers, armed services and police, and craftsmen and foremen; while the third category included shop assistants, process workers, drivers, personal domestic and other service workers, miners, farm rural workers, and labourers.

A measure of morale, was determined by a set of questions which closely correspond to the seventeen-item Philadelphia Geriatric Center Morale Scale (Lawton, 1975). The respondent was asked to agree or disagree with statements such as 'I have a lot to be sad about' and 'I get upset easily', and to answer yes or no to questions on depression and fears. In developing a morale score, responses to these questions scored one for disagreement with the statement, an indication of high morale, and scored zero for agreement. By the use of factor analysis, thirteen scored items were reduced to an eight-item scale, which predicted the morale score. The remaining five items were dropped from the scale.

Disability was measured by a series of seven questions designed to indicate the respondent's competence in performing specific activities. Four of the items were concerned with mobility—going out of doors alone, walking half a mile, using public transport, and going up and down stairs—while the last three addressed self-care—getting around inside the home, getting in and out of bed, and taking a bath or shower. Responses were coded as 'without any difficulty', 'on your own with difficulty', 'only with help', or 'not at all'. These seven items were combined to form a measure of overall disability; if help was required, or respondents could not perform any of the activities, they were classified as disabled. This measure corresponds closely with the measure of 'severe overall handicap' used by the Australian Bureau of Statistics Handicapped Persons Survey, (Australian Bureau of Statistics, 1982c), although not all items are identical (Gibson and Rowland, 1984). The Australian Bureau of Statistics (ABS) national sample produced 11 per cent in the disabled category, for non-institutionalised persons aged 60 or over, as compared to 15 per cent in the Sydney sample.

Appendix 2

Sample selection and characteristics of respondents in Chapter 6

This Appendix has two purposes. First, it identifies the selection and characteristics of the 23 respondents who provided the findings reported in Chapter 6. A more detailed report on the interview schedule and methodology is available in Day (1985: Appendices 1 to 4). Second, the Appendix reviews the network characteristics, as identified in the quantitative survey, of the four people reported in the case studies in Chapter 6.

A primary consideration in selecting people for re-interview was to illustrate the wide diversity of individual characteristics and social arrangements found in the larger survey. Respondents in the follow-up study were drawn from the earlier survey using a purposive sampling framework. The main purpose was to select a range of respondents in terms of gender, living arrangements, self-reported health.

Age was limited to the very-olds, those 75 years of age and over. This was done in order to focus on that segment of the older population for whom the issues of dependency and support are presumably of the most immediate concern (Job, 1983; Gibson and Rowland, 1984). The larger survey contained 404 such persons: 135 men and 269 women. Although women in these older age groups were much more numerous than men, both sexes were selected for re-interview in order to highlight important similarities and differences in family circumstances and personal responses to ageing. Table A2.1 shows the persons interviewed by selected social characteristics.

The Project's quantitative survey, although carried out five to six months before the qualitative follow-up study, provided similar

Table A2.1 Personal Characteristics of Respondents in Chapter 6

Men

Living condition and name*	Age	Marital status	Health	Housing tenure
Living alone				
Mr Forbes	80	Wid	a	1
Mr Graham	78	Wid@	a	4
Mr Gregory	77	Div	a	1
Mr McMahon	77	Wid	b	2
Mr O'Leary	75	NM@	b	1
Living with spouse				
Mr Fielding	75	Marr	b	4
Mr Grant	77	Marr	a	1
Mr Sherman	82	Marr	a	1
Mr Skinner	79	Marr	a	2
Living with family				
Mr Henderson	81	Wid	b	1

Women

Living condition	Age	Marital status	Health	Housing tenure
Living alone				
Mrs Ellis	84	Wid	b	1
Mrs Flemming	78	Wid	b	1
Mrs Ford	89	Div	a	3
Mrs Hercamm	75	Wid	a	1
Mrs Morley	83	Wid	a	1
Mrs Smart	83	Wid	b	
Mrs Williams	80	Wid@	b	1
Living with spouse				
Mrs Finlayson	76	Marr	b	1
Mrs Lindsay	77	Marr	b	1
Mrs Parsons	76	Marr	a	1
Mrs Perkins	77	Marr	a	1
Living with family				
Mrs Andrews	82	Wid	a	1
Mrs Kramer	82	Wid	b	5

@ Childless

* to ensure confidentiality for respondents and their families, all names are fictitious.

Health: (a) good/capable of self maintenance
(b) poor/needs assistance

Housing tenure: (1) owner-occupied
(2) leases from relative
(3) private renter
(4) Housing Commission flat
(5) lives in daughter's house

findings in terms of the basic structure and exchanges in the personal support networks of the four respondents presented in the case studies in Chapter 6.

Mrs Lindsay was classified, in the earlier quantitative survey findings, as having an 'intense' network (See Chapter 3) containing multiplex bonds with her spouse, son, and daughter-in-law. While her husband made no instrumental contribution in the household, he provided expressive support in confiding, acceptance, and reassurance of worth. Her son did all the gardening and minor house repairs, served as a confidant, provided reassurance of worth, and was seen as potentially providing financial help. Her daughter-in-law did all the shopping, provided transport, served as a confidant, and was seen as potentially providing care during illness in bed for a week. Home help did most of the housework, and services were seen as the primary support in the event of illness in bed for a month. While three friends had visited Mrs Lindsay at home in the last week, none were included in her expressive or instrumental support network.

Mrs Smart was identified in the quantitative survey as having a 'complex' network of eleven people, including two sons and two daughters, a daughter-in-law and a son-in-law, and five aged female friends (three widowed, one divorced, and one married). One of her daughters, and the daughter's husband and children, were visiting for a week's holiday at the time of the survey. In terms of instrumental support, one of Mrs Smart's daughters does most of the shopping and comes once a month to do heavy cleaning; dwelling repairs and gardening were handled by the manager of her home unit. In response to the expressive questions, she said she was close to her whole family but listed only friends in each of the specific dimensions of social and emotional bonds. A daughter and friends were nominated as potentially providing care if she were to be ill in bed for a week, while both daughters and a daughter-in-law were nominated as likely carers in the event of being bedbound for a month.

Mr Sherman was one of the people who was not assigned to any of the network types, because his overall pattern of social ties was midway between the 'intense' and 'balanced' categories. His support network included his wife, a widowed sister-in-law, a sister and her husband, and an aged woman friend; his son was noticeably absent in any of his support ties. Mr Sherman and his wife were very independent in terms of instrumental activities: they shared the shopping and cooking, while his wife did the housework and he did the minor house repairs. In terms of expressive support, he said he could confide in his wife and sister; was known well and accepted by his brother-in-law and wife; felt needed and appreciated by his wife and his sister and her husband; and shared common activities with his sister-in-law, friend and wife. He felt closest of all to his sister, not his wife, but his wife was expected to be the only provider of care during illness.

Mrs Kramer, as with most respondents who lived with a child, was classified as having an 'intense' network. The only members were her co-resident daughter and son-in-law, and two daughters living elsewhere in Sydney; her one living son who was living overseas, was a notable exclusion from the network, as were any friends (several of her friends were reported to have died in the last five years). Her co-resident daughter and son-in-law had primary responsibility for all of the household tasks, although Mrs Kramer did some shopping and housework. But it was her youngest, non-married daughter who assisted more with transport, and who was expected to provide care in the event of illness. This non-resident daughter was her only confidant, and Mrs Kramer's only other expressive link was to her co-resident daughter who was listed as knowing her well and accepting her. Nobody made her feel needed and appreciated, nor did she have anyone with whom to share common interests and activities.

Appendix 3

Methodology for Chapter 8

The sensitivity and complexity of the decision to enter a nursing home places special demands on the way a study is conducted. At every stage of the research design, it is essential to ensure that participation is voluntary. Another important criterion is to include a wide range of respondents in order to identify the diversity of social pathways into nursing homes. With these considerations in mind, it was decided to select a purposeful rather than random sample of nursing home patients (Minichiello, in progress).

An opportunity to identify nursing homes for the study arose when a group of matrons from the western suburbs in Sydney attended a seminar which I presented at Westmead Hospital. They were informed of the study and their co-operation was requested; a follow up letter and phone calls to 32 of the matrons yielded 20 who expressed interest in participating in the study. Of these, a range of types and sizes of homes were selected because of likely differences in their resident population and admission policies. These were four private nursing homes, two deficit funded voluntary nursing homes and two nursing homes operated by religious organisations; four of these having less than 40 beds and the other four more than 40 beds.

The eight selected nursing homes contained a total of 474 residents when inventoried early in 1982. Preliminary interviews to assess the patients' health prior to admission and their admission history were conducted with 182 patients who were able to hear the questions, comprehend and communicate their answers. The results of these interviews and follow-up discussions with matrons identified 90 patients who were mainly admitted because of social reasons, which represents 19 per cent of the total number of 474 patients in the eight nursing homes. Two residents, who were married and admitted primarily because of a medical problem, were also included to highlight the vulnerabilities of the married dyad.

The final data base for this study consists of personal interviews with 92 aged patients and their next-of-kin. The patient sample is predominantly female (74 per cent) and over-represents the widowed (60 per cent) and never-married (24 per cent). The age range of residents was 65 to 102 years old, with 72 per cent of the sample being over 75 years old. Over a third of the residents were admitted directly from private households; most living alone (26 per cent) or with others (10 per cent), usually a spouse or child. Hospitals accounted for the largest group of admission from an institution (37 per cent), while hostels and another nursing home accounted for 17 and 10 per cent respectively of the admission. In comparison to the 1976 New South Wales Nursing Home Census, the sample did not differ markedly with respect to the basic socio-demographic variables of sex, age, marital status and length of stay. The profile of a typical resident can be identified as female, aged between 80–89, widowed and living at the nursing home for 1 to 4 years (Minichiello, 1982).

A semi-structured questionnaire was used in conducting the interviews and follow-up conversational questions were asked to either clarify answers or extract more qualitative data. The interview schedule contained five areas of inquiry: (1) the aged person's ability to perform daily living activity tasks prior to being institutionalised; (2) help received from family and community services when living in the community; (3) the precipitating factors behind the institutionalisation decision and the issues surrounding the application; (4) feelings about living in a nursing home; and (5) social ties with family, friends and other patients since moving to the nursing home. The interviews averaged 80 minutes in length; were conducted at the nursing home; and were tape-recorded and later transcribed.

The patient identified the most important participant involved in the decision-making process to enter the nursing home and a total of 79 next-of-kin were interviewed. In 8 cases, the patients had no family, and in the remaining 5 cases permission to contact a relative or friend was refused by the patient. None of the relatives who were contacted refused to be interviewed. Of the 79 next-of-kin interviews conducted, 53 were with children or spouses, the remaining 26 were with siblings, nieces, nephews, grandchildren, cousins and friends.

The interview schedule for the next-of-kin sample consisted of both open-ended and closed-ended questions. Data were collected on four separate subject areas: (1) the family's involvement in the decision making process; (2) the factors leading to seeking nursing home care; (3) the details of the application; and (4) family visitation. The interviews were conducted on the telephone and the average call lasted approximately 25 minutes.

Endnotes

Chapter 1

1 The functionalist foundations of most social gerontological studies are subject to the extensive criticisms which for many years have plagued role theory (Coulson, 1972; Strauss, 1978; Connell, 1979; Russell, 1981; and Edwards, 1983). Foremost among these is the focus on social structure in determining behaviour, to the exclusion of individual action and meanings. The emphasis is on uniformity rather than diversity between different people acting within the same roles. Finally, there is the conservative assumption that social relationships reflect consensually derived and necessary 'functions', rather than unequal power and conflicting interests.

2 I have been collaborating with the Australian Institute of Multicultural Affairs (AIMA) in adapting our survey for application to older people from six ethnic groups. This second survey was carried out in 1984, and a preliminary comparison of the support networks of the foreign and Australian born is reported in AIMA (1985), Colson (1986, forthcoming), and Kendig (1986b, forthcoming).

3 Unfortunately the 1982 Family Survey conducted by the Australian Bureau of Statistics (ABS) was not available for analysis at the time of writing.

4 While our book reports some of the preliminary findings from this study, a full analysis is available in Carter (1985). The respondents included five daughters, five sons, five daughters-in-law, and two grand-daughters.

Chapter 3

1 These people are excluded from the subsequent analysis. The Chapter is based on the 904 cases for which full network data is available.

Chapter 4

1 See Conner et al., 1979; Lemon et al., 1972; Harel and Noelker, 1982; Hoyt et al., 1980; Strain and Chappell, 1982.

2 See Areno, 1982; Edwards and Klemmack, 1973; Graney, 1975; Okun
   et al., 1984; Parmalee, 1982; Tate, 1982; Wood and Robertson, 1978.

3 It should be noted that the network generating procedure yields two sets
   of results. Taking confiding as an example, the first set of results
   concerns whether or not someone claims to have a confident. Those who
   do not have one include both the respondents who said 'no' to the filter
   question and those who said 'no' (or refused or didn't know) when asked
   the specific question about confiding. Results of this type appear in
   Table 4.1. The second set of results (See Tables 4.2–4.4) concern who
   provided the dimension of support, such as confiding. In a few cases this
   was either not recorded or a very general answer (all my friends, all my
   family) was given. In such cases a respondent could be counted as having
   someone in the first set of results but not in the second. Anomalies
   resulting from this are trivial except for one category—the never-
   married males. Here, where the base number (16 cases) is very small
   there are a few anomalies in the data, anomalies which emerge on the
   most rigorous scrutiny of Table 4.1 versus Tables 4.2–4.4. These
   anomalies do not undermine the thrust of our argument and are ignored
   in the text, but should be noted.

4 For the married it would also be possible to discuss take-up rates for
   spouses. We have not done this for a variety of reasons. Important
   among these are that some of this reporting is unreliable. A number of
   respondents appeared (to our interviewers) to 'overlook' their spouse as
   someone needing mention. It was so 'obvious', apparently, that it wasn't
   said. On the other hand, for some couples, it was intentional. Interviewers reported respondents checking whether the spouse was in earshot
   before giving a reply that excluded the spouse from this list for that
   dimension. Thus no simple solution existed. A probe designed to elicit
   'overlooked' spouses would have boosted the number included for
   appearance sake. Since spouse-to-respondent multiplexity scores are
   very high overall, and since they correlate with a measure of marital
   satisfaction this is not a difficulty for most analysis, but is a problem in
   this special case.

5 A detailed illustration will help here. If we examine the responses of
   women on 'reassurance of worth' we find that 72 per cent of the married
   women list someone as providing reassurance, compared to 86 per cent
   (24 of 28 cases) for the divorced or separated women. When we ask,
   however, which people provide this support, the married women name
   an average of 3.34 (for those who have at least one), while divorced or
   separated women have an average of 2.04.

6 For reasons of space—six of the rows would be empty—the results for
   spouses do not appear in Tables 4.2 to 4.4. They are, however, reported
   in the text.

7 See Note 3 here. The identified confidants reported for never-married
   men are less than the number who, overall, claim to have some confidant.

8 The table from which the data is reported is not very informative, since
   little variation is observed, and is thus excluded for reasons of space.

9 These were measures on depression, anxiety, loneliness, desire to see
   more of people, a range of items from the Philadelphia Geriatric Center
   Morale Scale (Lawton, 1975) and general questions of happiness and life
   satisfaction.

10 Four simple measures were used to give a picture of social integration. These were the number of outings which respondents had made in the previous weeks with non-household members, the number of visitors they had received in the previous week, the number of visits they had made to see others in the previous week and whether or not, in the previous month, they had attended meetings or made visits to clubs and organisations.

11 Using chi square tests for assessing significance, a significant association ($p < .05$) existed between organisational visits and the following variables. In all cases the result was in the expected direction—greater visits linked with the 'better' answer. Items with a (P) next to them are from the Philadelphia Geriatric Center Morale Scale:

       Desire to see more of people.
(P) Take things hard as you get older.
(P) Feeling you have a lot to be sad about.
(P) Little things bother you a lot.
(P) Feel life is getting worse.
(P) Get upset easily.
       Happiness.
       Life satisfaction.

12 One should, of course, note an alternative hypothesis—namely that unhappy people are abandoned by significant others in exasperation. The argument cannot be discounted on our evidence, but there are other reasons to suggest that we should not lay too much stress upon it. First, at a more theoretical level, if we accept this argument, we must be faced with an entirely intrapsychic explanation for the original unhappiness. Secondly, longitudinal evidence should show the direction of causality. On both counts the general thrust of the literature emphasises the importance of happiness as outcome rather than cause, and it is this line we have taken here.

13 The variables where associations occurred (as defined in note 11) were the same as listed in note 11 except that (a) there was no association for the item 'Little things bother me', and (b) there was an association for an item not significant previously, namely (P) 'Life is not worth living'.

14 It should be noted that the existence of these 'loners' does not disturb the overall association between the number of expressive dimensions catered for, and well-being. Thus to be a 'loner' and to be so by choice may not, of itself, be sufficient to insulate a person from the negative effects of isolation. This finding raises interesting questions about the difference between subjective definitions of the situation and objective levels of provision. We attempted to explore these questions using multivariate techniques such as multiple correlation, but found that our data was being pushed close to its inherent limits.

Chapter 5

1 Following are the sample sizes for this analysis: living alone, 184 able and 31 disabled; living with a child only, 28 able and fourteen disabled; and living with a child and family, 20 able and ten disabled.

2   This analysis is restricted to disabled widows and widowers living alone. Twenty three had no community services, and thirteen had one or more.

Chapter 6

1   Fieldwork and travel costs were funded by a grant from the Institute of Family Studies, Melbourne, Victoria. Results are reported in A.T. Day, *'We can manage': Expectations about care and varieties of family support among persons 75 years of age and over* Melbourne, Institute of Family Studies, 1985. I also wish to acknowledge the support of the Population Reference Bureau, Inc., Washington, D.C. where I was an Andrew Mellon Scholar when I prepared this chapter.

Chapter 7

1   All analyses of a multivariate type use bivariate logit procedures available in the GLIM package (Baker and Nelder, 1978). Starting with a model containing all variables expected to predict the dependent variable, a decremental procedure was used in which the criterion for exclusion was the least 't-test' value. This procedure was completed when the removal of the next least important predictor would make a significant difference to the scaled deviance measure of goodness of fit. The final model was in all cases a parsimonious set of predictors which significantly improved the measure of scaled deviance from the baseline level in which only the constant in the equation was fitted.

Chapter 8

1   Only a small minority of aged persons live in nursing homes. In 1981, less than 3 per cent of persons aged 65 years or more in Australia were long term—but not necessarily permanent—patients in nursing homes and another 3 per cent were residents of other institutions, such as hospitals, homes for the aged or hostels (ABS, 1982c). Of all aged people admitted to nursing homes, 21 per cent are discharged back to the community, with almost three-quarters of the discharges occurring within two months of admission (Howe, 1983). Thus, most aged persons do not live in institutions. In Australia, the majority of the handicapped elderly, 82 per cent, live in private households (Gibson and Rowland, 1984).

2   As the great majority of nursing home patients are women, the female gender will be used throughout this chapter.

3   This study aims to be sensitive to the respondents' subjective interpretations, and makes use of their own words to develop categories and guide the analysis (Minichiello, in progress).

4   The interpersonal negotiations involved with seeking nursing home care are heavily influenced by the organisational structure of the institutions and broader public policies. While the findings presented here include respondents from each of the major kinds of nursing homes in New South Wales, the influence of the organisational structure in recruiting clients is not considered. A report of these effects on the admission process is available in Minichiello (forthcoming).

5   Interviews with family members support this claim. Although only one

kin member in the aged person's family was interviewed, respondents mentioned disagreements amongst family members over the decision to institutionalise or the selection of a nursing home. These family discussions occurred behind closed doors and rarely involved the aged person (Minichiello, in progress).

6 For a discussion of the family member's stories and a comparison with their aged relative's account see Minichiello, in progress

Chapter 9

1 Parts of this section have been taken from Kendig (1984c), with the permission of the Institute of Family Studies.

2 A more complete discussion of the social impact of population ageing in the future is available in Kendig and McCallum (1986a, forthcoming).

References

Adams, B.N. (1968) *Kinship in an Urban Setting* Chicago: Markham Publishing Company

Advisory Council for Inter-Government Relations (1983) *The Provision of Services for the Aged: A Report on Relations Among Governments in Australia* Canberra: AGPS

Allan, G. (1979) *A Sociology of Friendship and Kinship* London: Allen & Unwin

Andersen, R. and Newman, J.F. (1973) 'Societal and individual determinants of medical care utilisation in the United States' *Milbank Memorial Fund Quarterly* 51, pp. 95–124

Antonucci, T.C. (1985) 'Personal characteristics, social support and social behavior' in R.H. Binstock & E. Shanas (eds), 2nd edn, *Handbook of Ageing & the Social Sciences* New York: Van Nostrand Reinhold

Areno, D.A. (1982) 'Widowhood and well-being: an examination of sex differences within a causal model' *International Journal of Ageing and Human Development* 15 (1), pp. 27–40

Atchley, R.C. (1976) *The Sociology of Retirement* New York: Schenkman Publishing Company Inc

Australian Bureau of Statistics (1978) *Social Indicators, No. 2*

—— (1981–1982) *Income and Housing Survey of Individuals. Australia 1981–2*

—— (1982a) *Australia's Aged Population 1982*

—— (1982b) *Family Formation and Dissolution*

—— (1982c) *Handicapped Persons Australia 1981*

—— (1983a) *Cross-Classified Characteristics of Persons and Dwellings 1981 Census of Population and Housing*

—— (1983b) *Persons Retired from Full-time Work, Australia*

—— (1983c) *Provision of Welfare Services by Volunteers—Victoria, Year Ended November 1982*

—— (1984a) *Care for the Aged at Home October 1983 Queensland*

_____ (1984b) *Social Indicators No. 4*

_____ (1985) *Australian Demographic Statistics, June Quarter 1984*

Australian Council on the Ageing and Commonwealth Department of Community Services (1985) *Older People at Home; A Report of a 1981 Joint Survey Conducted in Melbourne and Adelaide* Canberra: AGPS

Australian Institute of Multicultural Affairs (1985) *Report on the Ethnic Aged in Australia* Melbourne: AIMA

Baker, R.J. and Nelder, J.A. (1978) *The GLIM System, Release 3* Oxford: Numerical Algorithms Group

Bankoff, E.A. (1983) 'Social support and adaptation to widowhood' *Journal of Marriage and the Family* November, pp. 827–839

Barnes, J.A. (1972) *Social Networks* Reading, Mass.: Addison-Wesley

Barrett, M. and Macintosh, M. (1982) *The Anti Social Family* London: Verso

Bassili, J.N. and Reil, J.E. (1981) 'On the dominance of the old age stereotype' *Journal of Gerontology* 36, pp. 682–688

Baur, P.A. and Okun, M.A. (1983) 'Stability of life satisfaction in late life' *The Gerontologist* 23 (3), pp. 261–265

Bengtson, V.L. (1979) 'Ethnicity and aging: problems and issues in current social science inquiry' in D.E. Gelfand and A.J. Kutzik (eds) *Ethnicity and Aging: Theory Research and Policy* New York: Spring Publishing Company

Bengtson, V.L., Cuellar, J.B. and Ragan, P.K. (1977) 'Stratum contrasts and similarities in attitudes towards death' *Journal of Gerontology* 32, pp. 204–216

Bengtson, V. and De Terre, E. (1980) 'Aging and family relations' *Marriage and Family Review* 3 (1/2), pp. 51–76

Bengtson, V.L. and Dowd, J.J. (1980) 'Sociological functionalism, exchange theory and life-cycle analysis: a call for more explicit theoretical bridges' *Journal on Aging and Human Development* 12(1), pp. 55–73

Bengtson, V.L. and Treas, J. (1980) 'The changing family context of mental health and aging' in J.E. Birren and R.B. Sloane (eds) *Handbook of Mental Health and Aging* Englewood Cliffs, N.J.: Prentice-Hall

Bernard, J. (1972) *The Future of Marriage* New York: The World Publishing Company

Bertaux, D. (1981) 'From the life-history approach to the transformation of sociological practice' in D. Bertaux (ed.) *Biography and Society: The Life History Approach in the Social Sciences* Beverly Hills, Cal.: Sage Publications

Blythe, R. (1979) *The View in Winter: Reflections on Old Age* London: Allen Lane

Boissevain, J. (1972) *Friends of Friends* Oxford: Basil Blackwell

Bongaarts, J. (1983) 'The formal demography of families and households' *IUSSP Newsletter* 17, pp. 27–42

Bott, E. (1971) *Family and Social Network: Roles, Norms and External Relationships in Ordinary Urban Families* 2nd edn, London: Tavistock

Braithwaite, V.A., Gibson, D.M. and Bosly-Crafth (1984) An Exploratory Study of Poor Adjustment Styles Among Retirees Working Paper No. 78 Ageing and the Family Project Canberra, ACT: ANU

Brennan, A.M. (1982) The Development in Australia up to 1975 of a National Home Care Program Primarily for the Aged, unpublished

Masters thesis, Department of Social Work Sydney: University of New South Wales

Brody, E. (1981) '"Women in the middle" and family help to older people' *The Gerontologist* 21, pp. 471–480

Brody, E.M., Johnsen, P.T., and Fulcomer, M.C. (1984) 'What should adult children do for elderly parents? opinions and preferences of three generations of women' *Journal of Geronotology* 39 (6), pp. 736–746

Brody, E.M., Johnsen, P.T., Fulcomer, M.C. and Lang, A.M. (1983) 'Women's changing roles and help to elderly parents: attitudes of three generations of women' *Journal of Gerontology* 38(5), pp. 597–607

Broom, L. and Jones, F. Lancaster. (1969) 'Career mobility in three societies: Australia, Italy and the United States' *American Sociological Review* 35 (5), pp. 650–658

Brubaker, T.H. ed. (1983) *Family Relationships in Later Life*, Beverly Hills, Cal.: Sage Publications Inc

Bureau of Labour Market Research (1983) *Retired, Unemployed or at Risk: Changes in the Australian Labour Market for Older Workers* Research Report No. 4. Canberra: AGPS

Burns, A., Bottomley, G. and Jools, P. eds (1983) *The Family in the World* North Sydney: Allen & Unwin

Butler, R.N. (1968) 'The life review: an interpretation of reminiscence in the aged' in B. Neugarten (ed.) *Middle Age and Aging* Chicago, Illinois: University of Chicago Press

Butler, R.N. (1980) 'Ageism: a foreword' *Journal of Social Issues* 36, pp. 8–11

Callahan, J., Diamond, L.D., Giele, J.Z. and Morris, R. (1980) 'Responsibility of families for their severely disabled elders' *Health Care Financing Review* 1, pp. 29–45

Cantor, M.H. (1979) 'Neighbors and friends' *Research on Aging* 1, pp. 434–463

—— (1980) 'The informal support system: its relevance in the lives of the elderly' in E. Borgatta and N. McCluskey (eds) *Aging and Society* Beverly Hills, California: Sage Publications

Cantor, M and Little, V. (1985) 'Aging and social care' in R. Binstock and E. Shanas (eds) *Handbook of Ageing and the Social Sciences* 2nd ed New York: Van Nostrand Reinhold

—— (1983) 'Strain among caregivers: a study of experience in the United States' *The Gerontologist* 23, pp. 597–604

Carter, J. (1985) Good Relations, unpublished Working Paper, Ageing and the Family Project, Canberra, ACT: ANU

Cath, S.H. (1972) 'The geriatric patient and his family: the institutionalisation of a parent—a nadir of life' *Journal of Geriatric Psychiatry* 5–6, pp. 25–46

Chappell, N.L. (1985) 'Social support and the receipt of home care services' *The Gerontologist* 25(1), pp. 47–54

Cicirelli, V.G. (1983) 'A comparison of helping behavior to elderly parents of adult children with intact and disrupted marriages' *The Gerontologist* 23 (6), pp. 619–625

Cohler, B. (1983) 'Autonomy and interdependence in adulthood: a psychological perspective' *The Gerontologist* 23, pp. 33–38

Colson, A (1986 forthcoming) 'Social isolation' in *Community and Institutional Care of Aged Migrants in Australia: Research Findings* Melbourne: Australian Institute of Multicultural Affairs

Congress of the United States, Congressional Budget Office (1977) *Long-Term Care for the Elderly and Disabled* Washington, DC: US Government Printing Office

Connell, R.W. (1979) 'The concept of role and what to do with it' *The Australian and New Zealand Journal of Sociology* 15 (3), pp. 7–17

Conner K.A., Powers, E.A. and Bultena, G.L. (1979) 'Social interaction and life satisfaction: an empirical assessment of late-life patterns' *Journal of Gerontology* 34 (1) pp. 116–121

Cooley, C.H. (1909) *Social Organization* New York: Scribner's

Coulson, M. (1972) 'Role: a redundant concept in sociology?' in J.A. Jackson (ed.) *Role* Cambridge: Cambridge University

Cowgill, D. and Holmes, L. eds (1972) *Ageing and Modernisation* New York: Appleton-Century-Crofts

Cox, P.R. (1970) *Demography* 4th edn, London: Cambridge University Press

Cumming, E. and Henry, W. (1961) *Growing Old* New York: Basic Books

D'Abbs, P. (1982) *Social support networks: a critical review of models and findings* Institute of Family Studies Monograph No. 1, Melbourne: Institute of Family Studies

—— (1983) Give and Take: A Study of Networks and Social Strategies, unpublished PhD thesis, University of Melbourne

—— (1984) 'Family support networks and public responsibility' in *Proceedings of XXth International CFR Seminar on Social Change and Family Policies* Melbourne: 2, pp. 509–535

Day, A.T. (1983) ' "I don't need more help at the moment": orientations of the frail aged toward future custodial care' in *Family Support Networks* Proceedings of the Family Research Conference, Vol. V, Melbourne, Victoria: Institute of Family Studies

—— (1985) *We Can Manage: Expectations about Care and Varieties of Family Support Among People 75 Years of Age and Over* Melbourne: Institute of Family Studies

—— (1986 forthcoming) 'Kinship networks and informal support in the later years: past approaches and new directions' in E. Grebnik, C. Hohn and R. MacKensen (eds) *The Demography of the Later Stages of the Family Life Cycle* London: Oxford University Press

Day, A.T. and Harley, A. (1985) ' "I hope something will come out of this": older women and government policies for the aged' La Trobe Working Papers in Sociology No. 72 Melbourne: Latrobe University

Dempsey, K. (1981) 'The rural aged' in A.L. Howe (ed.) *Towards an Older Australia* Queensland: Queensland University Press

Di Iullio, O.B. (1976) 'Household formation 1911–2001' *National Population Inquiry Paper No. 24* Canberra

Dobrof, R. and Litwak, E. (1979) *Maintenance of Family Ties of Long-Term Care Patients: Theory and Guide to Practice* Washington, DC: US Department of Health, Education and Welfare

Dobson, C. (1983) 'Sex-role and marital-role expectations' in T.H. Brubaker (ed.) *Family Relationships in Later Life* Beverly Hills, Cal.: Sage Publications Inc

Dono, J.E. et al. (1979) 'Primary groups in old age: structure and function'

Research on Aging 1 (4), pp. 403–33

Doobov, A. (1980) *Relative Costs of Home Care and Nursing Home and Hospital Care in Australia* Canberra: AGPS

Dowd, J.J. (1980) *Stratification Among the Aged* Monterey, California: Brooks/Cole Publishing Co

Dowd, J.J. and Bengtson, V.L. (1978) 'Aging in minority populations: an examination of the double jeopardy hypothesis' *Journal of Gerontology* 33, pp. 427–436

Dunkle, R.E. (1983) 'The effect of elders' household contributions on their depression' *Journal of Gerontology* 38 (6), pp. 732–737

Edwards, A.R. (1983) 'Sex roles: a problem for sociology and for women' *Australian and New Zealand Journal of Sociology* 19 (3), pp. 385–412

Edwards, J.N. and Klemmack, D.L. (1973) 'Correlates of life satisfaction: a re-examination' *Journal of Gerontology* 28(4), pp. 497–502

Ekerdt, D.J., Bosse, R. and Levkoff, S. (1985) 'An empirical test for phases of retirement: findings from the normative aging study' *Journal of Gerontology* 40(1), pp. 95–101

Elder, G.H. (1974) *Children of the Great Depression* Chicago: University of Chicago Press

―――― (1978a) 'Approaches to social change and the family' in J. Demos, and S.S. Boocock (eds) *Transitions* American Journal of Sociology Supplement, pp. 1–38

―――― (1978b) 'Family history and the life course' in T.K. Hareven (ed.) *Transitions: The Family and the Life Course in Historical Perspective* New York: Academic Press

Ell, K. (1984) 'Social networks, social support and health status: a review' *Social Service Review* pp. 131–149

Erickson, E.H. (1959) 'Identity and the life cycle' *Psychological Issues* Monograph No. 1. of Social Policy, 7 (3), pp. 257–84

―――― (1977) *Childhood and Society* 2nd edn, Frogmore, St. Albans: Triad/ Palladin

Facey, A.B. (1981) *A Fortunate Life* Fremantle, W.A.: The Fremantle Centre Press

Fengler, A. and Goodrich, N. (1979) 'Wives of elderly disabled men: the hidden patient' *The Gerontologist* 19 (2), pp. 175–183

Fillenbaum, G.G., George, L.K., and Palmore, E.B. (1985) 'Determinants and consequences of retirement among men of different races and economic levels' *Journal of Gerontology* 40 (1), pp. 85–94

Finch, J. and Groves, D. (1980) 'Community care and the family: a case for equal opportunities?' *Journal of Social Policy* 9 (4), pp. 487–511

Freud, S. (1917) 'Mourning and melancholia' in *Complete Works of Sigmund Freud* Standard Ed.5, Vol. 14, New York: Macmillan

Furestenberg, F.F. (1981) 'Remarriage and intergenerational relations' in R.W. Fogel, E. Hatfield, S.B. Kiesler and E. Shanas (eds). *Aging: Stability and Change in the Family* New York: Academic Press

George, L.K. (1980) *Role Transitions in Later Life* Monterey, CA: Brooks/ Cole Publishing Company

George, L.K. and Bearon, L.G. (1980) *Quality of Life in Older Persons* New York: Human Sciences Press

Gibson, D.M. (1983) 'Aging, the family and social interaction' in C. Dodd (ed.) *Education and the Ageing* Proceedings of the 18th Annual Conference of the Australian Association of Gerontology, Sydney

_____ (1984) 'Knowledge of community services amongst the aged' *Australian Journal of Social Issues* 19 (1), pp. 3–12

Gibson, D.M. and Aitkenhead, W. (1983) 'The elderly respondent' *Research on Ageing* 5, pp. 283–296

Gibson, D.M. and Kendig, H.L. (1982) 'Ageing, the family, and public policy' *Australian Journal on Ageing* 1(1), pp. 23–26

Gibson, D.M. and Rowland, D.T. (1984) 'Community vs institutional care: the case of the Australian aged' *Social Science and Medicine* 18, pp. 997–1004

Glazer, N. (1971) 'The limits of social policy' *Commentary* 52, pp. 51–58

Glenn, N.D. (1975) 'The contribution of marriage to the psychological well-being of males and females' *Journal of Marriage and the Family* August, pp. 594–600

Goffman, E. (1961) *Asylums: Essays on the Social Situation of Mental Patients and Other Inmates* Chicago: Aldine

Goldfarb, A.I. (1969) 'The psychodynamics of dependency and the search for aid' in R.A. Kalish (ed.) *The Dependencies of Old People* Ann Arbor: Institute of Gerontology, University of Michigan

Gorden, C., Gaitz, C. and Scott, J. (1976) 'Loves and lives: personal expressivity across the life span' in R. Binstock and E. Shanas (eds), *Handbook of Ageing and the Social Sciences* New York: Van Nostrand Reinhold

Graney, M.J. (1975) 'Happiness and social participation in aging' *Journal of Gerontology* 30 (6), pp. 701–706

Granovetter, M. (1973) 'The strength of weak ties' *American Journal of Sociology* 78, pp. 1360–1380

Green, V.L. (1983) 'Substitution between formally and informally provided care for the impaired elderly in the community' *Medical Care* 21, pp. 609–619

Gubrium, J.F. (1978) 'Notes on the social organization of senility' *Urban Life* 7, pp. 23–44

Hagestad, G.O. (1981) 'Problems and promises in the social psychology of intergenerational relations' in R.W. Fogel, E. Hatfield, S.B. Kiesler and E. Shanas (eds) *Aging: Stability and Change in the Family* New York: Academic Press

Hagestad, G.O. and Neugarten, B.L. (1985) 'Age and the life course' in R. Binstock and E. Shanas (eds) *Handbook of Ageing and the Social Sciences* 2nd edn, New York: Van Nostrand Reinhold

Harel, Z. and Noelker, L. (1982) 'Social integration, health and choice: their impact on the well-being of institutionalized aged' *Research on Ageing* 4(1), pp. 97–111

Hareven, T.K. ed. (1978) *Transitions: The Family and the Life Course in Historical Perspective* New York: Academic Press

Harris, C.C. (1983) *The Family and Industrial Society* London: Allen & Unwin

Helsing, K.J., Szklo, M. and Comstock, G.W. (1981) 'Factors associated with mortality after widowhood' *American Journal of Public Health* 71 (8), pp. 802–809

Hennon, C.B. (1983) 'Divorce and the elderly: a neglected area of research' in T.H. Brubaker (ed.) *Family Relationships in Later Life* Beverly Hills, Cal: Sage Publications

References 213

Hill, R. (1970) *Family Development in Three Generations* Cambridge, Mass., U.S.A.: Schenkman Publishing Co., Inc

Hiltz, S.R. (1978) 'Widowhood: a roleless role' *Marriage and Family Review* 1, pp. 2–10

Hochschild, A.R. (1973) *The Unexpected Community* Englewood Cliffs, N.J.: Prentice-Hall

Holmes, T.H. and Rahe, R.H. (1967) 'The social readjustment rating scale' *Journal of Psychosomatic Research*, 11, pp. 213–18

Holzberg, C.S. (1982) 'Ethnicity and aging: rejoinder' *The Gerontologist* 22, pp. 471–472

Horowitz, A. and Shindelman, L.W. (1981) 'Reciprocity and affection: past influences on current caregiving' paper presented at the 34th Annual Scientific Meeting of the Gerontological Society of America, Toronto, Canada

House of Representatives Standing Committee on Expenditure (1982) *In a Home or at Home: Accommodation and Home Care for the Aged* October, Canberra: Australian Government Publishing Service

Howe, A.L. (1979) 'Family support of the aged: some evidence and interpretation' *Australian Journal of Social Issues* 14 (4), pp. 259–73

——— (1981) *Towards an Older Australia* Queensland: University of Queensland Press

——— (1982), 'Review of C. Russell's the ageing experience' *Ageing and Society* 2(3), pp. 404–406

——— (1983) 'How long is long term care?' *Community Health Studies* 2, pp. 149–154

Hoyt, D. and Babchuk, N. (1983) 'Adult kinship networks: the selection and formation of intimate ties with kin' *Social Forces* 62, pp. 84–101

Hoyt, D.R., Kaiser, M.A., Peters, G.R. and Babchuck, N. (1980) 'Life satisfaction and activity theory: a multidimensional approach' *Journal of Gerontology* 35(6), pp. 935–941

Hunt, A. (1978) *The Elderly at Home: A Study of People Aged Sixty-five and Over Living in the Community in England in 1976* Social Survey Division, Office of Population Censuses and Surveys, HMSO

Hutchinson, B. (1954) *Old People in a Modern Australian Community: A Social Survey* Melbourne: Melbourne University Press

James, A., James, W.L. and Smith, H.L. (1984) 'Reciprocity as a coping strategy of the elderly: a rural Irish perspective' *The Gerontologist* 24 (5), pp. 483–489

Jarrett, W.H. (1985) 'Caregiving within kinship systems: is affection really necessary?' *The Gerontologist* 25(1), pp. 5–10

Jick, T.D. (1979) 'Mixing qualitative and quantitative methods: triangulation in action' *Administrative Science Quarterly* 24, pp. 602–611

Job, E. (1983) 'Retrospective life span analysis: a method for studying extreme old age' *Journal of Gerontology* 38 (3), pp. 369–374

——— (1984) *Eighty Plus: Outgrowing the Myths of Old Age* Queensland: University of Queensland Press

Johnson, C.L. and Catalano, D.G. (1981) 'Childless elderly and their family supports' *The Gerontologist* 21, pp. 610–618

Johnson, M. (1976) 'That was your life: a biographical approach to later life' in J.M.A. Munnichs and J.A. Wim (eds) *Dependency or Inter-dependency in Old Age* The Hague: Martinus Nijhoff

Johnson, M.L. and Cooper, S. (1983) *Informal Care and the Personal Social Services: An Interpretive Literature Review* Report for the Department of Health and Social Security Policy Studies Institute: London

Kahn, R.L. and Antonucci, T.C. (1981) 'Aging and the life course', in S.B. Kiesler, J.N. Morgan and V.K. Oppenheimer (eds) *Aging: Social Change* New York: Academic Press

Kalish, R. (1975) *Late Adulthood: Perspectives on Human Development* Monterey, California: Brooks-Cole

Kendig, H.L. (1983a) 'Blood ties and gender role: adult children who care for aged parents' *Support Networks, Volume 5: Proceedings of the Australian Family Research Conference* Melbourne: Institute of Family Studies

—— (1983b) 'Community care' in H.L. Kendig, D.M. Gibson, D.T. Rowland and J.M. Hemer (eds) *Health, Welfare and Family in Late Life* Canberra: Ageing and the Family Project, Research School of Social Sciences, Australian National University

—— (1983c) 'The providers of community care' in H.L. Kendig, D.M. Gibson, D.T. Rowland and J.M. Hemer (eds) *Health, Welfare and Family in Later Life* Canberra: Ageing and the Family Project, Research School of Social Sciences, Australian National University

—— (1984a) 'The cumulation of inequity: housing costs and income support in old age' *Australian Journal on Ageing* 3 (1), pp. 8–15

—— (1984b) 'Housing tenure and generational equity' *Ageing and Society* 4 (3), pp. 249–72

—— (1984c) 'Social change and support of the australian aged: individual, family and government responsibilities' in *Social Change and Family Policies* Proceedings of the XXth International CFR Seminar, International Sociological Association, Melbourne: Institute of Family Studies

—— (1985 forthcoming) 'Contributions of the aged' in *Proceedings of the Nineteenth Annual Conference of the Australian Association of Gerontology* Sydney:

—— (1986a forthcoming) 'Towards integrated community care for the frail aged' *Australian Journal of Social Issues* forthcoming

—— (1986b forthcoming) 'Informal support networks' in *Community and Institutional Care of Aged Migrants in Australia*, Research findings Melbourne: Australian Institute of Multicultural Affairs

Kendig, H.L., Gibson, D.M., Rowland, D.T. and Hemer, J.M. (1983) *Health, Welfare and Family in Later Life* Canberra: Ageing and the Family Project, Research School of Social Sciences, Australian National University

Kendig, H.L. and McCallum, J. (1986 forthcoming) *Ageing and Public Policy in Australia* Sydney: Allen & Unwin

Kendig, H.L. and McCallum, J. (1986b forthcoming) *Greying Australia: The Future Impact of Population Ageing* Canberra: National Population Council Report, AGPS

Kendig, H.L. and Rowland, D.T. (1983) 'Family support of the Australian aged: a comparison with the United States' *The Gerontologist* 23, pp. 643–649

Kinnear, D. and Graycar, A. (1982) 'Family care of elderly people' *Social Welfare Reports and Proceedings* No. 23 Sydney, NSW: Social Welfare

Research Centre, University of New South Wales

—— (1984) 'Ageing and family dependency' *Australian Journal of Social Issues* 19 (1), pp. 13–26

Kinnear, D. and Rossiter, C. (1983) 'Family care policies-findings from a survey of carers' *Support Networks, Vol. 5: Proceedings of the Australian Family Research Conference* Melbourne: Institute of Family Studies

Kuypers, J.A. and Bengtson, V.L. (1983) 'Toward competence in the older family' in T.H. Brubaker (ed.) *Family Relationships in Later Life* Beverly Hills, Cal.: Sage Publications Inc

Lancaster, H.O. (1959) 'Generation life tables for Australia' *Australian Journal of Statistics* 1, pp. 19–33

Laslett, P. (1977) *Family Life and Illicit Love in Earlier Generations* London: Cambridge University Press

—— (1984) 'The significance of the past in the study of ageing: introduction to the special issue on history and ageing' *Ageing and Society* 4 (4), pp. 379–389

Lawton, M.P. (1975) 'The Philadelphia geriatric center morale scale: A revision' *Journal of Gerontology* 30 (1), pp. 85–89

Lee, G.R. (1984) Kinship and social support of the elderly: the case of the United States, Seminar on The Demography of the Later Phases of The Family Life Cycle, September Berlin: International Union for the Scientific Study of Population

Lefroy, R.B. (1977) 'The elderly person and family life' *Australian Journal of Social Issues* 12 (1), pp. 33–42

Lemon, B.W., Bengtson, V.L. and Peterson, J.A. (1972) 'An exploration of the activity theory of ageing: activity types and life satisfaction among in-movers to a retirement community' *Journal of Gerontology* 24 (4), pp. 511–523

Litwak, E. (1960) 'Geographic mobility and extended family cohesion' *American Sociological Review* 25, pp. 385–394

—— (1965) 'Extended kin relations in an industrial society' in E. Shanas and G. Streib (eds) *Social Structure and Generational Family Relationships* Englewood Cliffs, J.J.: Prentice-Hall

—— (1977) 'Theoretical bases for practise' in R. Dobrov and E. Litwak (eds) *Maintenance of Family Ties of Long Term Care Patients* Washington DC: US Government Printing Office

—— (1985) *Helping Older People. The Complementary Roles of Informal Networks and Formal Systems* New York: The Guilford Press

Litwak, E. and Kulis, S. (1983) 'Changes in helping networks with changes in the health of older people: social policy and social theory' in S.E. Spiro and E. Yucktman-Yaar (eds) *Evaluating the Welfare State: Social and Political Perspective* New York: Academic Press

Lopata, H.Z. (1979) *Women as Widows. Support Systems* New York: Elsevier

Lowenthal, M.F. and Haven, C. (1968) 'Interaction and adaptation: intimacy as a critical variable' *American Sociological Review* 33, pp. 20–30

Maddison, D.C. and Viola, A. (1968) 'The Health of widows in the year following bereavement' *Journal of Psychomatic Research* 12, pp. 297–306

Maddison D.C. and Walker, W.L. (1967) 'Factors affecting the outcomes of conjugal bereavement' *British Journal of Psychiatry* 113, pp. 1057–67

Mangen, D.J. and Peterson, W.A. eds (1982) *Social Rules and Social*

Participation, Research Instruments in Social Gerontology Vol. 2, Minneapolis: University of Minnesota Press

Marshall, V.W. (1979) 'No exit: a symbolic interactionist perspective on aging' *International Journal of Aging and Human Development* 9, pp. 345–358

McAllister, L. and Fischer, C.S. (1978) 'A procedure for surveying research networks' *Sociological Methods and Research* 7 (2), pp. 131–148

McDonald, P. (1983) 'Can the family survive?' *Australan Society* 2(11), pp. 3–8

Minichiello, M.V. (1982) 'Perceptions of the Social Processes of Institutionalisation and Dying' Working Paper No. 18 Ageing and the Family Project Canberra, ACT: Australian National University.

Minichiello, M.V. (in progress) 'Beyond the Medical Admission: Social Pathways into Nursing Homes' unpublished PhD thesis Canberra: Research School of Social Sciences, Australian National University

—— (forthcoming) 'A patient's view of nursing homes' in H.L. Kendig and J.M. McCallum (eds), *Ageing and Public Policy* Sydney: Allen & Unwin.

Mitchell, J.C. ed. (1969) *Social Networks in Urban Situations* Manchester, UK: University of Manchester Press

Mitchell, J.C. and Trickett, E.J. (1980) 'Task force report: social networks as mediators of social support' *Community Mental Health Journal* 16, pp. 27–44

Moriwaki, S.Y. (1973) 'Self-disclosure, significant others and psychological well-being in old age' *Journal of Health and Social Behaviour* 14, pp. 226–232

Morris, J. (1981) 'Transport and mobility' in A.L. Howe (ed.) *Towards an Older Australia* Queensland: University of Queensland Press

Morris, J.N. and Sherwood, S. (1984) 'Informal support resources for vulnerable elderly persons: can they be counted on, why do they work?' *International Journal of Aging and Human Development* 18, pp. 81–98

Mueller, D.P. (1980) 'Social networks: a promising direction for research on the relationship of the social environment to psychiatric disorder' *Social Science and Medicine* 14, pp. 147–161

Neugarten, B.L. and Moore, J. (1968) 'The changing age status system' in B.L. Neugarten (ed.) *Middle Age and Aging* Chicago: University of Chicago Press

Neyland, B. and Shadbolt, B. (1985) 'The viability of singlehood in old age' Paper Presented at SAANZ Conference, Brisbane, August 1985

Nissel, M. (1984) 'The Family Costs of Looking After Handicapped Elderly Relatives' *Aging and Society* 4 (2), pp. 185–204

Nydegger, C.N. (1983) 'Family ties of the aged in cross-cultural perspective' *The Gerontologist* 23 (1), pp. 26–32

O'Connor, P. and Brown, G. (1984) '"Supportive relationships": fact or fancy?' *Journal of Social and Personal Relationships* 1, pp. 159–175

Okun, M.A., Stock, W.A., Haring, M.J. and Witter, R.A. (1984) 'Social activity/subjective well-being relation' *Research on Aging* 6 (1), pp. 45–65

Palmore, E. and Manton, K. (1973) 'Ageism compared to racism and sexism' *Journal of Gerontology*, 28, pp. 363–369

Parkes, C.M. (1971) 'Psycho-social transitions: a field for study' *Social Science and Medicine* 5, pp. 101–115

Parmalee, P.A. (1982) 'Social contacts, social instrumentality and adjustment of institutionalized aged' *Research on Aging* 4 (2), pp. 269–280

Parsons, T. (1955) 'The american family: its relations to personality and to the social structure' in T. Parsons and R.F. Bales *Family, Socialization and Interaction Process* Glencoe, Illinois: The Free Press

Penman, R. and Stolk, Y. (1984) *Not the Marrying Kind* Melbourne: Penguin

Philips, T.J. (1981) *A Comparative Cost Evaluation of Alternative Modes of Long Term Care for the Aged* Part II, Final Technical Report, Sydney: School of Health Administration, University of New South Wales

Pollitt, P. (1977) 'The aged' in J. McCaughey, S. Shaver and H. Ferber (eds) *Who Cares?* Melbourne: Sun Books

Raphael, B. (1983) *The Anatomy of Bereavement* New York: Basic Books, Inc

Reichardt, C.S. and Cook, T.D. (1979) 'Beyond qualitative versus quantitative methods' in T.D. Cook and C.S. Reichardt (eds) *Qualitative and Quantitative Methods in Evaluation Research* Beverly Hills: Sage Publications

Rice, D.P. and Feldman, J.J. (1983) 'Living longer in the United States: demographic changes and health needs of the elderly' *Health and Society* 61 (3)

Richards, L. (1985) 'Too close for comfort: neighbouring in a new estate', Paper Presented to Ageing and the Family Project Seminar, April Canberra, ACT: ANU

Riley, M.W. (1972) *Aging and Society, Vol. II: A Sociology of Age Stratification* New York: Russell Sage Foundation

___ ed., (1979) *Ageing from Birth to Death: Interdisciplinary Perspectives* Boulder, Colorado: Westview Press

Riley, M.W. and Foner, A. (1968) *Ageing and Society: An Inventory of Research Findings* 1, New York: Russell Sage Foundation

Rodin, J. and Langer, E. (1980) 'Aging labels: 'the decline of control and the fall of self-esteem' *Journal of Social Issues* 36, pp. 12–29

Rosenman, L., Shulman, A.D. and Penman, R. (1981) 'Support systems of widowed women in Australia' *Australian Journal of Social Issues* 16 (1), pp. 18–31

Rosenmayr, L. (1978) A view of multigenerational relations in the family, Paper Presented at the 9th World Congress of Sociology Uppsala, Sweden

Rosenmayr, L. and Kockeis, E. (1963) 'Propositions for a sociological theory of ageing and the family' *International Social Science Journal* 15 (3), pp. 410–26

Rosow, I. (1967) *Social Integration of the Aged* New York: Free Press

___ (1976) 'Status and role change through the life span' in R.H. Binstock and E. Shanas *Handbook of Aging and Social Sciences* New York: Van Nostrand Reinhold

___ (1977) *Socialization to Old Age* Berkeley: University of California Press

Rowland, D.T. (1979) *Internal Migration in Australia* Canberra: Australian Bureau of Statistics

___ (1982a) 'Living arrangements and the later family life cycle in Australia' *Australian Journal on Ageing* 1 (2), pp. 3–6

___ (1982b) 'The vulnerability of the aged in Sydney' *Australian and New Zealand Journal of Sociology* 18, pp. 229–247

—— (1983a) 'Beyond 2000' *Australian Society* 2 (10), pp. 17–23

—— (1983b) 'The family circumstances of the ethnic aged' in *Papers on the Ethnic Aged* Melbourne: Australian Institute of Multicultural Affairs

—— (1983c) 'Family structure' in H.L. Kendig, et al. *Health, Welfare and Family in Late Life* Canberra: Ageing and the Family Project, Research School of Social Sciences, Australian National University

—— (1984) 'Old age and the demographic transition' *Population Studies* 38, pp. 73–87

Rowland, D.T., Kendig, H.L. and Jones, R.G. (1984) 'Improving coverage and efficiency in a survey of the aged' *Australian Journal on Ageing* 3(2), pp. 34–38

Rundall, T.G. and Evashwick, C. (1982) 'Social networks and help-seeking among the elderly' *Research on Aging* 4, pp. 205–26

Russell, C. (1981) *The Aging Experience* Sydney: Allen & Unwin

Ryan, C.A. and Williams, L.S. (1984) 'A Microeconomic Analysis of the Labour Force Status of Older Males' Working Paper No. 37 Canberra: Bureau of Labour Market Research

Ryder, N. (1965) 'The cohort as a concept in the study of social change' *American Sociological Review* 30, pp. 843–861

Sax, S. (1985) *A Strife of Interests! Politics and Policies in Australian Health Services* Sydney: Allen & Unwin

Schaie, K.W. (1973) 'Methodological problems in descriptive developmental research on adulthood and aging' in J.R. Nesselrode and H.W. Reese (eds) *Life-Span Developmental Psychology: Methodological Issues* New York: Academic Press

Schoor, M. (1980) '. . . *Thy Father and Thy Mother* . . .: *A Second Look at Filial Responsibility and Family Policy*' Washington DC: US Government Printing Office

—— (1979) 'The family as a social support system in old age' *The Gerontologist* 19 (2), pp. 169–174

Shanas, E. and Hauser, P.M. (1974) 'Zero population growth and the family life of old people' *Journal of Social Issues* 30, pp. 79–92

Shanas, E. and Sussman, M.B. (1977) *Family, Bureaucracy and the Elderly* Durham N.C.: Duke University Press

Shanas, E., et al. (1968) *Old People in Three Industrial Societies* London: Routledge & Kegan Paul

Sieber, S. (1973) 'The integration of fieldwork and survey methods' *American Journal of Sociology* 78 (6), pp. 1335–1358

Simmel, G. (1950) *The Sociology of Georg Simmel*, K.H. Wolff (ed.), Glencoe, Ill.: Free Press

Simmons, R.L. (1983–84) 'Specificity and substitution in the social networks of the elderly' *International Journal on Aging and Human Development* 18 (2), pp. 121–39

Smith, K. and Bengtson, V.L. (1979) 'Positive consequences of institutionalisation: solidarity between elderly parents and their middle-aged children' *The Gerontologist*, 19, pp. 438–447

Snow, R. and Crapo, L. (1982) 'Emotional bondedness, subjective well-being, and health in elderly medical patients' *Journal of Gerontology* 37 (5), pp. 609–615

Social Welfare Policy Secretariat (1980) *Commonwealth Spending and Income Support Between 1968–69 and 1978–79 and Why it Increased*

Canberra: AGPS

Soldo, B.J. (1978) 'Living arrangements of the elderly: future trends and implications' in United States Congress, select committee on population *Domestic Consequences of United States Population Change*, Committee Serial E, Washington: Government Printing Office

Spanier, G.B. and Glick, P.C. (1980) 'The life cycle of American families: an expanded analysis' *Journal of Family History* 5, pp. 97–111

Steinmetz, S.K. and Amsden, D.J. (1983) 'Dependent elders, family stress and abuse' in T.H. Brubaker (ed.) *Family Relationships in Later Life* Beverly Hills, Cal.: Sage Publications Inc

Stoller, E.P. (1983) 'Parental caregiving by adult children' *Journal of Marriage and the Family* November pp. 851–858

Stokes, J.P. (1983) 'Predicting satisfaction with social support from social network structure' *American Journal of Community Psychology* 11 (2), pp. 141–152

Strain, L.A. and Chappell, N.A. (1982) 'Confidants. do they make a difference in quality of life?' *Research on Ageing* 4(4), pp. 479–502

Strauss, A. (1978) *Negotiations* San Francisco, California: Jossey-Bass

Streib, G.F. (1965) 'Intergenerational relations: Perspective of the two generations on the older parent' *Journal of Marriage and the Family* 27, pp. 496–476

_____ (1983) 'The frail elderly: research dilemmas and research opportunities' *The Gerontologist* 23 (1), pp. 40–44

Sussman, M.B. (1976) 'The family life of old people' in R. Binstock and E. Shanas (eds) *Handbook of Aging and the Social Sciences* New York: Van Nostrand Reinhold

Sussman, M.B. and Burchinall, L. (1962) 'Parental aid to married children: implications for family functioning' *Marriage and Family Living* 24, pp. 320–32

Sussman, M.B., Cates, J.N. and Smith, D.T. (1970) *The Family and Inheritance* New York: Russell Sage Foundation

Sweetser, D.A. (1983) 'Review of "the aging experience" by Cherry Russell (1981)' *The Gerontologist* 23 (4), pp. 439–440

Tate, L.A. (1982) 'Life satisfaction and death anxiety in aged women' *International Journal of Aging and Human Development* 15 (4), pp. 299–305

Taylor, R. and G. Ford (1983) 'Inequalities in old age: an examination of age, sex, and class differences in a community sample' *Ageing and Society* 3 (2), pp. 183–208

Tobin, S. and Kulys, R. (1980) 'The family services' *Annual Review of Gerontology and Geriatrics* New York: Springer Publishing

Tobin, S. and Leiberman, M.A. (1976) *Last Home for the Aged* San Francisco: Jossey-Bass

Townsend, P. (1963) *The Family Life of Old People: An Inquiry in East London* London: Penguin Books

_____ (1968) 'The structure of the family' in E. Shanas, P. Townsend, D. Wedderburn, H. Friis, P. Milhoj and J. Stehouver. *Old People in Three Industrial Societies* London: Routledge and Kegan Paul

_____ (1977) *The Family Life of Old People* Middlesex: Penguin Books

_____ (1981) 'The structured dependency of the elderly: a creation of social policy in the twentieth century' *Ageing and Society* 1 (1), pp. 5–28

Treas, J. (1975) 'Aging and the Family' in D.S. Woodruff and J.E. Birren (eds) *Aging: Scientific Perspectives and Social Issues* New York: Van Nostrand

Troll, L.E. (1971) 'The family in later life: a decade review' *Journal of Marriage and Family* 33, pp. 263–290

Troll, L.E., Miller, S.J. and Atchley, R.C. (1979) *Families in Later Life* Belmont, California: Wadsworth Publishing Company, Inc

Uhlenberg, P. (1977) 'Changing Structure of the Older Population of the USA During the Twentieth Century' *The Gerontologist* 17, pp. 197–202

Uhlenberg, P. (1978) 'Changing configurations of the Life Course' in T.K. Hareven (ed.) *Transitions: The Family and the Life Course in Historical Perspective* New York: Academic Press

Viney, L.L. (1980) *Transitions* Sydney: Cassell Australia

Walker, K.N., McBride, A. and Vachon, M.L. (1977) 'Social support networks and the crisis of bereavement' *Social Science and Medicine* 11, pp. 35–41

Weihl, H. (1977) 'The household, intergenerational relations and social policy' in E. Shanas and M.B.Sussman (eds) *Family, Bureaucracy and the Elderly* Durham, North Carolina: Duke University Press

Weiss, R.S. (1974) 'The provisions of social relationships' in Z. Rubin (ed.) *Doing Unto Others* Englewood Cliffs: Prentice-Hall

Weitz, S. (1977) *Sex Roles* New York: Oxford University Press

Wellman, B. and Hall, A. (1984) 'Social networks and social support: implications for late life' in V. Marshall and T. Harris (eds) *Later Life: A Microsociology* Norwood, N.J.: Ablex

Wenger, G. Clare (1984) *The Supportive Network. Coping with Old Age* London: Allen & Unwin

West, G.E. and Simmons, R.L. (1983) 'Sex differences in stress, coping resource and illness among the elderly' *Research on Aging* 5 (2), pp. 235–68

Wild, R.A. (1981) *Australian Community Studies and Beyond* Sydney: Allen & Unwin

Wood, V. and Robertson, J.F. (1978) 'Friendship and kinship interaction: differential effect on the morale of the elderly' *Journal of Marriage and the Family* 40, pp. 367–375

Woodfield, R.L. and Viney, L.L. (1984–1985) 'A personal construct approach to the conjugally bereaved woman' *Omega* 15 (1), pp. 1–13

Young, C.M. (1969) Population Growth and Mortality of Cohorts in Australia, PhD thesis in Demography, Canberra: Australian National University

Young, C.M. (1977) *The Family Life Cycle* Australian Family Formation Project, Monograph 6, Department of Demography, Canberra: Australian National University

Zanit, S.H., Reever, K.E. and Back-Peterson, J. (1980) 'Relatives of the impaired elderly: correlates of feelings of burden' *The Gerontologist* 20, pp. 649–655

Index

For Product Safety Concerns and Information please contact our EU
representative GPSR@taylorandfrancis.com
Taylor & Francis Verlag GmbH, Kaufingerstraße 24, 80331 München, Germany

www.ingramcontent.com/pod-product-compliance
Lightning Source LLC
Chambersburg PA
CBHW050422280326
41932CB00013BA/1959